COMPENDIUM OF THE CONFEDERATE ARMIES

VIRGINIA

COMPENDIUM OF THE CONFEDERATE ARMIES

VIRGINIA

Stewart Sifakis

WILLOW BEND BOOKS
2006

To the Memory of James Sifakis
1893-1961

WILLOW BEND BOOKS
AN IMPRINT OF HERITAGE BOOKS, INC.

Books, CDs, and more – Worldwide

For our listing of thousands of titles see our website
at
www.HeritageBooks.com

Published 2006 by
HERITAGE BOOKS, INC.
Publishing Division
65 East Main Street
Westminster, Maryland 21157-5026

Copyright © 1992 Stewart Sifakis

All rights reserved. No part of this book may be reproduced or transmitted in any form or by any means, electronic or mechanical, including photocopying, recording or by any information storage and retrieval system without written permission from the author, except for the inclusion of brief quotations in a review.

International Standard Book Number: 978-1-58549-701-0

To
the Memory of James Sifakis
1893–1961

CONTENTS

ACKNOWLEDGMENTS

I would like to thank the staffs of the National Archives, Library of Congress, the various state archives and the New York Public Library for their patience and assistance. Over the past decades the staff of the National Park Service, Edwin C. Bearss, chief historian, have proven very informative on my frequent visits to the various battlefields. To Shaun Potter, Christina Villano and Sally Gadsby I am indebted for keeping me at my work. For the logistical support of the management of the Hotel Post, Zermatt (Karl Ivarsson, Ursula Waeny and Leslie Dawkins), I am very grateful. And last, but certainly not least, I owe thanks to John Warren for his knowledge of computers, without which this project would have ground to a halt, and to his computer widow, Evelyne.

INTRODUCTION

This work is intended to be the companion set to Frederick H. Dyer's *Compendium of the War of the Rebellion* for the Confederacy. The Compendium was first published as a three-volume work in 1909. A study of all the Union regiments, battalions, batteries and independent companies, it has since been reprinted in two- and one-volume editions.

It has been estimated that for every day since the end of the American Civil War, one book, magazine or newspaper article has appeared dealing with some aspect of that fratricidal struggle. Many ask: If so much has been written on the Civil War, is there really a need for more? The answer is an emphatic yes. Many aspects of the conflict have been covered only superficially and require more in-depth research. But for such research a bedrock of reference works is essential.

There are many such works available, including the U.S. War Department's 128-volume *The War of the Rebellion: A Compilation of the Official Records of the Union and Confederate Armies* and the U.S. Navy Department's 31-volume *Official Records of the Union and Confederate Navies in the War of the Rebellion*. Registers of military personnel include: George W. Cullum's two-volume *Biographical Register of the Officers and Graduates of the United States Military Academy*, Francis B. Heitman's two-volume *Historical Register and Dictionary of the United States Army From Its Organization, September 29, 1789, to March 2, 1903*, Guy V. Henry's two-volume *Military Record of Civilian Appointments in the United States Army*, Robert K. Krick's *Lee's Colonels: A Biographical Register of the Field Officers of the Army of Northern Virginia* and Ezra J. Warner's *Generals in Gray: Lives of the Confederate Commanders* and *Generals in Blue: Lives of the Union Commanders*. Politics are covered in Jon L. Wakelyn's *Biographical Dictionary of the Confederacy* and Ezra J. Warner's and W. Buck Yearns' *Biographical Register of the Confederate Congress*. E. B. Long's *The Civil War Day by Day: An Almanac 1861–1865* provides an excellent chronology. Collective biographies include Mark M. Boatner's *The Civil War Dictionary*, Patricia L. Faust's *Historical Times Illustrated Encyclopedia of the Civil War* and Stewart

Sifakis' *Who Was Who in the Civil War*. Then, of course there is Dyer's Compendium.

To date there has not been a comprehensive equivalent to Dyer's work for the South as a whole. Basically work has been done by individual states. North Carolina has an excellent work currently nearing completion. Other commendable works have been done for Tennessee, Virginia and Texas. Works were begun for Georgia and South Carolina but did not proceed far. State government agencies in Florida and Kentucky made some efforts in the early years after the war. However, none of these draws a consolidated picture of the Confederate States Army. That is where the *Compendium of the Confederate Armies* comes in.

This work is organized into volumes by state. One volume includes the border state units—Kentucky, Maryland and Missouri; units organized directly by the Confederate authorities from various state companies; and those units from the Indian nations allied with the Confederacy. The final volume consists of the tables of organization of the various armies and departments throughout the war.

There are chapters in each volume on the artillery, cavalry and infantry. Those units having a numerical designation are listed first, followed by those units using the name of their commander, home region or some other name. Units are then broken down alphabetically by size—for example, battalions, batteries, companies and regiments. If two or more units still have the same sorting features, they are then further broken down alphabetically by any special designation—1st or 2nd Organization, Local Defense Troops, Militia, Provisional Army, Regulars, Reserves, Sharpshooters, State Guard, State Line, State Troops or Volunteers and so on. The company designation for artillery batteries that served within an artillery battalion or regiment is listed at the end of the battalion or regiment designation. If heavy artillery battalions or regiments served together as a unit through most of the war, they are treated as a whole with no breakdown of the companies.

Each entry starts with the unit's name. Any nicknames or other mistaken designations follow. Then comes a summary of its organizational details: its date and location of organization, mustering into service, the number of companies for battalion organizations, armament for artillery batteries, surrenders, paroles, exchanges and disbandment or mustering out. The next paragraph starts with the first commanding officer and continues with an alphabetical listing of the other field-grade officers. (Captains are listed chronologically for artillery batteries.) The next paragraph is the brigade and higher-level command assignments of the unit. This is followed by a listing of the battles and campaigns the unit engaged in. Note that the unit was not necessarily present on each date that is indicated for multiday actions. The final paragraph is the suggested further reading, if any.

Because records are incomplete, I have dropped the list of casualties of each unit that Dyer includes for the Northern units. But I have added to Dyer's format by including the first commanding officer and the field-grade officers of each unit. Selected bibliographies are included for each volume. Also, as available, unit histories and personal memoirs are listed with some units as suggested further reading.

VIRGINIA UNITS

Virginia seceded from the Union on April 17, 1861. On the same date the Virginia Convention authorized the governor to call into active service as many volunteers as he might deem necessary for the defense of the Old Dominion. The call was not formally issued for another three days. On April 24, 1861, Robert E. Lee was commissioned as the commander of the "military and naval forces of Virginia" with the rank of major general in both the Volunteers and the Provisional Army of Virginia.

The Provisional Army of Virginia was authorized on April 27, 1861. It was intended to be composed of two regiments of artillery, eight regiments of infantry, one regiment of riflemen and one regiment of cavalry. However, only one battalion of infantry and one battery of artillery were ever organized. They eventually became part of the fledgling Provisional Army of the Confederate States.

During April the Virginia forces were placed under the direction of the Confederate president, Jefferson Davis. While the governor transferred these troops formally to Confederate service on June 6, 1861, the order was not carried out until July 1, 1861.

Several specialized types of units were organized for the army. The Confederate Congress passed an act authorizing the creation of Local Defense Troops units on August 21, 1861. However, the Confederate Adjutant and Inspector General's Office did not issue its General Orders #86 outlining the regulations for their organization until June 23, 1863. These units were usually organized on the company and battalion level for defense of the areas in which they were raised. Frequently they were composed of employees of government arsenals, armories, bureaus and so on or from men detailed from regular line units for detached service. Toward the end of the war, some of these units were organized into regiments to be called into active service only when the situation in their vicinity required it.

The State Assembly organized the Virginia State Line on May 15, 1862. It was to be composed of not more than 10,000 men who were not otherwise subject to Confederate conscription, although it never reached this level. Designed to serve under Major General John B. Floyd, its goal was to retake the counties of western Virginia. As many men tried to avoid Confederate service by joining the State Line, there was much conflict between national and state authorities. It was finally disbanded in March 1863; a small remnant was transferred to Confederate service.

The Confederate Congress created the Reserves on February 17, 1864, when it expanded conscription to include all white males between 17 and 50 years of age. Those under 18 and those over 45 were to be organized in the Reserves, troops that did not have to serve beyond the boundaries of the state.

ARTILLERY

1. Virginia 1st Artillery Battalion

Organization: Organized by the change of designation of the 1st Artillery Regiment, which then comprised only Companies B, C and D (they retained these company letters) on September 2, 1864, per S.O. #208, Adjutant and Inspector General's Office. Battalion dissolved on January 18, 1865, per S.O. #14, Adjutant and Inspector General's Office.

First Commander: Edgar F. Moseley (Lieutenant Colonel)

Field Officer: Robert A. Hardaway (Lieutenant Colonel)

2. Virginia 1st Artillery Regiment

Nickname: Virginia 2nd Artillery Regiment

Organization: Organized in September 1861. Reduced to a battalion of three companies and designated as the 1st Artillery Battalion on September 2, 1864, per S.O. #208, Adjutant and Inspector General's Office.

First Commander: George Wythe Randolph (Colonel)

Field Officers: J. Thompson Brown (Major, Lieutenant Colonel, Colonel)
Henry Coalter Cabell (Lieutenant Colonel, Colonel)
Lewis M. Coleman (Major)
Robert A. Hardaway (Major, Lieutenant Colonel)
Edgar F. Moseley (Major, Lieutenant Colonel)
Robert M. Stribling (Major)
David Watson (Major)

See: VIRGINIA ALBEMARLE "EVERETTE" ARTILLERY BATTERY; VIRGINIA BEAUREGARD RIFLES (SCHAEFFER'S) ARTILLERY BATTERY; VIRGINIA HENRICO ARTILLERY; VIRGINIA JAMES CITY ARTILLERY BATTERY; VIRGINIA MONROE "DIXIE" ARTILLERY BATTERY, 2ND AND 3RD COMPANIES; VIRGINIA PENINSULA ARTILLERY BATTERY; VIRGINIA RICHMOND HOWITZERS ARTILLERY BATTALION; VIRGINIA RICHMOND "ORANGE" AND "FAYETTE" ARTILLERY BATTERIES; VIRGINIA WASHINGTON ARTILLERY BATTERY; VIRGINIA WILLIAMSBURG ARTILLERY BATTERY; AND GEORGIA PULASKI ARTILLERY BATTERY.

3. VIRGINIA 1ST (PENDLETON'S) ARTILLERY REGIMENT

Organization: Failed to complete organization and disbanded prior to April 26, 1862.

First Commander: William N. Pendleton (Colonel)

See: VIRGINIA WISE ARTILLERY BATTERY.

4. VIRGINIA 2ND ARTILLERY REGIMENT

Organization: Organized from 10 independent companies in February 1862. Broken up ca. May 23, 1862. Companies A, B, D, E, G and H reorganized as the 22nd Infantry Battalion. Company C became the Southside Artillery Battery. Company F became the Lunenburg Rebel Artillery Battery. Companies I and K disbanded.

First Commander: Robert Tansill (Colonel)

Field Officers: William P. Burwell (Major)

Joseph Panill (Lieutenant Colonel)

5. VIRGINIA 3RD ARTILLERY REGIMENT, LOCAL DEFENSE TROOPS

Also Known As: 2nd Artillery Regiment, Local Defense Troops

Organization: Organized on March 5, 1862. Disbanded in May 1862. Many members reenlisted in the 28th Infantry Battalion.

First Commander: John C. Porter (Colonel)

Field Officers: James B. Dorman (Major)

John C. Shields (Lieutenant Colonel)

Assignment: Field's Brigade, Aquia District, Department of Northern Virginia (April-May 1862)

6. VIRGINIA 4TH ARTILLERY REGIMENT

Organization: Failed to complete its organization.

7. VIRGINIA 4TH HEAVY ARTILLERY BATTALION

Organization: Organized with four companies. Increased to a regiment and designated as the 4th Heavy Artillery Regiment on May 15, 1863, per S.O. #112, Adjutant and Inspector General's Office.

First Commander: Thomas J. Page (Colonel)

8. VIRGINIA 4TH HEAVY ARTILLERY REGIMENT

Organization: Organized in part from the four companies of the 4th Heavy Artillery Battalion on May 15, 1862, per S. O. #112, Adjutant and Inspector General's Office. Converted to infantry service on May 23, 1862, per S.O. #118,

Adjutant and Inspector General's Office. Redesignated as the 34th Infantry Regiment on March 8, 1864, per S.O. #56, Adjutant and Inspector General's Office.

First Commander: John Thomas Goode (Colonel)

Field Officers: John R. Bagby (Major)

Randolph Harrison (Lieutenant Colonel)

J. Wickham Leigh (Major)

Assignments: Rodes' Brigade, D. H. Hill's Division, Department of Northern Virginia (May 1862)

Wise's Brigade, D. H. Hill's Division, Army of Northern Virginia (May-June 1862)

Wise's Brigade, Army of Northern Virginia (June-July 1862)

Wise's Brigade, D. H. Hill's Division, Army of Northern Virginia (July 1862)

Wise's Brigade, Unattached, Department of North Carolina and Southern Virginia (August-December 1862)

Wise's Brigade, Elzey's Command, Department of North Carolina and Southern Virginia (December 1862-April 1863)

Wise's Brigade, Department of Richmond (April-September 1863)

Wise's Brigade, 1st Military District of South Carolina, Department of South Carolina, Georgia and Florida (September-October 1863)

6th Military District of South Carolina, Department of South Carolina, Georgia and Florida (October-November 1863)

Wise's Brigade, 6th Military District of South Carolina, Department of South Carolina, Georgia and Florida (December 1863-March 1864)

Battles: Seven Days Battles (June 25-July 1, 1862)

Charleston Harbor (August-September 1863)

9. VIRGINIA 10TH HEAVY ARTILLERY BATTALION

Organization: Organized with five companies on April 4, 1862. Surrendered at Appomattox Court House, Virginia on April 9, 1865.

First Commander: William Allen (Major)

Field Officer: James O. Hensley (Major)

Assignments: Forces at Williamsburg (B. S. Ewell's Command), Magruder's Command, Department of Northern Virginia (April-May 1862)

1st Division, Inner Line, Richmond Defenses, Department of Richmond (May 1863-December 1864)

Artillery Defenses, Department of Richmond (December 1864-April 1865)

Crutchfield's Brigade, G. W. C. Lee's Division, Army of Northern Virginia (April 1865)

Battles: Yorktown Siege (April-May 1862)

Petersburg Siege (June 1864-April 1865)

Roper's Farm (September 30, 1864)
Sayler's Creek (April 6, 1865)
Appomattox Court House (April 9, 1865)

10. VIRGINIA 12TH LIGHT ARTILLERY BATTALION

Organization: Organized with four companies on May 15, 1862, per S.O.
#112, Adjutant and Inspector General's Office. 1st Company A became an
independent battery in the summer of 1862. Company C became an independent battery in the summer of 1862. 2nd Company A assigned prior to April
30, 1863. Company D became Company A, 13th North Carolina Light Artillery Battalion, on November 4, 1863. Dissolved on January 11, 1865, per S.O.
#8, Adjutant and Inspector General's Office.
First Commander: Francis J. Boggs (Major)

11. VIRGINIA 12TH LIGHT ARTILLERY BATTALION, COMPANY A (1ST)

See: VIRGINIA WARRENTON ARTILLERY BATTERY

12. VIRGINIA 12TH LIGHT ARTILLERY BATTALION, COMPANY A (2ND)

See: VIRGINIA ALBEMARLE ARTILLERY BATTERY

13. VIRGINIA 12TH LIGHT ARTILLERY BATTALION, COMPANY B

See: VIRGINIA RICHMOND "MARTIN" ARTILLERY BATTERY

14. VIRGINIA 12TH LIGHT ARTILLERY BATTALION, COMPANY C

See: VIRGINIA BATH ARTILLERY BATTERY

15. VIRGINIA 12TH LIGHT ARTILLERY BATTALION, COMPANY D

See: NORTH CAROLINA 13TH LIGHT ARTILLERY BATTALION, COMPANY A

16. VIRGINIA 13TH LIGHT ARTILLERY BATTALION

Organization: Organized with three companies in late 1863. Surrendered at
Appomattox Court House, Virginia, on April 9, 1865.
First Commander: J. Floyd King (Lieutenant Colonel)
Field Officers: Wade G. Gibbes (Major)
William M. Owen (Major)

17. VIRGINIA 13TH LIGHT ARTILLERY BATTALION, COMPANY A

Nickname: Virginia Richmond "Otey" Artillery Battery

Organization: Organized by the assignment of the Richmond "Otey" Artillery Battery in late 1863. Armed with four 12-lb. Napoleons on December 28, 1864. Also served three Coehorn mortars on December 30, 1864. Served as infantry during the Appomattox Campaign. Captured as part of Walker's artillery column on April 8, 1865. Part of the battery surrendered at Appomattox Court House, Virginia, on April 9, 1865.

First Commander: David Norvell Walker (Captain)

Assignments: King's Artillery Battalion, Ransom's Division, Department of Southwestern Virginia and East Tennessee (October 1863-February 1864)

King's Battalion, Artillery, Department of East Tennessee (February-April 1864)

Gibbes' Battalion, Artillery, Breckinridge's Division, Army of Northern Virginia (May-June 1864)

Gibbes'-Owen's Battalion, Artillery, 1st Corps, Army of Northern Virginia (June-October 1864)

Owen's-Walker's Battalion, Artillery, 3rd Corps, Army of Northern Virginia (October 1864-April 1865)

Battles: Cold Harbor (June 1864)

Petersburg Siege (June 1864-April 1865)

Appomattox Campaign (March-April 1865)

18. VIRGINIA 13TH LIGHT ARTILLERY BATTALION, COMPANY B

Nickname: Virginia Danville "Ringgold" Artillery Battery

Organization: Organized by the assignment of the Danville "Ringgold" Artillery Battery in late 1863. Armed with three 12-lb. Napoleons and one 3-inch Rifle on May 9, 1864. Armed with four 12-lb. Napoleons on December 28, 1865. Converted to heavy artillery in early 1865. Served armed as infantry during the Appomattox Campaign. Surrendered at Appomattox Court House, Virginia on April 9, 1865.

First Commander: Crispin Dickenson (Captain)

Assignments: Artillery Battalion, Ransom's Division, Department of Western Virginia and East Tennessee (December 1863-February 1864)

King's Battalion, Artillery, Department of East Tennessee (February-May 1864)

Artillery Battalion, Breckinridge's Division, Valley District, Department of Northern Virginia (May 1864)

Artillery Battalion, Breckinridge's Division, Army of Northern Virginia (May-June 1864)

Gibbes'-Owen's Battalion, Artillery, 1st Corps, Army of Northern Virginia (June-October 1864)

Gibbes'-Owen's Battalion, Artillery, 3rd Corps, Army of Northern Virginia
   (October 1864-February 1865)
King's Battalion, Artillery, 1st Corps, Army of Northern Virginia (February-
   April 1865)
Battles: Cloyd's Mountain (May 9, 1864)
New River Bridge (May 10, 1864)
Cold Harbor (June 1-3, 1864)
Petersburg Siege (June 1864-April 1865)
Appomattox Court House (April 9, 1865)

19.   VIRGINIA 13TH LIGHT ARTILLERY BATTALION, COMPANY C

Nickname: Virginia Lynchburg Artillery Battery
Organization: Organized in late 1863. Surrendered at Appomattox Court
House, Virginia, on April 9, 1865.
Battles: Petersburg Siege (June 1864-April 1865)
Appomattox Court House (April 9, 1865)

20.   VIRGINIA 18TH HEAVY ARTILLERY BATTALION

Organization: Organized with four companies on June 21, 1862, per S.O.
#143, Adjutant and Inspector General's Office. Alexandria Artillery assigned
as Company E on January 23, 1864, per S.O. #19, Adjutant and Inspector
General's Office, dated January 24, 1864. Surrendered at Appomattox Court
House, Virginia, on April 9, 1865.
First Commander: James Howard (Lieutenant Colonel)
Field Officer: Mark B. Hardin (Major)
Assignments: 2nd Division, Inner Line, Richmond Defenses, Department of
   Richmond (May 1863-December 1864)
Artillery Defenses, Department of Richmond (December 1864-April 1865)
Crutchfield's Brigade, G. W. C. Lee's Division, Army of Northern Virginia
   (April 1865)
Battles: Petersburg Siege (June 1864-April 1865)
Sayler's Creek (April 6, 1865)
Appomattox Court House (April 9, 1865)

21.   VIRGINIA 19TH HEAVY ARTILLERY BATTALION

Organization: Organized with four companies on June 21, 1862, per S.O.
#143, Adjutant and Inspector General's Office. 1st Company C detached as
the United Artillery on October 1, 1862, per S.O. #92, Headquarters, Richmond Defenses. Maryland Light Artillery assigned as 2nd Company C on
November 3, 1862. Whittington's Battery Light Artillery assigned to the
battalion on December 13, 1862, as Company E and eventually designated as

3rd Company C. 2nd Company C disbanded in February 1863. Surrendered at Appomattox Court House, Virginia, on April 9, 1865.

First Commander: John W. Atkinson (Major, Lieutenant Colonel)

Field Officer: Nathaniel R. Cary (Major)

Assignments: 1st Division, Inner Line, Richmond Defenses, Department of Richmond (May 1863-December 1864)

Artillery Defenses, Department of Richmond (December 1864-April 1865)

Crutchfield's Brigade, G. W. C. Lee's Division, Army of Northern Virginia (April 1865)

Battles: Petersburg Siege (June 1864-April 1865)

Roper's Farm (September 30, 1864)

Sayler's Creek (April 6, 1865)

Appomattox Court House (April 9, 1865)

22. VIRGINIA 20TH HEAVY ARTILLERY BATTALION

Organization: Organized with four companies on June 21, 1862, per S.O. #143, Adjutant and Inspector General's Office. Surrendered at Appomattox Court House, Virginia, on April 9, 1865.

First Commander: Arthur S. Cunningham (Lieutenant Colonel) (temporary)

Field Officers: Johnston DeLagnel (Major)

James E. Robertson (Major)

Assignments: 2nd Division, Inner Line, Richmond Defenses, Department of Richmond (May 1863-December 1864)

Artillery Defenses, Department of Richmond (December 1864-April 1865)

Crutchfield's Brigade, G. W. C. Lee's Division, Army of Northern Virginia (April 1865)

Battles: Petersburg Siege (June 1864-April 1865)

Sayler's Creek (April 6, 1865)

Appomattox Court House (April 9, 1865)

23. VIRGINIA 28TH HEAVY ARTILLERY BATTALION

See: VIRGINIA 28TH INFANTRY BATTALION

24. VIRGINIA 38TH LIGHT ARTILLERY BATTALION

Organization: Organized with four companies ca. June 1863. Surrendered at Appomattox Court House, Virginia, on April 9, 1865.

First Commander: James Dearing (Major, Lieutenant Colonel)

Field Officers: Joseph Grey Blount (Major)

John Postell Williamson Read (Major, Lieutenant Colonel)

Robert Mackey Stribling (Major, Lieutenant Colonel)

25. VIRGINIA 38TH LIGHT ARTILLERY BATTALION, COMPANY A

Nickname: Virginia Fauquier Artillery Battery

Organization: Organized by the assignment of the Fauquier Artillery Battery ca. June 1863. Armed with two 20-lb. Parrotts and four 12-lb. Napoleons from July 1, 1863, to December 28, 1864. Surrendered at Appomattox Court House, Virginia, on April 9, 1865.

First Commander: Robert M. Stribling (Captain)

Captain: William C. Marshall

Assignments: Artillery Battalion, Pickett's Division, 1st Corps, Army of Northern Virginia (June-July 1863)

Dearing's Battalion, Artillery, 1st Corps, Army of Northern Virginia (July-September 1863)

Artillery Battalion, Pickett's Division, Department of North Carolina (September-December 1863)

Dearing's Artillery Battalion, Department of North Carolina (December 1863-May 1864)

Artillery Battalion, Whiting's Division, Department of North Carolina and Southern Virginia (May 1864)

Artillery Battalion, Hoke's Division, Department of North Carolina and Southern Virginia (May-June 1864)

Read's Artillery Battalion, Department of North Carolina and Southern Virginia (June-October 1864)

Read's-Stribling's Artillery Battalion, 4th Corps, Army of Northern Virginia (October 1864-April 1865)

Battles: Gettysburg (July 1-3, 1863)

Plymouth Expedition (April 17-20, 1864)

Bermuda Hundred (May 17-June 14, 1864)

Cold Harbor (June 1-3, 1864)

Petersburg Siege (June 1864-April 1865)

Petersburg (June 17, 1864)

Appomattox Court House (April 9, 1865)

Further Reading: Chamberlayne, Edwin H., *War History and Roll of the Richmond Fayette Artillery, 38th Virginia Battalion Artillery, Confederate States Army, 1861-1865.*

26. VIRGINIA 38TH LIGHT ARTILLERY BATTALION, COMPANY B

Nickname: Virginia Richmond "Fayette" Artillery Battery

Organization: Organized by the assignment of the Richmond "Fayette" Artillery Battery ca. June 1863. Armed with two 10-lb. Parrotts and two 12-lb. Napoleons on July 1-3, 1863. Armed with two 10-lb. Parrotts and two 3-inch

Rifles on December 26, 1864. Surrendered at Appomattox Court House, Virginia, on April 9, 1865.

First Commander: Miles C. Macon (Captain)

Assignments: Artillery Battalion, Pickett's Division, 1st Corps, Army of Northern Virginia (June-July 1863)

Dearing's Battalion, Artillery, 1st Corps, Army of Northern Virginia (July-September 1863)

Artillery Battalion, Pickett's Division, Department of North Carolina (September-December 1863)

Dearing's Artillery Battalion, Department of North Carolina (December 1863-May 1864)

Artillery Battalion, Whiting's Division, Department of North Carolina and Southern Virginia (May 1864)

Artillery Battalion, Hoke's Division, Department of North Carolina and Southern Virginia (May-June 1864)

Read's Artillery Battalion, Department of North Carolina and Southern Virginia (June-October 1864)

Read's-Stribling's Artillery Battalion, 4th Corps, Army of Northern Virginia (October 1864-April 1865)

Battles: Gettysburg (July 1-3, 1863)
Plymouth Expedition (April 17-20, 1864)
Bermuda Hundred (May 17-June 14, 1864)
Cold Harbor (June 1-3, 1864)
Petersburg Siege (June 1864-April 1865)
Petersburg (June 17, 1864)
Appomattox Court House (April 9, 1865)

27. VIRGINIA 38TH LIGHT ARTILLERY BATTALION, COMPANY C

Nicknames: Virginia Richmond "Hampden" Artillery Battery
Virginia Richmond "Hampden" Light Artillery Battery

Organization: Organized by the assignment of the Richmond "Hampden" Artillery Battery ca. June 1863. Armed with one 10-lb. Parrott, one 3-inch Rifle, and two 12-lb. Napoleons on July 1-3, 1863. Armed with four 12-lb. Napoleons on December 26, 1864. Surrendered at Appomattox Court House, Virginia, on April 9, 1865.

First Commander: William Henderson Caskie (Captain)

Captain: John E. Sullivan

Assignments: Artillery Battalion, Pickett's Division, 1st Corps, Army of Northern Virginia (June-July 1863)

Dearing's Battalion, Artillery, 1st Corps, Army of Northern Virginia (July-September 1863)

Artillery Battalion, Pickett's Division, Department of North Carolina (September-December 1863)

Dearing's Artillery Battalion, Department of North Carolina (December 1863-May 1864)

Artillery Battalion, Whiting's Division, Department of North Carolina and Southern Virginia (May 1864)

Artillery Battalion, Hoke's Division, Department of North Carolina and Southern Virginia (May-June 1864)

Read's Artillery Battalion, Department of North Carolina and Southern Virginia (June-October 1864)

Read's-Stribling's Artillery Battalion, 4th Corps, Army of Northern Virginia (October 1864-April 1865)

Battles: Gettysburg (July 1-3, 1863)

Plymouth Expedition (April 17-20, 1864)

Bermuda Hundred (May 17-June 14, 1864)

Cold Harbor (June 1-3, 1864)

Petersburg Siege (June 1864-April 1865)

Petersburg (June 17, 1864)

Appomattox Court House (April 9, 1865)

28. VIRGINIA 38TH LIGHT ARTILLERY BATTALION, COMPANY D

Nickname: Virginia Lynchburg Artillery Battery

Organization: Organized by the assignment of the Lynchburg Artillery Battery ca. June 1863. Armed with four 12-lb. Napoleons from July 1, 1863, to December 26, 1864. Surrendered at Appomattox Court House, Virginia, on April 9, 1865.

First Commander: James Dearing (Captain)

Captains: Joseph Grey Blount

James Woodson Dickerson

Assignments: Artillery Battalion, Pickett's Division, 1st Corps, Army of Northern Virginia (June-July 1863)

Dearing's Battalion, Artillery, 1st Corps, Army of Northern Virginia (July-September 1863)

Artillery Battalion, Pickett's Division, Department of North Carolina (September-December 1863)

Dearing's Artillery Battalion, Department of North Carolina (December 1863-May 1864)

Artillery Battalion, Whiting's Division, Department of North Carolina and Southern Virginia (May 1864)

Artillery Battalion, Hoke's Division, Department of North Carolina and
Southern Virginia (May-June 1864)

Read's Artillery Battalion, Department of North Carolina and Southern Virginia (June-October 1864)

Read's-Stribling's Artillery Battalion, 4th Corps, Army of Northern Virginia
(October 1864-April 1865)

Battles: Gettysburg (July 1-3, 1863)
Suffolk Campaign (April-May 1863)
Plymouth Expedition (April 17-20, 1864)
Bermuda Hundred (May 17-June 14, 1864)
Cold Harbor (June 1-3, 1864)
Petersburg Siege (June 1864-April 1865)
Petersburg (June 17, 1864)
Appomattox Court House (April 9, 1865)

29. VIRGINIA ADAMS' ARTILLERY BATTERY

Organization: Organized on June 22, 1861. Surrendered at Fort Donelson on
February 16, 1862. Exchanged in the summer of 1862. Reorganized on August
24, 1862. Became Company A, 30th Sharpshooters Battalion, on September
1, 1862.

First Commander: Stephen Adams (Captain)

Assignment: Army of the Kanawha, Department of Northern Virginia (December 1861)

Battle: Fort Donelson (February 12-16, 1862)

30. VIRGINIA ALBEMARLE ARTILLERY BATTERY

Organization: Organized for the war in Albemarle County on March 19,
1862. Assigned as 2nd Company A, 12th Light Artillery Battalion, prior to
April 30, 1863. Armed with four 12-lb. Napoleons on December 28, 1864. Also
manned two 8-inch Mortars, seven 12-lb. Mortars and five 24-lb. Coehorn
Mortars on December 30, 1864. Again became an independent unit on January
11, 1865, per S.O. #8, Adjutant and Inspector General's Office. Captured as
part of Walker's artillery column on April 8, 1865.

First Commander: Nathaniel A. Sturdivant (Captain)

Assignments: Unattached Artillery, French's Command, Department of
North Carolina and Southern Virginia (February-April 1863)

Boggs' Artillery Battalion, Department of Southern Virginia (April-May 1863)

Boggs' Battalion, Artillery, Ransom's Division, Department of Richmond (July-
September 1863)

Boggs' Battalion, Artillery, Department of North Carolina (December 1863-
January 1864)

Boggs' Artillery Battalion, District of the Cape Fear (January-February 1864)

1st Military District, Department of North Carolina and Southern Virginia (June 1864)

Boggs' Battalion, Artillery, Department of North Carolina and Southern Virginia (June-October 1864)

Boggs'-Sturdivant's Battalion, Artillery, 4th Corps, Army of Northern Virginia (October 1864-April 1865)

Battles: Petersburg (June 9, 1864)

Petersburg Siege (June 1864-April 1865)

Appomattox Campaign (March-April 1865)

31. VIRGINIA ALBEMARLE "EVERETTE" ARTILLERY BATTERY

Organization: Organized at Charlottesville in June or early July 1861. Served as Company H, 1st Artillery Regiment, until December 31, 1862. Armed with two 3-inch Rifles, one 12-lb. Howitzer and one 10-lb. Parrott on July 1-3, 1863. Armed with two 10-lb. Parrotts and one 12-lb. Napoleon on December 28, 1864. Surrendered at Appomattox Court House, Virginia, on April 9, 1865.

First Commander: William H. Southall (Captain)

Captains: James Walter Wyatt

Charles F. Johnston

Assignments: Artillery, Department of the Peninsula (October 1861-January 1862)

Brown's Battalion, Reserve Artillery, Army of Northern Virginia (July 1862)

Artillery Battalion, Pender's Division, 3rd Corps, Army of Northern Virginia (June-July 1863)

Poague's Battalion, Artillery, 3rd Corps, Army of Northern Virginia (July 1863-April 1865)

Battles: Yorktown Siege (April-May 1862)

New Bern (March 14, 1862)

Gettysburg (July 1-3, 1863)

Falling Waters (July 14, 1863)

Bristoe Campaign (October 1863)

Mine Run Campaign (November-December 1863)

The Wilderness (May 5-6, 1864)

Spotsylvania Court House (May 8-21, 1864)

North Anna (May 23-26, 1864)

Cold Harbor (June 1-3, 1864)

Petersburg Siege (June 1864-April 1865)

Appomattox Court House (April 9, 1865)

32. VIRGINIA ALEXANDRIA ARTILLERY BATTERY

Organization: Organized at Alexandria March 15, 1861. Mustered into state service for one year on April 17, 1861. Armed with four 6-lb. Smoothbores from May 8, to June 17, 1861. Mustered into Confederate service for one year on June 30, 1861. Converted to heavy artillery service and assigned as Company E, 18th Heavy Artillery Battalion, on January 23, 1864, per S.O. #19, Adjutant and Inspector General's Office.

First Commander: Delaware Kemper (Captain)

Captain: David L. Smoot

Assignments: Department of Alexandria (April-June 1861)

Bonham's Brigade, Army of the Potomac (June-July 1861).

Bonham's Brigade, 1st Corps, Army of the Potomac (July-October 1861)

Bonham's Brigade, 3rd Division, 1st Corps, Army of the Potomac (October 1861)

Bonham's Brigade, 3rd Division, 1st Corps, October-November 1861

Bonham's Brigade, Van Dorn's Division, 1st Corps, Potomac District, Department of Northern Virginia (November 1861-January 1862)

Bonham's-Kershaw's Brigade, Van Dorn's Division, Potomac District, Department of Northern Virginia (January-March 1862)

Kershaw's Brigade, McLaws' Division, Magruder's Command, Army of Northern Virginia (April-July 1862)

Kershaw's Brigade, McLaws' Division, 1st Corps, Army of Northern Virginia (July 1862)

Lightfoot's Light Artillery Battalion, Richmond Defenses, Department of Richmond (July-September 1863)

Stark's Artillery Battalion, Chaffin's Farm Department of Richmond (October 1863-February 1864)

Battles: near Vienna [section] (June 17, 1861)

Blackburn's Ford (July 18, 1861)

1st Bull Run (July 21, 1861)

Yorktown Siege (April-May 1862)

Williamsburg (May 5, 1862)

Seven Days Battles (June 25-July 1, 1862)

Allen's Farm (June 26, 1862)

Savage Station (June 29, 1862)

Malvern Hill (July 1, 1862)

Suffolk Campaign (April-May 1863)

Fort Huger (April 13, 1863)

33. VIRGINIA ALLEGHANY ARTILLERY BATTERY

Nickname: Alleghany Roughs

Organization: Organized by the conversion of Company A, 27th Infantry Regiment, to artillery service ca. November 1861. Reorganized on April 22, 1862. Armed with four 3-inch Rifles in April and May 1862. Armed with two 3-inch Rifles and two 12-lb. Napoleons on September 17, 1862. Armed with two 3-inch Rifles and two 12-lb. Napoleons on July 1-3, 1863. Armed with two 12-lb. Napoleons on December 28, 1864. Surrendered at Appomattox Court House, Virginia, on April 9, 1865.

First Commander: Joseph Carpenter (Captain)

Captain: John C. Carpenter

Assignments: Artillery, Valley District, Department of Northern Virginia (November 1861-January 1862)

Stonewall Brigade, Valley District, Department of Northern Virginia (March-May 1862)

Artillery Battalion, Jackson's Division, Valley District, Department of Northern Virginia (May-June 1862)

Stonewall Brigade, Jackson's Division, 2nd Corps, Army of Northern Virginia (June-July 1862)

Artillery Battalion, Jackson's-Johnson's Division, 2nd Corps, Army of Northern Virginia (August 1862-July 1863)

Andrews'-Braxton's Battalion, Artillery, 2nd Corps, Army of Northern Virginia (July 1863-June 1864)

Braxton's Battalion, Artillery, Valley District, Department of Northern Virginia (June 1864-March 1865)

Braxton's Battalion, Artillery, 2nd Corps, Army of Northern Virginia (March-April 1865)

Battles: Shenandoah Valley Campaign of 1862 (May-June 1862)

Seven Days Battles (June 25-July 1, 1862)

White Oak Swamp (June 30, 1862)

Malvern Hill (July 1, 1862)

Cedar Mountain (August 9, 1862)

Cunningham's Ford (August 21, 1862)

2nd Bull Run (August 28-30, 1862)

Antietam (September 17, 1862)

near Kearneysville, Maryland (October 17, 1862)

Fredericksburg (December 13, 1862)

Chancellorsville (May 1-4, 1863)

2nd Winchester (June 14-15, 1863)

Gettysburg (July 1-3, 1863)

Bristoe Campaign (October 1863)

Mine Run Campaign (November-December 1863)

The Wilderness (May 5-6, 1864)

Spotsylvania Court House (May 8-21, 1864)
North Anna (May 23-26, 1864)
Cold Harbor (June 1-3, 1864)
Lynchburg Campaign (June 1864)
Monocacy (July 9, 1864)
3rd Winchester (September 19, 1864)
Fisher's Hill (September 22, 1864)
Cedar Creek (October 19, 1864)
Waynesborough (March 2, 1865)
Petersburg Siege (June 1864-April 1865)
Appomattox Court House (April 9, 1865)
Further Reading: Fonerden, Clarence A., *A Brief History of the Military Career of Carpenter's Battery.*

34.   VIRGINIA AMHERST ARTILLERY BATTERY

Organization: Organized for one year in Amherst County on July 24, 1861. Reorganized on May 15, 1862. Armed with two 12-lb. Howitzers and four 6-lb. Smoothbores on September 17-20, 1862. Hanover and Middlesex Artillery Batteries disbanded and some of the men transferred to this battery on October 4, 1862, per S.O. #209, Headquarters, Army of Northern Virginia. Armed with three 12-lb. Napoleons on July 1-3, 1863. Armed with two 12-lb. Napoleons and one 3-inch Rifle on December 28, 1864. No record after March 1865.

First Commander: Thomas Jellis Kirkpatrick (Captain)

Assignments: Reserve Artillery, Potomac District, Department of Northern Virginia (November 1861-March 1862)

Reserve Artillery, Department of Northern Virginia (March-June 1862)

Nelson's Battalion, Reserve Artillery, Army of Northern Virginia (June 1862-June 1863)

Nelson's Battalion, Reserve Artillery, 2nd Corps, Army of Northern Virginia (June-July 1863)

Nelson's Battalion, Artillery, 2nd Corps, Army of Northern Virginia (July 1863-June 1864)

Nelson's Battalion, Artillery, Valley District, Department of Northern Virginia (June 1864-March 1865)

Battles: Yorktown Siege (April-May 1862)

Seven Days Battles (June 25-July 1, 1862)

Shepherdstown Ford (September 20, 1862)

Fredericksburg (December 13, 1862)

Chancellorsville (May 1-4, 1863)

Gettysburg (July 1-3, 1863)

Bristoe Campaign (October 1863)

Mine Run Campaign (November-December 1863)
The Wilderness (May 5-6, 1864)
Spotsylvania Court House (May 8-21, 1864)
North Anna (May 23-26, 1864)
Cold Harbor (June 1-3, 1864)
Lynchburg Campaign (June 1864)
Monocacy (July 9, 1864)
3rd Winchester (September 19, 1864)
Fisher's Hill (September 22, 1864)
Cedar Creek (October 19, 1864)
Waynesborough (March 2, 1865)

35. VIRGINIA AMHERST-NELSON LIGHT ARTILLERY BATTERY

Organization: Organized for one year in Amherst and Nelson counties on September 3, 1861. Reorganized May 7, 1862. Unarmed during the early part of October 1863. Armed with 26 mortars on December 28, 1864. Surrendered at Appomattox Court House, Virginia, on April 9, 1865.

First Commander: Woodville Latham (Captain)

Captain: James Nelson Lamkin

Assignments: Cocke's [old] Brigade, Longstreet's Division, Potomac District, Department of Northern Virginia (January 1862)

2nd Military District of South Carolina, Department of South Carolina and Georgia (April-July 1862)

1st Military District of South Carolina, Department of South Carolina, Georgia and Florida (July-December 1862)

3rd Military District of South Carolina, Department of South Carolina, Georgia and Florida (December 1862-September 1863)

Henry's-Haskell's Battalion, Reserve Artillery, Army of Northern Virginia (October 1863)

Cabell's Battalion, Reserve Artillery, Army of Northern Virginia (October-November 1863)

Haskell's Battalion, Artillery, 3rd Corps, Army of Northern Virginia (December 1863-April 1864)

Haskell's Battalion, Artillery, 1st Corps, Army of Northern Virginia (April 1864-April 1865)

Battles: Bristoe Campaign (October 1863)

Mine Run Campaign (November-December 1863)

The Wilderness (May 5-6, 1864)

Spotsylvania Court House (May 8-21, 1864)

North Anna (May 23-26, 1864)

Cold Harbor (June 1-3, 1864)

Petersburg Siege (June 1864-April 1865)
Appomattox Court House (April 9, 1865)

36. VIRGINIA ARNOLD'S ARTILLERY BATTERY

Organization: Organized on February 10, 1862. Mustered into Confederate service as a cavalry company and designated as Company C,. 15th Cavalry Battalion. Does not appear in the *Official Records*.
First Commander: Mark Arnold (Captain)

37. VIRGINIA ASHBY HORSE ARTILLERY BATTERY

Organization: Organized at Flowing Spring, Jefferson County, on November 13, 1861. Reorganized on May 19, 1862. Temporarily disbanded on January 16, 1865, with orders to reassemble on April 1, 1865, at Lynchburg. Armed with one 3-inch Rifle, one 12-lb. Howitzer, and one 3.1-inch Blakely Rifle from March 23, 1862, to April 9, 1865. Surrendered at Appomattox Court House, Virginia, on April 9, 1865.
First Commander: Roger Preston Chew (Captain)
Captains: James Walton Thomson
John W. Carter
Assignments: Cavalry, Valley District, Department of Northern Virginia (December 1861-May 1862)
Cavalry, Jackson's Division, Valley District, Department of Northern Virginia (May-June 1862)
Cavalry Brigade, Valley District, Department of Northern Virginia (June-July 1862)
Horse Artillery Battalion, Cavalry Division, Army of Northern Virginia (August 1862-September 1863)
Horse Artillery Battalion, Cavalry Corps, Army of Northern Virginia (September 1863-May 1864)
Horse Artillery Battalion, Rosser's Cavalry Division, Valley District, Department of Northern Virginia (September 1864-March 1865)
Thomson's Battalion, Horse Artillery, Cavalry Corps, Army of Northern Virginia (March 1865)
Breathed's Battalion, Horse Artillery, Cavalry Corps, Army of Northern Virginia (March-April 1865)
Battles: Kernstown (March 23, 1862)
Shenandoah Valley Campaign of 1862 (May-June 1862)
2nd Bull Run (August 28-30, 1862)
Antietam (September 17, 1862)
Charlestown, West Virginia (October 16, 1862)
Fredericksburg (December 13, 1862)

Chancellorsville (May 1-4, 1863)
Brandy Station (June 9, 1863)
Gettysburg (July 1-3, 1863)
Funkstown and Boonesborough (July 6-10, 1863)
Stanardsville, Virginia (February 29, 1864)
Petersburg Siege (June 1864-April 1865)
Cedar Creek (October 19, 1864)
Expedition to Moorefield and Petersburg, West Virginia (January 2-5, 1865)
Appomattox Court House (April 9, 1865)
Further Reading: Neese, George Michael, *Three Years in the Confederate Horse Artillery.*

38.   VIRGINIA ASHLAND ARTILLERY BATTERY

Organization: Organized for one year in Hanover County on August 14, 1861. Reorganized in the spring of 1862. Some of the men of the disbanded Nelson Artillery Battery and the Middlesex Artillery Battery transferred to this battery on October 4, 1862, per S.O. #209, Headquarters, Army of Northern Virginia. Armed with two 20-lb. Parrotts and two 12-lb. Napoleons from July 1, 1863, to December 26, 1864. Reenlisted for the war on January 12, 1864. Surrendered at Appomattox Court House, Virginia, on April 9, 1865.

First Commander: Pichegru Woolfolk, Jr. (Captain)

Assignments: Reserve Artillery, Potomac District, Department of Northern Virginia (January-March 1862)

Reserve Artillery, Army of Northern Virginia (March-June 1862)

Richardson's Battalion, Reserve Artillery, Army of Northern Virginia (June-July 1862)

Lee's-Alexander's Battalion, Reserve Artillery, 1st Corps, Army of Northern Virginia (September 1862-July 1863)

Alexander's Battalion, Artillery, 1st Corps (July-September 1863)

Alexander's Artillery Battalion, Longstreet's Corps, Army of Tennessee (September-November 1863)

Alexander's Artillery Battalion, Department of East Tennessee (November 1863-April 1864)

Alexander's-Huger's Battalion, Artillery, 1st Corps, Army of Northern Virginia (April 1864-April 1865)

Battles: Yorktown Siege (April-May 1862)

Seven Days Battles (June 25-July 1, 1862)

Antietam (September 17, 1862)

Fredericksburg (December 13, 1862)

Chancellorsville (May 1-4, 1863)

Gettysburg (July 1-3, 1863)

Chattanooga Siege (September-November 1863)
Knoxville Siege (November 1863)
Campbell's Station (November 16, 1863)
The Wilderness (May 5-6, 1864)
Spotsylvania Court House (May 8-21, 1864)
North Anna (May 23-26, 1864)
Cold Harbor (June 1-3, 1864)
Petersburg Siege (June 1864-April 1865)
Appomattox Court House (April 9, 1865)

39. VIRGINIA BAPTIST COLLEGE ARTILLERY BATTALION

Organization: Organized as a temporary command with three companies at Richmond in 1861. Was soon broken up.
First Commander: Thomas Henry Carter (Captain)
See: VIRGINIA FLUVANNA ARTILLERY BATTERY, NO. 1; VIRGINIA KING WILLIAM ARTILLERY BATTERY; VIRGINIA RICHMOND "COURTNEY" ARTILLERY BATTERY

40. VIRGINIA BATH ARTILLERY BATTERY

Organization: Organized for three years or the war on March 22, 1862. Assigned as Company C, 12th Artillery Battalion, on May 15, 1862 per S.O. #112, Adjutant and Inspector General's Office. Regained its independent status during the late summer of 1862. Armed with one 3-inch Rifle, one 12-lb. Howitzer and one 6-lb. Smoothbore in August and September 1862. Men from the disbanded Wise Artillery Battery transferred to this battery on October 4, 1862, per S.O. #209, Headquarters Army of Northern Virginia. Armed with four 12-lb. Napoleons from July 1, 1863, to December 28, 1864. Surrendered at Appomattox Court House, Virginia, on April 9, 1865.
First Commander: John Lewis Eubank (Captain)
Captain: Osmond B. Taylor
Assignments: Lee's-Alexander's Battalion, Reserve Artillery, 1st Corps, Army of Northern Virginia (August 1862-July 1863)
Alexander's Battalion, Artillery, 1st Corps (July-September 1863)
Alexander's Artillery Battalion, Longstreet's Corps, Army of Tennessee (September-November 1863)
Alexander's Artillery Battalion, Department of East Tennessee (November 1863-April 1864)
Alexander's-Huger's Battalion, Artillery, 1st Corps, Army of Northern Virginia (April 1864-April 1865)
Battles: 2nd Bull Run (August 28-30, 1862)
Antietam (September 17, 1862)

Fredericksburg (December 13, 1862)
Chancellorsville (May 1-4, 1863)
Gettysburg (July 1-3, 1863)
Chattanooga Siege (September-November 1863)
Knoxville Siege (November 1863)
The Wilderness (May 5-6, 1864)
Spotsylvania Court House (May 8-21, 1864)
North Anna (May 23-26, 1864)
Cold Harbor (June 1-3, 1864)
Petersburg Siege (June 1864-April 1865)
Appomattox Court House (April 9, 1865)

41. VIRGINIA BAYLEY'S HEAVY ARTILLERY BATTERY

Organization: Organized on April 28, 1862. Disbanded and the men transferred to the King William Artillery Battery on June 17, 1862, per S.O. #136, Headquarters, Department of Northern Virginia. Does not appear in the *Official Records.*
First Commander: Samuel T. Bayley (Captain)

42. VIRGINIA BEAUREGARD RIFLES ARTILLERY BATTERY

See: VIRGINIA LYNCHBURG "BEAUREGARD RIFLES" ARTILLERY BATTERY

43. VIRGINIA BEAUREGARD RIFLES (SCHAEFFER'S) ARTILLERY BATTERY

Organization: Organized by the conversion of Company F, 1st Infantry Regiment, to artillery service in September 1861 per order of General Joseph E. Johnston, commanding the Army of the Potomac. Served as 1st Company C, 1st Artillery Regiment. Disbanded on November 5, 1861. Does not appear in the *Official Records.*
First Commander: Frank B. Schaeffer (Captain)

44. VIRGINIA BEDFORD ARTILLERY BATTERY

Organization: Organized by the conversion of 1st Company C, 28th Infantry Regiment, to artillery service in August 1861. Reorganized on April 12, 1862. Disbanded with some men transferred to the Richmond "Purcell" Artillery Battery and some to the Lynchburg Artillery Battery on October 4, 1862, per S.O. #209, Headquarters, Army of Northern Virginia.
First Commander: Thomas M. Bowyer (Captain)
Captain: John Richard Johnson
Assignments: Department of the Peninsula (January-February 1862)

Taylor's Brigade, E. K. Smith's-Ewell's Division, Potomac District, Department
  of Northern Virginia (January-March 1862)
Artillery Battalion, Ewell's Division, 2nd Corps, Army of Northern Virginia
  (July-October 1862)
Battles: Cedar Mountain (August 9, 1862)
2nd Bull Run (August 28-30, 1862)
Antietam (September 17, 1862)

45. VIRGINIA BEDFORD LIGHT ARTILLERY BATTERY

Organization: Organized in Bedford County on January 22, 1861. Enlisted for
one year on May 8, 1861. Reorganized during the spring of 1862. Armed with
three 24-lb. Howitzers and one 12-lb. Napoleon on June 24, 1862. Some men
from the disbanded "Magruder" Artillery transferred to this battery on October
4, 1862, per S.O. #209, Headquarters, Army of Northern Virginia. Armed with
four 3-inch Rifles from July 1, 1863, to December 28, 1864. Surrendered at
Appomattox Court House, Virginia, on April 9, 1865.
First Commander: Tyler C. Jordan (Captain)
Captain: John Donnell Smith
Assignments: Cobb's Brigade, Magruder's Division, Army of Northern Vir-
  ginia (June 1862)
Early's Brigade, Ewell's Division, 2nd Corps, Army of Northern Virginia
  (July-August 1862)
Lee's-Alexander's Battalion, Reserve Artillery, 1st Corps, Army of Northern
  Virginia (August 1862-July 1863)
Alexander's Battalion, Artillery, 1st Corps (July-September 1863)
Alexander's Artillery Battalion, Longstreet's Corps, Army of Tennessee (Sep-
  tember-November 1863)
Alexander's Artillery Battalion, Department of East Tennessee (November
  1863-April 1864)
Alexander's-Huger's Battalion, Artillery, 1st Corps, Army of Northern Virginia
  (April 1864-April 1865)
Battles: Yorktown Siege (April-May 1862)
Lee's Mill (April 16, 1862)
Cedar Mountain (August 9, 1862)
2nd Bull Run (August 28-30, 1862)
Antietam (September 17, 1862)
Fredericksburg (December 13, 1862)
Chancellorsville (May 1-4, 1863)
Gettysburg (July 1-3, 1863)
Chattanooga Siege (September-November 1863)
Knoxville Siege (November 1863)

The Wilderness (May 5-6, 1864)
Spotsylvania Court House (May 8-21, 1864)
North Anna (May 23-26, 1864)
Cold Harbor (June 1-3, 1864)
Petersburg Siege (June 1864-April 1865)
Appomattox Court House (April 9, 1865)
Further Reading: Graves, Joseph A., *The History of the Bedford Light Artillery.*

46. VIRGINIA BETHEL ARTILLERY BATTERY
See: LOUISIANA 12TH ARTILLERY BATTALION, COMPANY D

47. VIRGINIA BOTETOURT ARTILLERY BATTERY

Organization: Organized by the conversion of Company H, 28th Infantry Regiment, to artillery service on December 24, 1861. Reorganized for the war in the spring of 1862. Battery surrendered at Vicksburg, Warren County, Mississippi, on July 4, 1863. Paroled there later in the month. Declared exchanged on September 12, 1863. Reorganized in the fall of 1863. Unarmed in October and November 1863. Armed with six guns in February and March 1864. Captured as part of Walker's artillery column on April 8, 1865.

First Commander: Joseph W. Anderson (Captain)

Captains: John W. Johnston

Henry Clay Douthat

Assignments: Johnson's Brigade, Army of the Northwest (December 1861-January 1862)

Barton's Brigade, Department of East Tennessee (May-July 1862)

Barton's Brigade, Stevenson's Division, Department of East Tennessee (July-December 1862)

Barton's Brigade, Stevenson's Division, Department of Mississippi and East Louisiana (December 1862-January 1863)

Barton's Brigade, Stevenson's Division, 2nd Military District, Department of Mississippi and East Louisiana (January-February 1863)

Artillery Battalion, Stevenson's Division, 2nd Military District, Department of Mississippi and East Louisiana (April 1863)

Artillery Battalion, Stevenson's Division, Department of Mississippi and East Louisiana (April-July 1863)

Unattached Artillery, Department of Western Virginia and East Tennessee (October 1863-February 1864)

Artillery Battalion, Department of Western Virginia (February-April 1864)

Unattached, Department of Western Virginia (April-May 1864)

Artillery Battalion, Department of Southwestern Virginia and East Tennessee (April 1864-March 1865)

King's Battalion, Artillery, 1st Corps, Army of Northern Virginia (March-April 1865)

Battles: Cumberland Gap (June 17-18, 1862)
Chickasaw Bayou [detachment] (December 27-29, 1862)
Vicksburg Company (May-July 1863)
Port Gibson (May 1, 1863)
Champion's Hill (May 16, 1863)
Vicksburg Siege (May-July 1863)
Cloyd's Mountain (May 9, 1864)
New River Bridge (May 10, 1864)
Petersburg Siege [from March 1865] (July 1864-April 1865)
Appomattox Campaign (March-April 1865)

48.   VIRGINIA BOTETOURT HEAVY ARTILLERY BATTERY

Organization: Organized as a heavy artillery company for the war in Botetourt County on March 10, 1862. Intended to be assigned to Harris' proposed Heavy Artillery Battalion. Disbanded, with some of the men going to Company C, 20th Heavy Artillery Battalion, and the rest transferred to the light artillery on June 21, 1862, per S.O. #143, Adjutant and Inspector General's Office. Does not appear in the *Official Records.*
First Commander: Edmund F. Bowyer (Captain)

49.   VIRGINIA BRANCH FIELD ARTILLERY BATTERY
See: VIRGINIA PETERSBURG ARTILLERY BATTERY

50.   VIRGINIA BRANDON ARTILLERY BATTERY
Also Known As: Jamestown Heavy Artillery Battery
Organization: Organized for one year in Prince George and Surry counties on May 10, 1861. Served as Company E, 1st Artillery Regiment. Reorganized on March 25, 1862. Became Company D, 10th Heavy Artillery Battalion, on April 4, 1862.
First Commander: William Allen (Captain)
Captain: Charles S. Harrison

51.   VIRGINIA CAMPBELL ARTILLERY COMPANY
Organization: Organized for the war on March 5, 1862. Originally intended to form part of the 1st (Fitzgerald's) Confederate Artillery Regiment, which failed to complete its organization. Then assigned to Harris' Heavy Artillery Battalion, which also failed to complete its organization. Battery disbanded with men transferred to Company D, 18th Artillery Battalion, and Company

D, 20th Artillery Battalion, on June 21, 1862, per S.O. #143, Adjutant and Inspector General's Office. Does not appear in the *Official Records*.
First Commander: William N. Patteson (Captain)

52. VIRGINIA CAMPBELL "LONG ISLAND" LIGHT ARTILLERY BATTERY

Organization: Organized for three years or the war in Campbell County on March 15, 1862. Mustered into Confederate service for three years or the war on March 20, 1862. Intended to become Company E, 1st (Fitzgerald's) Confederate Artillery Regiment, which failed to complete its organization. Battery was disbanded and the men transferred to the Richmond "Orange" Artillery Battery and the Louisa "Morris" Artillery Battery on October 4, 1862, per S.O. #209, Headquarters, Army of Northern Virginia.
First Commander: Patrick Henry Clark (Captain)
Assignment: Jones' Battalion, Reserve Artillery, Army of Northern Virginia (June-October 1862)
Battles: Seven Days Battles (June 25-July 1, 1862)
White Oak Swamp (June 30, 1862)
Antietam (September 17, 1862)

53. VIRGINIA CAROLINA LIGHT ARTILLERY BATTERY

Organization: Organized for the war in Caroline County on July 23, 1861. Surrendered at Appomattox Court House, Virginia, on April 9, 1865.
First Commander: Thomas Rowe Thornton (Captain)
Assignments: Department of South Carolina and Georgia (December 1861-April 1862)
6th Military District of South Carolina, Department of South Carolina, Georgia and Florida (April-June 1862)
4th Military District of South Carolina, Department of South Carolina, Georgia and Florida (June-July 1862)
Lightfoot's Light Artillery Battalion, Richmond Defenses, Department of Richmond (July 1863-April 1865)
Battles: Petersburg Siege (June 1864-April 1865)
Appomattox Court House (April 9, 1865)

54. VIRGINIA CENTREVILLE RIFLES ARTILLERY BATTERY

Nickname: Virginia Wise Legion Artillery Battalion
Organization: Organized by the detachment of Company C, Wise Legion, on May 15, 1862. Armed with two 12-lb. Napoleons on December 28, 1864. Ordered to turn all of its equipment over to other batteries and report to

Richmond on March 17, 1865, where it was presumably included in Lee's surrender at Appomattox Court House on April 9, 1865.

First Commander: William M. Lowrey (Captain)

Assignments: Artillery Battalion, District of Lewisburg ["Army of New River"], Department of Southwestern Virginia (May 1862)

Artillery Battalion, Department of Western Virginia (September 1862-March 1863)

Williams' Brigade, Department of Western Virginia (April-May 1863)

Artillery Battalion, Department of Western Virginia (May-October 1863)

Artillery Battalion, Ransom's Division, Department of Western Virginia and East Tennessee (October 1863-February 1864)

King's Battalion, Artillery Department of East Tennessee (February-May 1864)

Artillery Battalion, Department of Southwestern Virginia (May-June 1864)

King's-McLaughlin's Battalion, Artillery, Valley District, Department of Northern Virginia (June 1864-March 1865)

Battles: Kanawha Campaign (September 1862)

Fayetteville, West Virginia (September 10, 1862)

Charleston, West Virginia (September 13, 1862)

Knoxville Campaign (November 1863)

New Market (May 15, 1864)

Lynchburg Campaign (June 1864)

Monocacy (July 9, 1864)

3rd Winchester (September 19, 1864)

Fisher's Hill (September 22, 1864)

Cedar Creek (October 19, 1864)

Waynesborough (March 2, 1865)

Petersburg Siege [from March 1865] (June 1864-April 1865)

55. VIRGINIA CHARLOTTE "STAUNTON HILL" ARTILLERY BATTERY

Organization: Organized for one year in Charlotte County on September 23, 1861. Mustered in on September 28, 1861. Reorganized on May 23, 1862. Surrendered by General Joseph E. Johnston at Durham Station, Orange County, North Carolina, on April 26, 1865.

First Commander: Charles Bruce (Captain)

Captain: Andrew Bailey Paris

Assignments: J. R. Anderson's Brigade, Department of North Carolina [section] (April 1862)

Department of North Carolina [section] (April-May 1862)

Mercer's Brigade, District of Georgia, Department of South Carolina, Georgia and Florida [section] (April-May 1862)

Harrison's Brigade, District of the Cape Fear, Department of North Carolina (January-February 1863)

Artillery, District of the Cape Fear, Department of North Carolina and Southern Virginia (February-April 1863)

Artillery, District of the Cape Fear, Department of North Carolina (April-September 1863)

Light Artillery, District of the Cape Fear (September 1863-April 1864)

Light Artillery, District of the Cape Fear, Department of North Carolina (April-June 1864)

Light Artillery, District of the Cape Fear, Department of North Carolina and Southern Virginia (June 1864-January 1865)

Light Artillery, 3rd Military District, Department of North Carolina (January-February 1865)

Artillery Battalion, Hoke's Division, Department of North Carolina (March 1865)

Manly's Battalion, Artillery, Hardee's Corps (March-April 1865)

Artillery Battalion, 1st Corps, Army of Tennessee (April 1865)

Battles: New Bern Expedition (February 1864)

1st Fort Fisher (December 24-25, 1865)

Carolinas Campaign (February-April 1865)

56.   VIRGINIA CHARLOTTESVILLE ARTILLERY BATTERY

Organization: Organized for the war at Charlottesville, Albemarle County, on March 15, 1862. Armed with two 3-inch Rifles, two 12-lb. Howitzers and two 6-lb. Smoothbores in August and September 1862. Armed with four 12-lb. Napoleons on July 1-3, 1863. Most of the battery captured at Spotsylvania Court House on May 12, 1864. Remnants of the company transferred to the Staunton Artillery.

First Commander: James McDowell Carrington (Captain)

Assignments: Artillery Battalion, Jackson's Division, Valley District, Department of Northern Virginia (June 1862)

Taylor's Brigade, Jackson's Division, 2nd Corps, Army of Northern Virginia (June-July 1862)

Nelson's Battalion, Reserve Artillery, Army of Northern Virginia (July-August 1862)

Artillery Battalion, Ewell's-Early's Division, 2nd Corps, Army of Northern Virginia (August 1862-July 1863)

Jones'-Cutshaw's Battalion, Artillery, 2nd Corps, Army of Northern Virginia (July 1863-May 1864)

Battles: Shenandoah Valley Campaign of 1862 (May-June 1862)

Port Republic (June 9, 1862)

Seven Days Battles (June 25-July 1, 1862)
Gaines' Mill (June 27, 1862)
Malvern Hill (July 1, 1862)
Fredericksburg (December 13, 1862)
Chancellorsville (May 1-4, 1863)
2nd Winchester (June 14-15, 1863)
Gettysburg (July 1-3, 1863)
Bristoe Campaign (October 1863)
Mine Run Campaign (November-December 1863)
The Wilderness (May 5-6, 1864)
Spotsylvania Court House (May 8-21, 1864)

57. VIRGINIA CHARLOTTESVILLE HORSE ARTILLERY BATTERY

Organization: Organized on May 2, 1863. Apparently disbanded in April 1865.

First Commander: Thomas E. Jackson (Captain)

Assignments: Jenkins' Cavalry Brigade, Department of Southwestern Virginia (June 1863)

Jenkins' Brigade, Cavalry Division, Army of Northern Virginia (June-July 1863)

Horse Artillery Battalion, Cavalry Division, Army of Northern Virginia (July-August 1863)

Unattached, Department of Western Virginia and East Tennessee (August 1863-January 1864)

Unattached, Department of Western Virginia (February-June 1864)

Horse Artillery Battalion, Lomax's Cavalry Division, Valley District, Department of Northern Virginia (October 1864-March 1865)

Johnston's Battalion [assigned to Lomax's Cavalry Division, in the Valley district], Horse Artillery, Cavalry Corps, Army of Northern Virginia (March-April 1865)

Battles: Harrisburg, Pennsylvania (June 28-29, 1863)

Gettysburg (July 1-3, 1863)

Droop Mountain (November 6, 1863)

Lynchburg Campaign (June 1864)

Cedar Creek (October 19, 1864)

58. VIRGINIA CHESTERFIELD ARTILLERY BATTERY

Nickname: Virginia Johnston Artillery Battery

Organization: Organized for one year in Dinwiddie County on September 2, 1861. Reorganized in the spring of 1862. Surrendered at Appomattox Court House, Virginia, on April 9, 1865.

First Commander: Branch Jones Epes (Captain)

Assignments: Drewry's Bluff, Department of Richmond (July 1863-May 1864)

Drewry's Bluff, Department of North Carolina (May 1864)

Smith's Artillery Battalion, Drewry's Bluff, Department of North Carolina and Southern Virginia (May-October 1864)

Smith's Battalion, Artillery, 4th Corps, Army of Northern Virginia (October 1864-April 1865)

Battles: Drewry's Bluff (May 16, 1864)

Petersburg Siege (June 1864-April 1865)

Appomattox Court House (April 9, 1865)

59. VIRGINIA COURTNEY ARTILLERY BATTERY

See: VIRGINIA RICHMOND "COURTNEY" ARTILLERY BATTERY

60. VIRGINIA DANVILLE ARTILLERY BATTERY

Organization: Organized for one year in Pittsylvania County on April 22, 1861. Reorganized on April 21, 1862. Armed with two 10-lb. Parrotts, one 3-inch Rifle and one 12-lb. Napoleon on September 17, 1862. Men from the disbanded Page-Shenandoah "Eighth Star" Artillery Battery were assigned to this battery on September 26, 1862. Armed with four 12-lb. Napoleons from July 1, 1863, to December 28, 1864. Surrendered at Appomattox Court House, Virginia, on April 9, 1865.

First Commander: Lindsay M. Shumaker (Captain)

Captains: George Washington Wooding

Robert Sidney Rice

Berryman Zirkie Price

Assignments: Army of the Northwest (June-September 1861)

H. R. Jackson's Brigade, Army of the Northwest (September-December 1861)

S. R. Anderson's Brigade, Army of the Northwest (December 1861-January 1862)

Fulkerson's Brigade, Valley District, Department of Northern Virginia, March-May 1862)

Artillery Battalion, Jackson's Division, Valley District, Department of Northern Virginia (May-June 1862)

Fulkerson's-Warren's-Hampton's Brigade, Jackson's Division, 2nd Corps, Army of Northern Virginia (June-July 1862)

Artillery Battalion, Jackson's Division, Valley District, Department of Northern Virginia (August 1862-February 1863)

Hardaway's-McIntosh's Battalion, Reserve Artillery, 2nd Corps, Army of Northern Virginia (February-June 1863)

McIntosh's Battalion, Artillery Reserve, 3rd Corps, Army of Northern Virginia (June-July 1863)

McIntosh's Battalion, Artillery, 3rd Corps, Army of Northern Virginia (July 1863-April 1865)

Battles: Corrick's Ford, West Virginia (July 13-14, 1861)
Greenbrier River (October 3, 1861)
Kernstown (March 23, 1862)
Shenandoah Valley Campaign of 1862 (May-June 1862)
Seven Days Battles (June 25-July 1, 1862)
Gaines' Mill (June 27, 1862)
Malvern Hill (July 1, 1862)
Cunningham's Ford (August 21, 1862)
2nd Bull Run (August 28-30, 1862)
Harpers Ferry (September 12-15, 1862)
Antietam (September 17, 1862)
Fredericksburg (December 13, 1862)
Chancellorsville (May 1-4, 1863)
Gettysburg (July 1-3, 1863)
Bristoe Campaign (October 1863)
Mine Run Campaign (November-December 1863)
The Wilderness (May 5-6, 1864)
Spotsylvania Court House (May 8-21, 1864)
North Anna (May 23-26, 1864)
Cold Harbor (June 1-3, 1864)
Petersburg Siege (June 1864-April 1865)
Appomattox Court House (April 9, 1865)

61. VIRGINIA DANVILLE "RINGGOLD" ARTILLERY BATTERY

Organization: Organized for three years or the war on February 15, 1862. Briefly designated as Company B, 1st (Fitzgerald's) Confederate Artillery Regiment, which failed to complete its organization. Became Company B, 13th Light Artillery Battalion in late 1863.

First Commander: Timothy H. Stamps (Captain)

Captain: Crispin Dickenson

Assignments: Artillery Battalion, Department of Southwestern Virginia (May-November 1862)

Artillery Battalion, Department of Western Virginia (November 1862-March 1863)

Wharton's Brigade, Department of Western Virginia (April-May 1863)

Artillery Battalion, Department of Western Virginia (May-September 1863)

Artillery Battalion, Ransom's Division, Department of Western Virginia and East Tennessee (October 1863)
Battles: Kanawha Campaign (September 1862)
Fayetteville, West Virginia (September 10, 1862)
Charleston, West Virginia (September 13, 1862)

62. VIRGINIA DAVIS ARTILLERY BATTERY
See: VIRGINIA LOUISA "MORRIS" ARTILLERY BATTERY

63. VIRGINIA DIXIE ARTILLERY BATTERY
See: VIRGINIA MONROE "DIXIE" ARTILLERY BATTERY

64. VIRGINIA DIXIE (PAGE COUNTY) ARTILLERY BATTERY
Organization: Organized for one year in Page County on June 21, 1861. Armed with four 6-lb. Smoothbores in June and July 1862. Disbanded and men transferred to the Richmond "Purcell" Artillery Battery on October 4, 1862, per S.O. #209, Headquarters, Army of Northern Virginia.
First Commander: John Kaylor Booton (Captain)
Captain: William Henry Chapman
Assignments: Artillery, Department of the Peninsula (October 1861-January 1862)
Rains' Division, Department of the Peninsula (January-April 1862)
Artillery Battalion, Longstreet's Division, Army of Northern Virginia (June 1862)
Artillery Battalion, Longstreet's Division, 1st Corps, Army of Northern Virginia (June-August 1862)
Featherston's Brigade, Wilcox's Division, 1st Corps, Army of Northern Virginia (August-September 1862)
Unattached, Reserve Artillery, Army of Northern Virginia (September-October 1862)
Battles: Yorktown Siege (April-May 1862)
Seven Days Battles (June 25-July 1, 1862)
2nd Bull Run (August 28-30, 1862)
Antietam (September 17, 1862)

65. VIRGINIA EIGHTH STAR ARTILLERY BATTERY
See: VIRGINIA PAGE-SHENANDOAH "EIGHTH STAR" ARTILLERY BATTERY

66. VIRGINIA EVERETTE ARTILLERY BATTERY
See: VIRGINIA ALBEMARLE "EVERETTE" ARTILLERY BATTERY

67. VIRGINIA FAUQUIER ARTILLERY BATTERY

Organization: Organized by the conversion of 1st Company G, 49th Infantry Regiment, to artillery service in September or October 1861. Reorganized on May 12, 1862. Armed with two 24-lb. Howitzers and four 12-lb. Napoleons in August and September 1862. Loudoun Aritllery and part of the Bedford Artillery assigned to this battery on October 4, 1862, per S.O. #209, Headquarters, Army of Northern Virginia. Became Company A, 38th Artillery Battalion, ca. June 1863.

First Commander: Robert M. Stribling (Captain)

Assignments: Jones'-R. H. Anderson's Brigade, Longstreet's Division, Potomac District, Department of Northern Virginia (January-April 1862)

R. H. Anderson's Brigade, Longstreet's Division, Department of Northern Virginia (April-June 1862)

Armistead's Brigade, Huger's-R. H. Anderson's Division, Army of Northern Virginia (June-July 1862)

Jenkins' Brigade, Kemper's Division, 1st Corps, Army of Northern Virginia (August-September 1862)

Artillery Battalion, D. R. Jones' Division, 1st Corps, Army of Northern Virginia (September-October 1862)

Artillery Battalion, Pickett's Division, 1st Corps, Army of Northern Virginia (October 1862-February 1863)

Artillery Battalion, Pickett's Division, Department of Virginia and North Carolina (February-April 1863)

Artillery Battalion, Pickett's Division, Department of Southern Virginia (April-May 1863)

Artillery Battalion, Pickett's Division, 1st Corps, Army of Northern Virginia (May-June 1863)

Battles: Yorktown Siege (April-May 1862)

Williamsburg (May 5, 1862)

Seven Pines (May 31-June 1, 1862)

Seven Days Battles (June 25-July 1, 1862)

2nd Bull Run (August 28-30, 1862)

Fredericksburg (December 13, 1862)

Suffolk Campaign (April-May 1863)

Battery Huger (April 19, 1863)

68. VIRGINIA FAYETTE ARTILLERY BATTERY

See: VIRGINIA RICHMOND "FAYETTE" ARTILLERY BATTERY

69. VIRGINIA FLUVANNA ARTILLERY BATTERY, No. 1

Nickname: Sons of Fluvanna

Organization: Organized for one year in Fluvanna County on June 20, 1861. Reorganized on May 16, 1862. Consolidated with the Fluvanna Artillery No. 2 and designated as the Fluvanna Artillery Battery Consolidated on October 4, 1862, per S.O. #209, Headquarters, Army of Northern Virginia.

First Commander: William Henry Holman (Captain)

Captain: Charles T. Huckstep

Assignments: Reserve Artillery, Potomac District, Department of Northern Virginia (November 1861-March 1862)

Reserve Artillery, Department of Northern Virginia (March-June 1862)

Nelson's Battalion, Reserve Artillery, Army of Northern Virginia (June-October 1862)

Battles: Yorktown Siege (April-May 1862)

Seven Days Battles (June 25-July 1, 1862)

Shepherdstown Ford (September 20, 1862)

70.   VIRGINIA FLUVANNA ARTILLERY BATTERY, NO. 2

Organization: Organized for one year in Fluvanna county on August 6, 1861. Reorganized on May 16, 1862. Consolidated with the Fluvanna Artillery No. 1 and designated as the Fluvanna Artillery Battery Consolidated on October 4, 1862, per S.O. #209, Headquarters, Army of Northern Virginia.

First Commander: Cary Charles Cocke (Captain)

Captain: John J. Ancell

Assignments: Reserve Artillery, Potomac District, Department of Northern Virginia (November 1861-March 1862)

Reserve Artillery, Department of Northern Virginia (March-June 1862)

Richardson's Battalion, Reserve Artillery, Army of Northern Virginia (June-July 1862)

Nelson's Battalion, Reserve Artillery, Army of Northern Virginia (September-October 1862)

Battles: Yorktown Siege (April-May 1862)

Seven Days Battles (June 25-July 1, 1862)

Shepherdstown Ford (September 20, 1862)

71.   VIRGINIA FLUVANNA ARTILLERY BATTERY
CONSOLIDATED

Organization: Organized by the consolidation of the Fluvanna Artillery No. 1 and No. 2 batteries on October 4, 1862, per S.O. #209, Headquarters, Army of Northern Virginia. Armed with one 3-inch Rifle and three 12-lb. Napoleons on July 1-3, 1863. Armed with two 12-lb. Howitzers on December 28, 1864. No record after March 1865.

First Commander: John L. Massie (Captain)

Captain: Charles G. Snead

Assignments: Nelson's Battalion, Reserve Artillery, Army of Northern Virginia (October 1862-June 1863)

Nelson's Battalion, Reserve Artillery, 2nd Corps, Army of Northern Virginia (June-July 1863)

Nelson's Battalion, Artillery, 2nd Corps, Army of Northern Virginia (July 1863-June 1864)

Nelson's Battalion, Artillery, Valley District, Department of Northern Virginia (June 1864-March 1865)

Battles: Fredericksburg (December 13, 1862)

Chancellorsville (May 1-4, 1863)

Gettysburg (July 1-3, 1863)

Bristoe Campaign (October 1863)

Mine Run Campaign (November-December 1863)

Kelly's Ford (November 7, 1863)

The Wilderness (May 5-6, 1864)

Spotsylvania Court House (May 8-21, 1864)

North Anna (May 23-26, 1864)

Cold Harbor (June 1-3, 1864)

Lynchburg Campaign (June 1864)

Monocacy (July 9, 1864)

3rd Winchester (September 19, 1864)

Fisher's Hill (September 22, 1864)

Cedar Creek (October 19, 1864)

Waynesborough (March 2, 1865)

72. VIRGINIA FREDERICKSBURG ARTILLERY BATTERY

Organization: Organized at Fredericksburg for one year on April 23, 1861. Armed with two 10-lb. Parrotts and two 12-lb. Napoleons on July 1-3, 1863. Armed with four 12-lb. Napoleons on December 28, 1864. Reorganized on April 1, 1862. Surrendered at Appomattox Court House, Virginia, on April 9, 1865.

First Commander: Carter M. Braxton (Captain)

Field Officers: Edward A. Marye (Captain)

John G. Pollock

Assignments: French's Brigade, Aquia District, Department of Northern Virginia (January 1862)

S. R. Anderson's-Hatton's Brigade, G. W. Smith's-Whiting's Division, Department of Northern Virginia (March-June 1862)

Artillery Battalion, A. P. Hill's Division, Army of Northern Virginia (June-July 1862)

Archer's Brigade, A. P. Hill's Division, 1st Corps, Army of Northern Virginia (July 1862)

Artillery Battalion, A. P. Hill's Division, 2nd Corps, Army of Northern Virginia (August 1862-May 1863)

Pegram's Battalion, Reserve Artillery, 3rd Corps, Army of Northern Virginia (May-July 1863)

Pegram's Battalion, Artillery, 3rd Corps, Army of Northern Virginia (July-September 1863)

M. Johnson's Battalion, Artillery, 1st Corps, Army of Northern Virginia (October 1864-March 1865)

M. Johnson's Battalion, Artillery, 2nd Corps, Army of Northern Virginia (March-April 1865)

Battles: Seven Days Battles (June 25-July 1, 1862)

Beaver Dam Creek (June 26, 1862)

Gaines' Mill (June 27, 1862)

Frayser's Farm (June 30, 1862)

Cedar Mountain (August 9, 1862)

2nd Bull Run (August 28-30, 1862)

Harpers Ferry (September 12-15, 1862)

Fredericksburg (December 13, 1862)

Chancellorsville (May 1-4, 1863)

Gettysburg (July 1-3, 1863)

Mine Run Campaign (November-December 1863)

The Wilderness (May 5-6, 1864)

Spotsylvania Court House (May 8-21, 1864)

North Anna (May 22-26, 1864)

Cold Harbor (June 1-3, 1864)

Petersburg Siege (June 1864-April 1865)

Sayler's Creek (April 6, 1865)

Appomattox Court House (April 9, 1865)

Further Reading: Krick, Robert E., *Fredericksburg Artillery*.

73. VIRGINIA FREDERICKSBURG ARTILLERY BATTERY, 2ND ORGANIZATION

Organization: Organized for one year at Fredericksburg on June 22, 1861. Disbanded when it failed to receive its guns and refused to serve as infantry in September 1861. Not listed in the *Official Records*.

First Commander: Thomas A. Curtis (Captain)

74. VIRGINIA GILES LIGHT ARTILLERY BATTERY

Nicknames: McComas Artillery

Pearlsburg Reserves

Organization: Organized by the detachment of Company B, Wise Legion, in early 1862. Armed with four 12-lb. Napoleons on December 28, 1864. Surrendered at Appomattox Court House, Virginia on April 9, 1865.

First Commander: David Alexander French (Captain)

Captain: Alexander Martin

Assignments: Artillery Battalion, Floyd's Division, Central Army of Kentucky, Department #2 (January-February 1862)

Artillery Battalion, Floyd's Division, Fort Donelson, Department #2 (February 1862)

Stark's Artillery Battalion, Wise's Brigade, Elzey's Command, Department of North Carolina and Southern Virginia (December 1862-April 1863)

Stark's Artillery Battalion, Wise's Brigade, Department of Richmond (April-September 1863)

Stark's Artillery Battalion, Hunton's Command, Department of Richmond (September-October 1863)

Stark's Light Artillery Battalion, Chaffin's Farm, Department of Richmond (December 1863-May 1864)

Stark's Light Artillery Battalion, Chaffin's Farm, Artillery Defenses, Department of Richmond (May-October 1864)

Stark's Battalion, Artillery, 1st Corps, Army of Northern Virginia (October 1864-February 1865)

Stark's Battalion, Artillery, 2nd Corps, Army of Northern Virginia (March-April 1865)

Battles: Fort Donelson (February 12-16, 1862)

Blake's Farm, near Deep Bottom, James River (August 6, 1863)

Petersburg Siege (June 1864-April 1865)

Chaffin's Farm (September 29, 1864)

Fort Gilmer (September 29-30, 1864)

Appomattox Court House (April 9, 1865)

75. VIRGINIA GOOCHLAND ARTILLERY

Organization: Organized by the detachment of Company D, Wise Legion Artillery Battalion, in March or April 1862. Armed with four guns on July 23, 1862. Disbanded and men transferred to the Richmond "Orange" Artillery on October 4, 1862, per S.O. #209, Headquarters, Army of Northern Virginia.

First Commander: William H. Turner (Captain)

Assignments: Armistead's Brigade, Huger's-R. H. Anderson's Division, Army of Northern Virginia (June-July 1862)

Artillery Battalion, R. H. Anderson's Division, 1st Corps, Army of Northern Virginia (July-August 1862)

Jones' Battalion, Reserve Artillery, Army of Northern Virginia (August-October 1862)

Battles: Seven Days Battles (June 25-July 1, 1862)
Antietam (September 17, 1862)

76. VIRGINIA GOOCHLAND LIGHT ARTILLERY BATTERY

Organization: Organized and mustered into Confederate service for one year in Goochland County on June 6, 1861. Temporarily attached to the 45th Infantry Regiment in 1861. Armed with four guns on December 14, 1861. Surrendered at Fort Donelson on February 16, 1862. Declared exchanged on November 10, 1862. Reorganized on November 19, 1862. Served as heavy artillery in 1864-1865. Served as infantry in the Appomattox Campaign. Surrendered at Appomattox Court House, Virginia on April 9, 1865.

First Commander: John H. Guy (Captain)

Captain: Jonathan Talley

Assignments: Army of the Kanawha (December 1861-January 1862)
Artillery Battalion, Floyd's Division, Central Army of Kentucky, Department #2 (January-February 1862)
Artillery Battalion, Floyd's Division, Fort Donelson, Department #2 (February 1862)
Moseley's Battalion, Artillery, Department of North Carolina (June-July 1863)
Moseley's Artillery Battalion, Ransom's Division, Department of Richmond (July-September 1863)
Chaffin's Bluff, Department of Richmond (September 1863-May 1864)
Chaffin's Bluff, Artillery Defenses, Department of Richmond (May 1864-February 1865)
Chaffin's Bluff, Crutchfield's Artillery Brigade, Department of Richmond (February-March 1865)
Chaffin's Bluff, Crutchfield's Artillery Brigade, G. W. C. Lee's Division, Department of Richmond (March-April 1865)
Crutchfield's Artillery Brigade, G. W. C. Lee's Division, Army of Northern Virginia (April 1865)

Battles: Fort Donelson (February 12-16, 1862)
Petersburg Siege (June 1864-April 1865)
Fort Harrison (September 29, 1864)
Chaffin's Farm (September 29, 1864)
Fort Gilmer (September 29, 1864)
Sayler's Creek (April 6, 1865)
Appomattox Court House (April 9, 1865)

77. VIRGINIA GOOCHLAND "TURNER" ARTILLERY BATTERY

See: VIRGINIA TURNER ARTILLERY BATTERY.

78. VIRGINIA HALE'S-JACKSON'S ARTILLERY BATTERY

See: VIRGINIA KANAWHA ARTILLERY BATTERY

79. VIRGINIA HALIFAX HEAVY ARTILLERY BATTERY

Organization: Organized for three years or the war in Halifax County on March 18, 1862. Mustered in on March 22, 1862. Served as Company C, 12th Louisiana Heavy Artillery Battalion. Armed with four 12-lb. Napoleons on December 28, 1864. Surrendered at Appomattox Court House, Virginia, on April 9, 1865.

First Commander: Samuel T. Wright (Captain)

Assignments: Unattached, French's Command, Department of North Carolina and Southern Virginia (September-December 1862)

Pryor's Brigade, French's Command, Department of North Carolina and Southern Virginia (December 1862-February 1863)

Forces on the Blackwater, French's Command, Department of North Carolina and Southern Virginia (February-April 1863)

Department of Southern Virginia (April-May 1863)

Branch's Battalion, Artillery, Department of North Carolina (June-July 1863)

Branch's Artillery Battalion, Ransom's Division, Department of Richmond (July-September 1863)

Branch's-Coit's Battalion, Artillery, Department of North Carolina (September 1863-June 1864)

Branch's-Coit's Battalion, Artillery, Department of North Carolina and Southern Virginia (June-October 1864)

Branch's-Coit's Battalion, Artillery, 4th Corps, Army of Northern Virginia (October 1864-April 1865)

Battles: Kelly's Store (January 30, 1863)

Swift Creek (May 9, 1864)

Drewry's Bluff (May 16, 1864)

Petersburg Siege (June 1864-April 1865)

Appomattox Court House (April 9, 1865)

80. VIRGINIA HALIFAX LIGHT ARTILLERY BATTERY

Also Known As: Virginia Yorktown Artillery Battery

Organization: Organized by the conversion of 1st Company G, 14th Infantry Regiment, to artillery service on May 1, 1862. Served as Company G (subsequently Company C), 1st Artillery Regiment, and later as Company C, 1st Artillery Battalion, until January 18, 1865. Then served independently. Armed with two 12-lb. Napoleons on June 24, 1862. There was some consideration in October 1862 of either returning the company to infantry service or relieving the officers and distributing the enlisted men to the other batteries of the 1st Artillery Regiment. Neither appears to have been carried out. Armed with four 12-lb. Napoleons on December 28, 1864. Surrendered at Appomattox Court House, Virginia, on April 9, 1865.

First Commander: Edward Rush Young (Captain)

Assignments: McLaws' Brigade, McLaws' Division, Magruder's Command, Department of Northern Virginia (April-May 1862)

McLaws' Brigade, Magruder's Division, Army of Northern Virginia (May-June 1862)

Toombs' Brigade, McLaws' Division, Army of Northern Virginia (June 1862)

Brown's Battalion, Reserve Artillery, Army of Northern Virginia (July-October 1862)

Moseley's Battalion, Artillery, Department of North Carolina (June-July 1863)

Moseley's Battalion, Artillery, Ransom's Division, Department of Richmond (July-September 1863)

Moseley's Battalion, Artillery, Department of North Carolina (September 1863-June 1864)

Moseley's Battalion, Aritllery, Department of North Carolina and Southern Virginia (June-October 1864)

Moseley's-Caskie's-Blount's Battalion, Artillery, 4th Corps, Army of Northern Virginia (October 1864-April 1865)

Battles: Yorktown Siege (April-May 1862)

Drewry's Bluff (May 16, 1864)

Bermuda Hundred (May 17-June 14, 1864)

Petersburg (June 9, 1864)

Petersburg Siege (June 1864-April 1865)

Appomattox Court House (April 9, 1865)

81.   VIRGINIA HAMPDEN ARTILLERY BATTERY

See: VIRGINIA RICHMOND "HAMPDEN" ARTILLERY BATTERY

82.   VIRGINIA HAMPTON ARTILLERY BATTERY

See: VIRGINIA WASHINGTON ARTILLERY BATTERY

83.   VIRGINIA HANOVER LIGHT ARTILLERY BATTERY

Organization: Organized for one year at Hanover Junction in April 1861. Mustered into state service for one year on May 21, 1861. Reorganized April 30, 1862. Armed with six guns on July 23, 1862. Disbanded and men transferred to the Amherst Artillery Battery and Ashland Artillery Battery on October 4, 1862, per S.O. #209, Headquarters, Army of Northern Virginia.

First Commander: William Nelson (Captain)

Assignments: Rains' Division, Department of the Peninsula (January-April 1862)

Unattached Artillery, D. H. Hill's Division, Army of Northern Virginia (June-July 1862)

Artillery Battalion, D. H. Hill's Division, Army of Northern Virginia (July 1862)

Yorktown Siege (April-May 1862)

Seven Days Battles (June 25-July 1, 1862)

84. VIRGINIA HARRIS' HEAVY ARTILLERY BATTALION

Organization: Organization authorized per S.O. #113, Adjutant and Inspector General's Office, dated May 17, 1862. Never actually organized. Authorization revoked per S.O. #133, Adjutant and Inspector General's Office, dated June 10, 1862. Two companies disbanded. One company assigned to the 19th Heavy Artillery Battalion and three companies assigned to the 20th Heavy Artillery per S.O. #143, dated June 21, 1862.

First Commander: Nicholas C. Harris (Lieutenant Colonel)

85. VIRGINIA HENRICO ARTILLERY BATTERY

See: VIRGINIA RICHMOND "COURTNEY" ARTILLERY BATTERY

86. VIRGINIA HENRICO ARTILLERY BATTERY, COMPANY B

Organization: Organized in Henrico County in the fall of 1861. Served as 2nd Company C, 1st Artillery Regiment. Reorganized on April 30, 1862. Armed with one 10-lb. Parrott and three 6-lb. Smoothbores on June 24, 1862. Disbanded and men assigned to the other companies of the regiment on October 4, 1862, per S.O. #209, Headquarters, Army of Northern Virginia.

First Commander: Johnson H. Sands (Captain)

Captain: William Bailey Ritter

Assignments: Artillery Battalion, Department of the Peninsula (October 1861-April 1862)

Griffith's Brigade, McLaws' Division, Magruder's Command, Department of Northern Virginia (April-May 1862)

Cabell's Artillery Battalion, Magruder's Division, Army of Northern Virginia (May-June 1862)

Toombs' Brigade, Magruder's Division, Army of Northern Virginia (June 1862)

Brown's Regiment, Reserve Artillery, Army of Northern Virginia (July-October 1862)

Battle: Yorktown Siege (April-May 1862)

87.   VIRGINIA HOWITZERS ARTILLERY BATTERY

Organization: Organized on November 9, 1859. Increased to a battalion of three companies and designated as the Richmond Howitzers prior to May 11, 1861.

First Commander: George Wythe Randolph (Captain)

88.   VIRGINIA JACKSON'S ARTILLERY BATTALION, STATE LINE

Organization: Organized with two companies and one section probably in late 1862. Disbanded ca. March 31, 1863.

First Commander: Thomas E. Jackson (Major)

89.   VIRGINIA JACKSON ARTILLERY BATTERY

See: VIRGINIA WINCHESTER ARTILLERY BATTERY

90.   VIRGINIA JAMES CITY ARTILLERY BATTERY

Organization: Organized by the conversion of Company H, 32nd Infantry Regiment, to artillery service ca. September 1861. Served as Company B (AKA: A), 1st Artillery Regiment, and as Company B, 1st Artillery Battalion, until January 18, 1865. Armed with two 32-lb. Smoothbores from June 24, 1862, to July 1, 1862. Served as heavy artillery in 1864-1865. Armed with three heavy guns on December 30, 1864. Surrendered at Appomattox Court House, Virginia, on April 9, 1865.

First Commander: Alex Hamilton Hankins (Captain)

Captain: Lucien W. Richardson

Assignments: Artillery Battalion, Department of the Peninsula (October 1861-April 1865)

Forces at Williamsburg [B. S. Ewell's], Magruder's Command, Department of Northern Virginia (April-May 1862)

Toombs' Brigade, Magruder's Division, Army of Northern Virginia (June 1862)

Lee's Artillery Battalion, Magruder's Command, Army of Northern Virginia (June-July 1862)

Brown's Regiment, Reserve Artillery, Army of Northern Virginia (July-October 1862)

Artillery, French's Command, Department of North Carolina and Southern Virginia (September 1862-February 1863)

Moseley's Artillery Battalion, French's Command, Department of North Carolina and Southern Virginia (February-April 1863)

Moseley's Battalion, Artillery, Department of North Carolina (April-July 1863)

Moseley's Artillery Battalion, Ransom's Division, Department of Richmond (July-September 1863)

Chaffin's Bluff, Department of Richmond (September 1863-May 1864)

Chaffin's Bluff, Artillery Defenses, Department of Richmond (May 1864-February 1865)

Chaffin's Bluff, Crutchfield's Artillery Brigade, Department of Richmond (February-March 1865)

Chaffin's Bluff, Crutchfield's Artillery Brigade, G. W. C. Lee's Division, Department of Richmond (March-April 1865)

Crutchfield's Artillery Brigade, G. W. C. Lee's Division, Army of Northern Virginia (April 1865)

Battles: Yorktown Siege (April-May 1862)

Seven Days Battles (June 25-July 1, 1862)

Petersburg Siege (June 1864-April 1865)

Fort Harrison (September 29, 1864)

Chaffin's Farm (September 29, 1864)

Fort Gilmer (September 29-30, 1864)

Sayler's Creek (April 6, 1865)

Appomattox Court House (April 9, 1865)

91. VIRGINIA JAMESTOWN HEAVY ARTILLERY BATTERY

See: VIRGINIA BRANDON ARTILLERY BATTERY

92. VIRGINIA JOHNSTON ARTILLERY BATTERY

See: VIRGINIA CHESTERFIELD ARTILLERY BATTERY

93. VIRGINIA KANAWHA ARTILLERY BATTERY

Organization: Organized by detachment of the Kanawha Artillery from the 22nd Infantry Regiment in July or August 1861. Surrendered at Fort Donelson on February 16, 1862. Does not appear in the *Official Records*.

First Commander: John P. Hale (Captain)

Captain: Thomas E. Jackson

Assignment: Artillery Battalion, Buckner's Division, Fort Donelson, Department #2 (February 1862)

Battle: Fort Donelson (February 12-16, 1862)

94. VIRGINIA KING WILLIAM ARTILLERY BATTERY

Organization: Organized for one year in King William County on June 1, 1861. Reorganized on June 1, 1862. Bayley's Heavy Artillery Company disbanded and men assigned to this company on June 17, 1862, per S.O. #136, Headquarters, Department of Northern Virginia. Armed with one 10-lb.

Parrott, two 12-lb. Howitzers and two 6-lb. Smoothbores in August and September 1862. Turner Light Artillery Battery disbanded and men transferred to this company on October 4, 1862, per S.O. #209, Headquarters, Army of Northern Virginia. Armed with two 10-lb. Parrotts and two 12-lb. Napoleons on July 1-3, 1863. Apparently merged into the batteries of Cutshaw's Artillery Battalion in November 1864. Surrendered at Appomattox Court House, Virginia, on April 9, 1865.

First Commander: Thomas Hill Carter (Captain)

Captain: William P. Carter

Assignments: Rodes' Brigade, Van Dorn's-D. H. Hill's Division, Potomac District, Department of Northern Virginia (January-March 1862)

Rodes' Brigade, D. H. Hill's Division, Army of Northern Virginia (March-June 1862)

Rodes' Brigade, D. H. Hill's Division, 2nd Corps, Army of Northern Virginia (June-July 1862)

Artillery Battalion, D. H. Hill's Division, Army of Northern Virginia (July-September 1862)

Artillery Battalion, D. H. Hill's-Rodes' Division, 2nd Corps, Army of Northern Virginia (September 1862-July 1863)

Carter's-Page's Battalion, Artillery, 2nd Corps, Army of Northern Virginia (July 1863-June 1864)

Page's Battalion, Artillery, Valley District, Department of Northern Virginia (September-November 1864)

Cutshaw's Battalion, Artillery, Valley District, Department of Northern Virginia (November 1864-March 1865)

Cutshaw's Battalion, Artillery, 2nd Corps, Army of Northern Virginia (March-April 1865)

Battles: Yorktown Siege (April-May 1862)

Seven Pines (May 31-June 1, 1862)

Seven Days Battles (June 25-July 1, 1862)

Gaines' Mill (June 27, 1862)

Antietam (September 17, 1862)

Port Royal (December 4, 1862)

Fredericksburg (December 13, 1862)

Chancellorsville (May 1-4, 1863)

Gettysburg (July 1-3, 1863)

Bristoe Campaign (October 1863)

Mine Run Campaign (November-December 1863)

The Wilderness (May 5-6, 1864)

Spotsylvania Court House (May 8-21, 1864)

North Anna (May 23-26, 1864)

Cold Harbor (June 1-3, 1864)
Cedar Creek (October 19, 1864)
Wayesborough (March 2, 1865)
Petersburg Siege (June 1864-April 1865)
Appomattox Court House (April 9, 1865)

95. VIRGINIA KYLE'S HEAVY ARTILLERY BATTERY

Organization: Organized for the war on March 6, 1862. Intended to form part of Roberson's Heavy Artillery Battalion, which failed to complete its organization. This battery was disbanded, with the men transferred to Companies A and D, 19th Heavy Artillery Battalion, and Company B, 20th Heavy Artillery Battalion, on June 21, 1862, per S.O. #143, Adjutant and Inspector General's Office.

First Commander: Robert R. Kyle (Captain)
Assignment: Department of Norfolk (April 1862)

96. VIRGINIA LEE ARTILLERY BATTERY

See: VIRGINIA LYNCHBURG "LEE" ARTILLERY BATTERY

97. VIRGINIA LEVI'S-BARR'S ARTILLERY BATTERY

Organization: Organized by the change of designation of the Artillery Battery, Thomas' North Carolina Legion, on February 29, 1864. Surrendered by Brigadier General James G. Martin, commanding the District of North Carolina, Department of East Tennessee, on May 10, 1865.

First Commander: John T. Levi (Captain)
Captain: John W. Barr
Assignments: Artillery, Department of Western Virginia (February 1864)
Jackson's Brigade, Buckner's Division, Department of East Tennessee (April 1864)
Artillery, Department of Western Virginia and East Tennessee (July-August 1864)
Page's Artillery Battalion, Department of Western Virginia and East Tennessee (November 1864)
Unattached, District of Western North Carolina, Department of East Tennessee (November 1864-March 1865)
Further Reading: Crow, Vernon H., *Storm in the Mountains: Thomas' Confederate Legion of Cherokee Indians and Mountaineers.*

98. VIRGINIA LEWISBURG ARTILLERY BATTERY

See: VIRGINIA MONROE ARTILLERY BATTERY

99. VIRGINIA LONG ISLAND LIGHT ARTILLERY BATTERY

See: VIRGINIA CAMPBELL "LONG ISLAND" LIGHT ARTILLERY BATTERY

100. VIRGINIA LOUDOUN ARTILLERY BATTERY

Organization: Organized at Leesburg, Loudoun County, on December 13, 1859. Enlisted for one year in state service on April 21, 1861. Mustered into Confederate service on June 12, 1861. Armed with four 6-lb. Smoothbores on July 21, 1861. Reorganized in the spring of 1862. Disbanded and men transferred to the Fauquier Artillery Battery on October 4, 1862, per S.O. #209, Headquarters, Army of Northern Virginia.

First Commander: Arthur Lee Rogers (Captain)

Assignments: Evans' Brigade, Army of the Potomac (July 1861)

Evans' Brigade, 1st Corps, Army of the Potomac (July 1861)

Longstreet's Brigade, 1st Corps, Army of the Potomac (July-October 1861)

Clark's Brigade, Longstreet's Division, 1st Corps, Army of the Potomac (October 1861)

Clark's-Griffith's Brigade, Longstreet's Division, 1st Corps, Potomac District, Department of Northern Virginia (October-November 1861)

Griffith's-Ewell's Brigade, Longstreet's Division, 1st Corps, Potomac District, Department of Northern Virginia (November 1861-January 1862)

Ewell's-A. P. Hill's Brigade, Longstreet's Division, Potomac District, Department of Northern Virginia (January-March 1862)

A. P. Hill's-Kemper's Brigade, Longstreet's Division, Army of Northern Virginia (March-June 1862)

Kemper's Brigade, Longstreet's Division, 1st Corps, Army of Northern Virginia (June-August 1862)

Kemper's Brigade, Kemper's Division, 1st Corps, Army of Northern Virginia (August-September 1862)

Artillery Battalion, D. R. Jones' Division, 1st Corps, Army of Northern Virginia (September-October 1862)

Battles: 1st Bull Run (July 21, 1861)

Yorktown Siege (April-May 1862)

Seven Days Battles (June 25-July 1, 1862)

2nd Bull Run (August 28-30, 1862)

101. VIRGINIA LOUISA "MORRIS" ARTILLERY BATTERY

Nickname: Davis Artillery

Organization: Organized for one year in Louis County on August 19, 1861. Armed with two 3-inch Rifles, one 12-lb. Howitzer and three 6-lb. Smoothbores in August and September 1862. Some members of the Campbell "Long Island" Artillery Battery transferred to this battery when that unit was disbanded on October 4, 1862, per S.O. #209, Headquarters, Army of Northern Virginia. Armed with four 12-lb. Napoleons on July 1-3, 1863. Apparently merged into the batteries of Cutshaw's Artillery Battalion in November 1864. Surrendered at Appomattox Court House, Virginia, on April 9, 1865.

First Commander: Lewis M. Coleman (Captain)

Captains: Richard C. M. Page

Charles R. Montgomery

Assignments: Reserve Artillery, Potomac District, Department of Northern Virginia (January-March 1862)

Reserve Artillery, Department of Northern Virginia (April-May 1862)

Nelson's Battalion, Reserve Artillery, Army of Northern Virginia (June-July 1862)

Artillery Battalion, D. H. Hill's-Rodes' Division, 2nd Corps, Army of Northern Virginia (September 1862-July 1863)

Carter's-Page's Battalion, Artillery, 2nd Corps, Army of Northern Virginia (July 1863-June 1864)

Page's Battalion, Artillery, Valley District, Department of Northern Virginia (September-November 1864)

Cutshaw's Battalion, Artillery, Valley District, Department of Northern Virginia (November 1864-March 1865)

Cutshaw's Battalion, Artillery, 2nd Corps, Army of Northern Virginia (March-April 1865)

Battles: Yorktown Siege (April-May 1862)

Seven Days Battles (June 25-July 1, 1862)

Harpers Ferry (September 12-15, 1862)

Antietam (September 17, 1862)

Fredericksburg (December 13, 1862)

Chancellorsville (May 1-4, 1863)

Gettysburg (July 1-3, 1863)

Bristoe Campaign (October 1863)

Mine Run Campaign (November-December 1863)

The Wilderness (May 5-6, 1864)

Spotsylvania Court House (May 8-21, 1864)

North Anna (May 23-26, 1864)

Cold Harbor (June 1-3, 1864)

Cedar Creek (October 19, 1864)

Waynesborough (March 2, 1865)

Petersburg Siege (June 1864-April 1865)

Appomattox Court House (April 9, 1865)

Further Reading: Page, Richard Channing Moore, *Sketch of Page's Battery or, Morris Artillery, 2nd Corps, Army of Northern Virginia.*

102.   VIRGINIA LUNENBURG "REBEL" ARTILLERY BATTERY

Organization: Organized for one year in Lunenburg County on January 25, 1862. Served as Company F, 2nd Artillery Regiment, until reorganized as an independent company on June 5, 1862. Served as heavy artillery in 1864-1865. Armed with four heavy guns on December 30, 1864. Surrendered at Appomattox Court House, Virginia, on April 9, 1865.

First Commander: Samuel W. Hawthorne (Captain)

Captain: Cornelius Tacitus Allen

Assignments: Chaffin's Bluff, Department of North Carolina and Southern Virginia (September-December 1862)

Chaffin's Bluff, Elzey's Command, Department of North Carolina and Southern Virginia (December 1862-April 1863)

Chaffin's Bluff, Department of Richmond (April 1863-May 1864)

Chaffin's Bluff, Artillery Defenses, Department of Richmond (May 1864-February 1865)

Chaffin's Bluff, Crutchfield's Artillery Brigade, Department of Richmond (February-March 1865)

Chaffin's Bluff, Crutchfield's Artillery Brigade, G. W. C. Lee's Division, Department of Richmond (March-April 1865)

Crutchfield's Artillery Brigade, G. W. C. Lee's Division, Army of Northern Virginia (April 1865)

Battles: Petersburg Siege (June 1864-April 1865)

Fort Harrison (September 29, 1864)

Chaffin's Farm (September 29, 1864)

Fort Gilmer (September 29-30, 1864)

Sayler's Creek (April 6, 1865)

Appomattox Court House (April 9, 1865)

103.   VIRGINIA LYNCHBURG ARTILLERY BATTERY

Organization: Organized for one year at Lynchburg on April 23, 1861. Armed with four 6-lb. Smoothbores on July 21, 1861. Reorganized on April 3, 1862. Armed with one 10-lb. Parrott, one 12-lb. Howitzer and two 6-lb. Smoothbores in August and September 1862. Part of Bedford Artillery was merged into this battery on October 4, 1862, per S.O. #209, Headquarters, Army of Northern Virginia. Became Company D, 38th Artillery Battalion, ca. June 1863.

First Commander: Henry Grey Latham (Captain)

Captain: James Dearing

Assignments: Cocke's Brigade, Army of the Potomac (July 1861)

Cocke's Brigade, 1st Corps, Army of the Potomac (July-October 1861)

Cocke's Brigade, Longstreet's Division, 1st Corps, Army of the Potomac (August-November 1861)

Cocke's Brigade, Longstreet's Division, 1st Corps, Potomac District, Department of Northern Virginia (November 1861-January 1862)

Cocke's (old) Brigade, Longstreet's Division, Potomac District, Department of Northern Virginia (January-April 1862)

Pickett's Brigade, Longstreet's Division, Army of Northern Virginia (April-June 1862)

Artillery Battalion, Longstreet's Division, Army of Northern Virginia (June 1862)

Artillery Battalion, Longstreet's Division, 1st Corps, Army of Northern Virginia (June-July 1862)

Pickett's Brigade, Longstreet's Division, 1st Corps, Army of Northern Virginia (July-August 1862)

Artillery Battalion, Pickett's Division, 1st Corps, Army of Northern Virginia (October 1862-February 1863)

Artillery Battalion, Pickett's Division, Department of Virginia and North Carolina (February-April 1863)

Artillery Battalion, Pickett's Division, Department of Southern Virginia (April-May 1863)

Artillery Battalion, Pickett's Division, 1st Corps, Army of Northern Virginia (May-June 1863)

Battles: 1st Bull Run (July 21, 1861)
Yorktown Siege (April-May 1862)
Williamsburg (May 5, 1862)
Seven Pines (May 31-June 1, 1862)
Seven Days Battles (June 25-July 1, 1862)
Frayser's Farm (June 30, 1862)
Fredericksburg (December 13, 1862)
Suffolk Campaign (April-May 1863)

104. VIRGINIA LYNCHBURG "BEAUREGARD RIFLES" ARTILLERY BATTERY

Nickname: Lynchburg Beauregards

Organization: Organized in Campbell County on April 19, 1861. Enlisted for one year on May 16, 1861. Reorganized during the spring of 1862. Portsmouth Light Artillery disbanded and some of the men transferred to this battery on October 4, 1862, per S.O. #209, Headquarters, Army of Northern Virginia. Converted to horse artillery during the fall of 1862. Armed with four guns on July 1-3, 1863. Surrendered at Appomattox Court House, Virginia, on April 9, 1865.

First Commander: Marcellus Newton Moorman (Captain)

Captain: John Jordan Shoemaker

Assignments: Artillery Battalion, Department of Norfolk (July 1861-April 1862)

Mahone's Brigade, Huger's-R. H. Anderson's Division, Army of Northern Virginia (June-July 1862)

Artillery Battalion, R. H. Anderson's Division, 1st Corps, Army of Northern Virginia (July-September 1862)

Horse Artillery Battalion, Cavalry Division, Army of Northern Virginia (December 1862-September 1863)

Horse Artillery Battalion, Cavalry Corps, Army of Northern Virginia (September 1863-May 1864)

Horse Artillery Battalion, Rosser's Cavalry Division, Valley District, Department of Northern Virginia (September 1864-March 1865)

Breathed's Battalion, Horse Artillery, Cavalry Corps, Army of Northern Virginia (March-April 1865)

Battles: Seven Days Battles (June 25-July 1, 1862)

Brackett's (June 30, 1862)

Malvern Hill (July 1, 1862)

2nd Bull Run (August 28-30, 1862)

Harpers Ferry (September 12-15, 1862)

Antietam (September 17, 1862)

Port Royal (December 4, 1862)

Fredericksburg (December 13, 1862)

Rappahannock Bridge (April 14-15, 1863)

Chancellorsville (May 1-4, 1863)

Brandy Station (June 9, 1863)

Gettysburg (July 1-3, 1863)

Funkstown and Boonesborough (July 6-10, 1863)

Stanardsville, Virginia (February 29, 1864)

Petersburg Siege (June 1864-April 1865)

Appomattox Court House (April 9, 1865)

Further Reading: Shoemaker, John J., *Shoemaker's Battery, Stuart Horse Artillery, Pelham's Battalion, Afterwards commanded by Col. R. P. Chew, Army of Northern Virginia.*

105. VIRGINIA LYNCHBURG "LEE" ARTILLERY BATTERY

Organization: Organized at Lynchburg on May 28, 1861. Mustered into state service for the war at Lynchburg on June 7, 1861. Transferred to Confederate service on July 1, 1861. Armed with three 3-inch Rifles and one 12-lb. Howitzer from August 20, 1862, to September 24, 1862; two 20-lb. Parrotts, one 10-lb. Parrott and one 3-inch Rifle on July 1-3, 1863; two 12-lb. Napoleons on

December 26, 1864. Surrendered at Appomattox Court House, Virginia, on April 9, 1865.

First Commander: James Deshler (Captain)

Captains: Pierce B. Anderson
William W. Hardwicke
Charles I. Raine

Assignments: Army of the Northwest (July 1861)
Taliaferro's Brigade, Army of the Northwest (September-November 1861)
Johnson's Brigade, Jackson's Division, Army of the Northwest (November-December 1861)
Army of the Northwest (December 1861-March 1862)
Baldwin's Brigade, Army of the Northwest (May 1862)
Artillery, Ewell's Division, Valley District, Department of Northern Virginia (May-June 1862)
Artillery Battalion, Jackson's-Trimble's-Johnson's Division, 2nd Corps, Army of Northern Virginia (August 1862-July 1863)
Andrews'-Braxton's Battalion, Artillery, 2nd Corps, Army of Northern Virginia (July 1863-June 1864)
Braxton's Battalion, Artillery, Valley District, Department of Northern Virginia (June 1864-March 1865)
Braxton's Battalion, Artillery, 2nd Corps, Army of Northern Virginia (March-April 1865)

Battles: Rich Mountain (July 11, 1861)
Greenbrier River (October 3, 1861)
Camp Alleghany, West Virginia (December 13, 1861)
Shenandoah Valley Campaign of 1862 (May-June 1862)
Cross Keys (June 8, 1862)
2nd Bull Run (August 28-30, 1862)
Harpers Ferry (September 12-15, 1862)
Antietam (September 17, 1862)
Fredericksburg (December 13, 1862)
Chancellorsville (May 1-4, 1863)
2nd Winchester (June 14-15, 1863)
Gettysburg (July 1-3, 1863)
Bristoe Campaign (October 1863)
Mine Run Campaign (November-December 1863)
The Wilderness (May 5-6, 1864)
Spotsylvania Court House (May 8-21, 1864)
North Anna (May 22-26, 1864)
Cold Harbor (June 1-3, 1864)
Monocacy (July 9, 1864)

3rd Winchester (September 19, 1864)
Fisher's Hill (September 22, 1864)
Cedar Creek (October 19, 1864)
Waynesborough (March 2, 1865)
Petersburg Siege [from March 1865] (June 1864-April 1865)
Appomattox Court House (April 9, 1865)

106. Virginia Magruder Light Artillery Battery

See: VIRGINIA YORKTOWN "MAGRUDER" LIGHT ARTILLERY BATTERY

107. Virginia Manchester Artillery Battery

Organization: Organized and mustered into state service for one year at Manchester, Chesterfield County, on May 1, 1861. Initially served as part of the 6th and 16th Infantry Regiments. Reorganized as an independent company in May 1862. Armed with four guns on July 31, 1862. Consolidated with the Richmond "Courtney" Artillery Battery ca. August 1862. Disbanded and men transferred to that battery on April 15, 1863, per S.O. #92, Adjutant and Inspector General's Office.
First Commander: Emmett Washington Weisiger (Captain)
Assignment: Trimble's Brigade, Ewell's Division, 2nd Corps, Army of Northern Virginia (July-August 1862)
Battle: Cedar Mountain [not engaged] (August 9, 1862)

108. Virginia Marion, Company A, Artillery Battery

Nickname: Richmond Local Guards, Company A
Organization: Organized and mustered into Confederate service as a heavy artillery company for three years or the war at Richmond on December 15, 1861. Disbanded and mustered out of service on February 14, 1862, per S.O. #37, Adjutant and Inspector General's Office. Does not appear in the *Official Records.*
First Commander: Thomas P. Wilkinson (Captain)

109. Virginia Mathews Light Artillery Battery

Organization: Organized from Company H, 61st Infantry Regiment Militia, in Mathews County on July 5, 1861. Mustered into Confederate service for one year on July 18, 1861. Reorganized on March 22, 1862. Continued to serve in the militia regiment until May 14, 1862. Intended to be made one of the companies of the 4th Artillery Regiment. Surrendered at Appomattox Court House, Virginia, on April 9, 1865.
First Commander: Andrew D. Armistead (Captain)

Assignments: Gloucester Point (Crump's Command), Rains' Division, D. H. Hill's Command, Department of Northern Virginia (April-May 1862)

Crump's Brigade, D. H. Hill's Division, Army of Northern Virginia (May 1862)

Stark's Artillery Battalion, Wise's Brigade, Elzey's Command, Department of North Carolina and Southern Virginia (December 1862-April 1863)

Stark's Artillery Battalion, Wise's Brigade, Department of Richmond (April-September 1863)

Stark's Artillery Battalion, Hunton's Command, Department of Richmond (September-October 1863)

Stark's Light Artillery Battalion, Chaffin's Farm, Department of Richmond (December 1863-May 1864)

Stark's Light Artillery Battalion, Chaffin's Farm, Artillery Defenses, Department of Richmond (May-October 1864)

Stark's Battalion, Artillery, 1st Corps, Army of Northern Virginia (October 1864-February 1865)

Stark's Battalion, Artillery, 2nd Corps, Army of Northern Virginia (March-April 1865)

Battles: Yorktown Siege (April-May 1862)

Blake's Farm, near Deep Bottom, James River (August 6, 1863)

Petersburg Siege (June 1864-April 1865)

Chaffin's Farm (September 29, 1864)

Fort Gilmer (September 29-30, 1864)

Appomattox Court House (April 9, 1865)

110. VIRGINIA MIDDLESEX ARTILLERY BATTERY

Organization: Organized by the conversion of Company B, 55th Infantry Regiment, to artillery service in early 1862. Disbanded and men assigned to the Richmond "Johnson" Artillery Battery and to the Ashland Artillery Battery on October 4, 1862, per S.O. #209, Headquarters, Army of Northern Virginia.

First Commander: William C. Fleet (Captain)

Assignments: Field's Brigade, A. P. Hill's Division, 1st Corps, Army of Northern Virginia (July 1862)

Artillery Battalion, A. P. Hill's Division, 2nd Corps, Army of Northern Virginia (August-October 1862)

Battles: Cedar Mountain (August 9, 1862)

2nd Bull Run (August 28-30, 1862)

Harpers Ferry (September 12-15, 1862)

111. VIRGINIA MONROE ARTILLERY BATTERY

Nickname: Lewisburg (West Virginia) Artillery

Organization: Organized at Lewisburg, Monroe County (now in West Virginia), on March 27, 1862. Armed with two 3-inch Rifles on December 28, 1864. Ordered to turn over its equipment to other batteries and report to Richmond, Virginia, on March 17, 1865, where it was presumably included in Lee's surrender at Appomattox Court House on April 9, 1865.

First Commander: Thomas A. Bryan (Captain)

Assignments: Artillery Battalion, District of Lewisburg ("Army of New River"), Department of Southwestern Virginia (May 1862)

Artillery Battalion, Department of Western Virginia (September 1862-March 1863)

McCausland's Brigade, Department of Western Virginia (April-May 1863)

Artillery Battalion, Department of Western Virginia (May-October 1863)

Artillery Battalion, Ransom's Division, Department of Western Virginia and East Tennessee (October 1863-February 1864)

King's Battalion, Artillery, Department of East Tennessee (February-May 1864)

Artillery Battalion, Department of Southwestern Virginia (May-June 1864)

King's-McLaughlin's Battalion, Artillery, Valley District, Department of Northern Virginia (June 1864-March 1865)

Battles: Kanawha Campaign (September 1862)

Fayetteville, West Virginia (September 10, 1862)

Charleston, West Virginia (September 13, 1862)

Knoxville Campaign (November 1863)

Cloyd's Mountain (May 9, 1864)

New Market (May 15, 1864)

Lynchburg Campaign (June 1864)

Monocacy (July 9, 1864)

3rd Winchester (September 19, 1864)

Fisher's Hill (September 22, 1864)

Cedar Creek (October 19, 1864)

Waynesborough (March 2, 1865)

Petersburg Siege (from March 1865) (June 1864-April 1865)

Further Reading: Scott, J. L., *Lowry's, Bryan's and Chapman's Batteries of Virginia Artillery.*

112. VIRGINIA MONROE "DIXIE" ARTILLERY BATTERY

Organization: Organized in Monroe County on April 25, 1862. Armed with two 3-inch Rifles, one 12-lb. Howitzer and one 24-lb. Howitzer on August 26-27, 1863. Ordered to turn over its equipment to other batteries and report to Richmond, Virginia, on March 17, 1865, where it was presumably included in Lee's surrender at Appomattox Court House on April 9, 1865.

First Commander: George Beirne Chapman (Captain)

Captain: William A. Deas (never served)

Assignments: Artillery Battalion, District of Lewisburg ("Army of New River"), Department of Southwestern Virginia (May 1862)

Artillery Battalion, Department of Western Virginia (September 1862-March 1863)

Echols' Brigade, Department of Western Virginia (April-May 1863)

Artillery Battalion, Department of Western Virginia (May-October 1863)

Artillery Battalion, Ransom's Division, Department of Western Virginia and East Tennessee (October 1863-February 1864)

King's Battalion, Artillery, Department of East Tennessee (February-May 1864)

Artillery Battalion, Department of Southwestern Virginia (May-June 1864)

King's-McLaughlin's Battalion, Artillery, Valley District, Department of Northern Virginia (June 1864-March 1865)

Battles: Giles Court House, West Virginia (May 10, 1862)

Kanawha Campaign (September 1862)

Fayetteville, West Virginia (September 10, 1862)

Charleston, West Virginia (September 13, 1862)

Expedition to Beverly, West Virginia (June 29-July 4, 1863)

White Sulphur Springs (August 26-27, 1863)

Droop Mountain (November 6, 1863)

Knoxville Campaign (November 1863)

New Market (May 15, 1864)

Lynchburg Campaign (June 1864)

Monocacy (July 9, 1864)

3rd Winchester (September 19, 1864)

Fisher's Hill (September 22, 1864)

Cedar Creek (October 19, 1864)

Waynesborough (March 2, 1865)

Petersburg Siege (from March 1865) (June 1864-April 1865)

Further Reading: Scott, J. L., *Lowry's, Bryan's, and Chapman's Batteries of Virginia Artillery.*

113. VIRGINIA MORRIS ARTILLERY BATTERY

See: VIRGINIA LOUISA "MORRIS" ARTILLERY BATTERY

114. VIRGINIA NEBLETT'S-COLEMAN'S HEAVY ARTILLERY BATTERY

Organization: Organized for the war on March 1, 1862. Surrendered at Appomattox Court House, Virginia, on April 9, 1865.

First Commander: James H. M. Neblett (Captain)

Captain: Wiley G. Coleman

Assignments: Drewry's Bluff, Department of Richmond (July 1863-May 1864)

Drewry's Bluff, Department of North Carolina and Southern Virginia (May-October 1864)

Drewry's Bluff, Department of Richmond (October 1864-March 1865)

Smith's Battalion, Artillery, 4th Corps, Army of Northern Virginia (March-April 1865)

Battles: Drewry's Bluff (May 16, 1864)

Petersburg Siege (June 1864-April 1865)

Appomattox Court House (April 9, 1865)

115.   VIRGINIA NELSON LIGHT ARTILLERY BATTERY

Also Known As: Nelson Artillery, Company B

Nelson Artillery, No. 2

Organization: Organized for the war in Nelson County on August 1, 1861. Mustered into Confederate service August 31, 1861. Surrendered at Appomattox Court House, Virginia, on April 9, 1865.

First Commander: James Henry Rives (Captain)

Assignments: Unattached, Forces near Dumfries (Whiting's) Command, Potomac District, Department of Northern Virginia (January-March 1862)

Wise's Brigade, Department of Northern Virginia (June-July 1862)

1st Military District of South Carolina, Department of South Carolina, Georgia and Florida (July-September 1862)

Lightfoot's Light Artillery Battalion, Richmond Defenses, Department of Richmond (July 1863-March 1865)

Lightfoot's Battalion, Artillery, 2nd Corps, Army of Northern Virginia (April 1865)

Battles: Seven Days Battles (June 25-July 1, 1862)

Malvern Hill (July 1, 1862)

Coosawhatchie, South Carolina (October 22-23, 1862)

Destruction of the *George Washington*, near Beaufort, South Carolina (section) (April 9, 1863)

Petersburg Siege (June 1864-April 1865)

Fort Harrison (September 29-30, 1864)

Appomattox Court House (April 9, 1865)

116.   VIRGINIA NEW MARKET ARTILLERY BATTERY

See: VIRGINIA PAGE-SHENANDOAH "EIGHTH STAR" ARTILLERY BATTERY

117. VIRGINIA NORFOLK ARTILLERY BATTERY

Organization: Organized for one year by the division of the Norfolk "Light Artillery Blues" on June 8, 1861. Reorganized for the war on March 26, 1862. Armed with one 3-inch Rifle, one 10-lb. Parrott and two 6-lb. Smoothbores in August and September 1862. Portsmouth Light Artillery Battery disbanded and some of men transferred to this battery on October 4, 1862, per S.O. #209, Headquarters, Army of Northern Virginia. Armed with one 3-inch Rifle, one 10-lb. Parrott and two 12-lb. Napoleons on July 1-3, 1863. Armed with four 12-lb. Napoleons on December 28, 1864. Captured as part of Walker's artillery column on April 8, 1865.

First Commander: Frank Huger (Captain)

Captain: Joseph D. Moore

Assignments: Artillery Battalion, Department of Norfolk (July 1861-April 1862)

Artillery Battalion, Huger's Division, Department of Northern Virginia (April-June 1862)

Wright's Brigade, Huger's-R. H. Anderson's Division, Army of Northern Virginia (June-July 1862)

Artillery Battalion, R. H. Anderson's Division, 1st Corps, Army of Northern Virginia (July 1862-June 1863)

Artillery Battalion, Heth's Division, 3rd Corps, Army of Northern Virginia (June-July 1863)

Garnett's-Richardson's Battalion, Artillery, 3rd Corps, Army of Northern Virginia (July 1863-April 1865)

Battles: Seven Days Battles (June 25-July 1, 1862)

2nd Bull Run (August 28-30, 1862)

Harpers Ferry (September 12-15, 1862)

Antietam (September 17, 1862)

Fredericksburg (December 13, 1862)

Chancellorsville (May 1-4, 1863)

Gettysburg (July 1-3, 1863)

Williamsport (July 6, 1863)

Falling Waters (July 14, 1863)

Bristoe Campaign (October 1863)

Mine Run Campaign (November-December 1863)

The Wilderness (May 5-6, 1864)

Spotsylvania Court House (May 8-21, 1864)

North Anna (May 23-26, 1864)

Cold Harbor (June 1-3, 1864)

Petersburg Siege (June 1864-April 1865)

Appomattox Campaign (March-April 1865)

118. VIRGINIA NORFOLK "LIGHT ARTILLERY BLUES" BATTERY

Organization: Organized by the conversion of 1st Company H, 16th Infantry, to artillery service on March 25, 1862. In May 1862 the battery's armament comprised two 12-lb. Napoleons, two 12-lb. Howitzers and two 3-inch Rifles. Between July 1, 1863 and December 28, 1864, it comprised two 12-lb. Napoleons and two 3-inch Rifles. Captured as part of Walker's artillery column on April 8, 1865.

First Commander: Charles R. Grandy (Captain)

Assignments: Department of Norfolk (March-April 1862)

Artillery, Department of North Carolina (July 1862)

Artillery Battalion, Anderson's Division, 1st Corps, Army of Northern Virginia (December 1862-May 1863)

Artillery Battalion, Heth's Division, 3rd Corps, Army of Northern Virginia (May-July 1863)

Garnett's-Richardson's Battalion, Artillery, 3rd Corps, Army of Northern Virginia (July 1863-April 1865)

Battles: Fredericksburg (December 13, 1862)

Chancellorsville (May 1-4, 1863)

Gettysburg (July 1-3, 1863)

Falling Waters (July 14, 1863)

Mine Run Campaign (November-December 1863)

The Wilderness (May 5-6, 1864)

Spotsylvania Court House (May 8-21, 1864)

North Anna (May 22-26, 1864)

Cold Harbor (June 1-3, 1864)

Petersburg Siege (June 1864-April 1865)

Appomattox Campaign (March-April 1865)

119. VIRGINIA NOTTOWAY ARTILLERY

Organization: Organized for one year on June 24, 1861. Reorganized on May 24, 1862. On March 29, 1864, its armament comprised four 10-lb. Parrotts. No record subsequent to September 20, 1864.

First Commander: William C. Jeffress (Captain)

Assignments: Marshall's Brigade, Department #2 (November 1861-February 1862)

Marshall's Brigade, Army of Eastern Kentucky, Department #2 (February-May 1862)

District of Abingdon (May-November 1862)

District of Abingdon, Department of Western Virginia (November 1862-January 1863)

District of Abingdon, Department of East Tennessee (January-July 1863)

Preston's Brigade, Army of East Tennessee, Department of Tennessee (July-August 1863)

Artillery Battalion, Preston's Division, Buckner's Corps, Army of Tennessee (September 1863)

Artillery Battalion, Buckner's-Preston's Division, Longstreet's Corps, Army of Tennessee (September-October 1863)

Artillery Battalion, Buckner's Division, 1st Corps, Army of Tennessee (October-November 1863)

Williams' Battalion, Reserve Artillery, Army of Tennessee (November 1863-July 1864)

Williams' Battalion, Artillery, 2nd Corps, Army of Tennessee (July-September 1864)

Williams' Artillery Battalion, Macon, Georgia (presumably the army's reserve artillery), Army of Tennessee (September 1864)

Battles: Prestonburg (January 10, 1862)

Princeton, West Virginia (May 1862)

Chickamauga (September 19-20, 1863)

Chattanooga Siege (September-November 1863)

Chattanooga (November 23-25, 1863)

Atlanta Campaign (May-September 1864)

New Hope Church (May 25-June 4, 1864)

Atlanta Siege (July-September 1864)

120.   VIRGINIA ORANGE ARTILLERY BATTERY
See: VIRGINIA RICHMOND "ORANGE" ARTILLERY BATTERY

121.   VIRGINIA OTEY ARTILLERY BATTTERY
See: VIRGINIA RICHMOND "OTEY" ARTILLERY BATTERY

122.   VIRGINIA PAGE-SHENANDOAH "EIGHTH STAR" ARTILLERY BATTERY

Nickname: New Market Artillery

Organization: Organized for one year in Page and Shenandoah counties on April 22, 1861. Reorganized in the spring of 1862. Merged into the Danville Artillery Battery on September 26, 1862.

First Commander: William H. Rice (Captain)

Captain: Robert Sidney Rice

Assignments: Taliaferro's Brigade, Army of the Northwest (August-October 1861)

Johnson's Brigade, H. R. Jackson's Division, Army of the Northwest (November-December 1861)

Johnson's Brigade, Army of the Northwest (December 1861-January 1862)
Army of the Northwest (March-May 1862)
Artillery Battalion, Ewell's Division, Valley District, Department of Northern
    Virginia (May-June 1862)
Unattached, Reserve Artillery, Army of Northern Virginia (September 1862)
Battles: Greenbrier River (October 3, 1861)
Shenandoah Valley Campaign of 1862 (May-June 1862)
Antietam (September 17, 1862)

123. VIRGINIA PAMUNKEY ARTILLERY BATTERY

Nicknames: Pamunkey Guards
Pamunkey Rescuers
Organization: Organized for one year in New Kent County on May 21, 1861.
Served as heavy artillery. Armed with nine heavy guns on December 30, 1864.
Surrendered at Appomattox Court House, Virginia, on April 9, 1865.
First Commander: Robert T. Ellett (Captain)
Captain: Andrew Judson Jones
Assignments: Chaffin's Bluff, Department of Richmond (July 1863-May 1864)
Chaffin's Bluff, Artillery Defenses, Department of Richmond (May 1864-February 1865)
Chaffin's Bluff, Crutchfield's Artillery Brigade, Department of Richmond (February-March 1865)
Chaffin's Bluff, Crutchfield's Artillery Brigade, G. W. C. Lee's Division, Department of Richmond (March-April 1865)
Crutchfield's Artillery Brigade, G. W. C. Lee's Division, Army of Northern
    Virginia (April 1865)
Battles: Petersburg Siege (June 1864-April 1865)
Fort Harrison (September 29, 1864)
Chaffin's Farm (September 29, 1864)
Fort Gilmer (September 29-30, 1864)
Harman Road (October 2, 1864)
Sayler's Creek (April 6, 1865)
Appomattox Court House (April 9, 1865)

124. VIRGINIA PEARLSBURG RESERVES ARTILLERY BATTERY

See: VIRGINIA GILES LIGHT ARTILLERY BATTERY; VIRGINIA WISE LEGION
ARTILLERY BATTALION, COMPANY B

125. VIRGINIA PENINSULA ARTILLERY BATTERY

Organization: Organized for the war in York County on May 18, 1861. Served
as Company G, 1st Artillery Regiment. Armed with one 12-lb. Napoleon on

June 24, 1862. Disbanded and men transferred to the other companies of the regiment in June 1862.

First Commander: Joseph B. Cosnahan (Captain)

Captain: William B. Jones

Assignments: Artillery, Department of the Peninsula (October 1861-January 1862)

McLaws' Division, Department of the Peninsula (January 1862)

Griffith's Brigade, McLaws' Division, Magruder's Command, Department of Northern Virginia (April-May 1862)

Cabell's Artillery Battalion, Magruder's Division, Army of Northern Virginia (May-June 1862)

Anderson's Brigade, Magruder's Division, Army of Northern Virginia (June 1862)

Battles: Yorktown Siege (April-May 1862)

Lee's Mill (April 5, 1862)

126. VIRGINIA PETERSBURG ARTILLERY BATTERY

Nicknames: Branch Field Artillery

Lee's Life Guard

Organization: Organized by the conversion of 1st Company K, 16th Infantry Regiment, to artillery service on March 18, 1862, per S.O. #62, Adjutant and Inspector General's Office. Armed with three 12-lb. Howitzers, one 10-lb. Parrott and two 3-inch Rifles in August and September 1862. Armed with four 12-lb. Napoleons on December 28, 1864. Surrendered at Appomattox Court House, Virginia, on April 9, 1865.

First Commander: James Read Branch (Captain)

Captain: Richard Gregory Pegram

Assignments: Artillery Battalion, Holmes' Division, Army of Northern Virginia (June-July 1862)

Artillery Battalion, Department of North Carolina (July 1862)

Ransom's Brigade, Walker's-Ransom's Division, 1st Corps, Army of Northern Virginia (September 1862-January 1863)

Ransom's Brigade, French's Command, Department of North Carolina and Southern Virginia (February 1863)

Ransom's Brigade, District of the Cape Fear, D. H. Hill's Command, Department of North Carolina and Southern Virginia (February-March 1863)

Unattached, District of the Cape Fear, Department of North Carolina and Southern Virginia (March-April 1863)

Unattached, District of the Cape Fear, Department of North Carolina (April-May 1863)

Ransom's Brigade, Department of North Carolina (May-June 1863)

Branch's Battalion, Artillery, Department of North Carolina (June-July 1863)

Branch's Artillery Battalion, Ransom's Division, Department of North Carolina (July-September 1863)

Branch's Battalion, Artillery, Department of North Carolina (September 1863-May 1864)

Coit's Battalion, Artillery, Department of North Carolina and Southern Virginia (May-June 1864)

Artillery Battalion, Johnson's Division, Department of North Carolina and Southern Virginia (June 1864)

Branch's-Coit's Battalion, Artillery, Department of North Carolina and Southern Virginia (June-October 1864)

Branch's-Coit's Battalion, Artillery, 4th Corps, Army of Northern Virginia (October 1864-April 1865)

Battles: Seven Days Battles (June 25-July 1, 1862)

Antietam (September 17, 1862)

Fredericksburg (December 13, 1862)

Swift Creek (May 9, 1864)

Drewry's Bluff (May 16, 1864)

Petersburg Siege (June 1864-April 1865)

The Crater (July 30, 1864)

Appomattox Court House (April 9, 1865)

127. VIRGINIA PETERSBURG "COCKADE" ARTILLERY BATTERY

Organization: Organized at Petersburg on May 14, 1861. Mustered into state service for one year at Petersburg on June 1, 1861. Mustered into Confederate service on June 30, 1861. Temporarily attached to the 10th Heavy Artillery Battalion and to the 1st Light Artillery Regiment. Reorganized on May 10, 1862. Became Company C, 18th Heavy Artillery Battalion, on June 21, 1862, per S.O. #143, Adjutant and Inspector General's Office.

First Commander: Gilbert V. Rambaut (Captain)

Captain: Bernard J. Black

Assignment: Jamestown Island (Carter's Command), Department of the Peninsula (January-February 1862)

128. VIRGINIA PETERSBURG HORSE ARTILLERY BATTERY

Organization: Organized in Petersburg on April 25, 1843. Enlisted for one year in the 4th Infantry Battalion Volunteers (Militia) on April 19, 1861. Detached from the battalion in April 1861. Reorganized as a horse artillery unit in May 1862. Apparently armed with rockets in late 1862. Armed with two 12-lb. Howitzers and two 3-inch Rifles on December 28, 1864. Surrendered at Appomattox Court House, Virginia, on April 9, 1865.

First Commander: James Nathaniel Nichols (Captain)

Captain: Edward Graham

Assignments: Clarke's (5th) Brigade, Department of Norfolk (February-April 1862)

Light Artillery, Department of North Carolina (July 1862-July 1863)

District of North Carolina, Department of North Carolina (July-September 1863)

Unattached Artillery, Department of North Carolina (December 1863-January 1864)

Branch's-Coit's Battalion, Artillery, Department of North Carolina and Southern Virginia (May-June 1864)

Dearing's Cavalry Brigade, Department of North Carolina and Southern Virginia (August-September 1864)

Chew's Battalion, Artillery, Cavalry Corps, Army of Northern Virginia (September 1864-April 1865)

Battles: near Franklin, Virginia, on the Blackwater (October 3, 1862)

near Franklin, Virginia, on the Blackwater (December 2, 1862)

Petersburg (June 9, 1864)

Petersburg Siege (June 1864-April 1865)

Peebles' Farm (September 29-October 2, 1864)

Harman Road (October 2, 1864)

Appomattox Court House (April 9, 1865)

129. VIRGINIA PITTSYLVANIA ARTILLERY BATTERY

Organization: Organized for three years or the war in Pittsylvania County on April 3, 1862. Intended to be assigned to the 1st (Fitzgerald's) Confederate Artillery Regiment, which failed to complete its organization. Armed with two 3-inch Rifles and two 10-lb. Parrotts in September 1862. Armed with two 3-inch Rifles and two 12-lb. Napoleons on July 1-3, 1863. Armed with two 3-inch Rifles and two 10-lb. Parrotts on December 28, 1864. Surrendered at Appomattox Court House, Virginia, on April 9, 1865. Note: This battery is alleged to have fired the last artillery round of the Army of Northern Virginia.

First Commander: Benjamin H. Motley (Captain)

Captains: John W. Lewis

Nathan Penick

Assignments: Artillery Battalion, R. H. Anderson's Division, 1st Corps, Army of Northern Virginia (September 1862-June 1863)

Artillery Battalion, Heth's Division, 3rd Corps, Army of Northern Virginia (June-July 1863)

Garnett's-Richardson's Battalion, Artillery, 3rd Corps, Army of Northern Virginia (July 1863-September 1864)

Poague's Battalion, Artillery, 3rd Corps, Army of Northern Virginia (September 1864-April 1865)
Battles: Fredericksburg (December 13, 1862)
Chancellorsville (May 1-4, 1863)
Gettysburg (July 1-3, 1863)
Falling Waters (July 14, 1863)
Bristoe Campaign (October 1863)
Mine Run Campaign (November-December 1863)
The Wilderness (May 5-6, 1864)
Spotsylvania Court House (May 8-21, 1864)
North Anna (May 23-26, 1864)
Cold Harbor (June 1-3, 1864)
Petersburg Siege (June 1864-April 1865)
Appomattox Court House (April 9, 1865)

130. VIRGINIA PORTSMOUTH LIGHT ARTILLERY

Organization: Organized at Portsmouth, Norfolk County, in 1808. Mustered into Confederate service for one year on April 20, 1861. Reorganized on April 1, 1862. Disbanded and the men were transferred to the Norfolk Artillery Battery and to the Lynchburg "Beauregard Rifles" Artillery Battery on October 4, 1862, per S.O. #209, Headquarters, Army of Northern Virginia.
First Commander: Carey F. Grimes (Captain)
Captain: John H. Thompson
Assignments: Artillery Battalion, Department of Norfolk (July 1861-April 1862)
Mahone's Brigade, Department of Norfolk (April 1862)
Mahone's Brigade, Huger's-R. H. Anderson's Division, Army of Northern Virginia (April-July 1862)
Artillery Battalion, R. H. Anderson's Division, 1st Corps, Army of Northern Virginia (July-October 1862)
Battles: near Hoffler's Creek (October 7, 1861)
Hoffler's Creek (April 23, 1862)
Pasquotank Creek vs. USS *Lockwood* (May 2, 1862)
Seven Days Battles (June 25-July 1, 1862)
French's Farm (June 25, 1862)
Malvern Hill (July 1, 1862)
City Point (vs. U.S. Navy) (July 28, 1862)
Warrenton Springs (August 26, 1862)
2nd Bull Run (August 28-30, 1862)
South Mountain (September 14, 1862)
Antietam (September 17, 1862)

131. VIRGINIA POWHATAN ARTILLERY BATTERY

Organization: Organized for one year in Powhatan County on July 16, 1861. Reorganized in the spring of 1862. Temporarily served as part of the 1st Artillery Regiment and the 1st Artillery Battalion, Armed with one 3-inch Rifle, one 6-lb. Smoothbore and two 12-lb. Howitzers in August and September 1862. Armed with four 3-inch Rifles from July 1, 1863, to December 28, 1864. Surrendered at Appomattox Court House, on April 9, 1865.

First Commander: Willis Jefferson Dance (Captain)

Assignments: Reserve Artillery, Potomac District, Department of Northern Virginia (November 1861-March 1862)

Reserve Artillery, Army of Northern Virginia (April-June 1862)

Brown's Battalion, Reserve Artillery, Army of Northern Virginia (June 1862-February 1863)

Brown's Battalion, Reserve Artillery, 2nd Corps, Army of Northern Virginia (February-July 1863)

Brown's-Hardaway's Battalion, Artillery, 2nd Corps, Army of Northern Virginia (July 1863-June 1864)

Hardaway's Battalion, Artillery, 1st Corps, Army of Northern Virginia (June 1864-March 1865)

Hardaway's Battalion, Artillery, 2nd Corps, Army of Northern Virginia (March-April 1865)

Battles: Yorktown Siege (April-May 1862)

Seven Days Battles (June 25-July 1, 1862)

Antietam (September 17, 1862)

Fredericksburg (December 13, 1862)

Chancellorsville (May 1-4, 1863)

Gettysburg (July 1-3, 1863)

Bristoe Campaign (October 1863)

Mine Run Campaign (November-December 1863)

The Wilderness (May 5-6, 1864)

Spotsylvania Court House (May 8-21, 1864)

North Anna (May 23-26, 1864)

Cold Harbor (June 1-3, 1864)

Petersburg Siege (June 1864-April 1865)

Chaffin's Farm (September 29, 1864)

Fort Gilmer (September 29-30, 1864)

Appomattox Court House (April 9, 1865)

132. VIRGINIA PRICE'S HEAVY ARTILLERY BATTERY

Organization: Organized for three years or the war in Fluvanna and Albemarle counties on April 3, 1862. Intended to be assigned to Harris' Heavy

Artillery Battalion, which failed to complete its organization. Battery disbanded and men assigned to Company B, 18th Heavy Artillery Battalion, on June 21, 1862, per S.O. #143, Adjutant and Inspector General's Office. Does not appear in the *Official Records*.

First Commander: Henry Monroe Price (Captain)

133. VIRGINIA READ'S HEAVY ARTILLERY BATTERY

Organization: Organized on April 12, 1862. Disbanded and men transferred to Company B, 19th Heavy Artillery Battalion, on June 21, 1862, per S.O. #143, Adjutant and Inspector General's Office.

First Commander: Alvan E. Read (Captain)

Assignment: Department of Norfolk (April 1862)

134. VIRGINIA RICHMOND "COURTNEY" ARTILLERY BATTERY

Also Known As: Courtney Artillery Battery

Nickname: Henrico Artillery

Organization: Organized for one year in Henrico County on July 8, 1861. Intended to form part of the 4th Artillery Regiment, which failed to complete its organization. Reorganized on April 28, 1862. Armed with two 3-inch Rifles and two 12-lb. Napoleons in August and September 1862. Manchester Light Artillery Battery transferred to this battery on September 1, 1862, by order of Major General Thomas J. Jackson. Order confirmed on April 15, 1863, per S.O. #92, Adjutant and Inspector General's Office. Armed with four 3-inch Rifles on July 1-3, 1863. It apparently was consolidated with other batteries of Cutshaw's Artillery Battalion some time in late 1864.

First Commander: Alfred R. Courtney (Captain)

Captains: Joseph W. Latimer

William A. Tanner

Assignments: Trimble's Brigade, E. K. Smith's-Ewell's Division, Potomac District, Department of Northern Virginia (January-May 1862)

Artillery Battalion, Ewell's Division, Valley District, Department of Northern Virginia (May-June 1862)

Trimble's Brigade, Ewell's Division, 2nd Corps, Army of Northern Virginia (June-July 1862)

Artillery Battalion, Ewell's-Early's Division, 2nd Corps, Army of Northern Virginia (August 1862-February 1863)

Artillery Battalion, Jackson's (old) Division, 2nd Corps, Army of Northern Virginia (February-June 1863)

Artillery Battalion, Early's Division, 2nd Corps, Army of Northern Virginia (June-July 1863)

Jones'-Cutshaw's Battalion, Artillery, 2nd Corps, Army of Northern Virginia (July 1863-May 1864)

Cutshaw's Battalion, Artillery, Valley District, Department of Northern Virginia (October-November 1864)

Battles: Shenandoah Valley Campaign of 1862 (May-June 1862)
Cross Keys (June 8, 1862)
Seven Days Battles (June 25-July 1, 1862)
Gaines' Mill (June 27, 1962)
Cedar Mountain (August 9, 1862)
2nd Bull Run (August 28-30, 1862)
Chantilly (September 1, 1862)
Harpers Ferry (September 12-15, 1862)
Fredericksburg (December 13, 1862)
Chancellorsville (May 1-4, 1863)
Gettysburg (July 1-3, 1863)
Bristoe Campaign (October 1863)
Mine Run Campaign (November-December 1863)
The Wilderness (May 5-6, 1864)
Spotsylvania Court House (May 8-21, 1864)
North Anna (May 23-26, 1864)
Cold Harbor (June 1-3, 1864)
Cedar Creek (October 19, 1864)

135. VIRGINIA RICHMOND "CRENSHAW" ARTILLERY BATTERY

Organization: Organized in Richmond for three years or the war on March 14, 1862. Armed on that date with two 10-lb. Parrotts, two 12-lb. Howitzers and two 6-lb. Smoothbores. From July 1, 1863, to December 28, 1864, armed with four 12-lb. Napoleons. Disbanded on April 9, 1865.

First Commander: William G. Crenshaw (Captain)

Captain: Thomas Ellet

Assignments: Artillery Battalion, A. P. Hill's Division, Army of Northern Virginia (June 1862)

Artillery Battalion, A. P. Hill's Division, 1st Corps, Army of Northern Virginia (June-July 1862)

J. R. Anderson's Brigade, A. P. Hill's Division, 1st Corps, Army of Northern Virginia (July 1862)

Artillery Battalion, A. P. Hill's Division, 2nd Corps, Army of Northern Virginia (August 1862-May 1863)

Pegram's Battalion, Reserve Artillery, 3rd Corps, Army of Northern Virginia (May-July 1863)

Pegram's Battalion, Artillery, 3rd Corps, Army of Northern Virginia (July 1863-April 1865)

Battles: Seven Pines (May 31-June 1, 1862)
Seven Days Battles (June 25-July 1, 1862)
Beaver Dam Creek (June 26, 1862)
Gaines' Mill (June 27, 1862)
Frayser's Farm (June 30, 1862)
Malvern Hill (July 1, 1862)
Cedar Mountain (August 9, 1862)
Warrenton Springs (August 23, 1862)
2nd Bull Run (August 28-30, 1862)
Chantilly (September 1, 1862)
Harpers Ferry (September 12-15, 1862)
Antietam (September 17, 1862)
Shepherdstown Ford (September 20, 1862)
Fredericksburg (December 13, 1862)
Chancellorsville (May 1-4, 1863)
Gettysburg (July 1-3, 1863)
Bristoe Campaign (October 1863)
Bristoe Station (October 14, 1863)
Rixeyville (November 9, 1863)
Mine Run Campaign (November-December 1863)
The Wilderness (May 5-6, 1864)
Spotsylvania Court House (May 8-21, 1864)
North Anna (May 22-26, 1864)
Cold Harbor (June 1-3, 1864)
Turkey Ridge (June 9, 1864)
Petersburg Siege (June 1864-April 1865)
Reams' Station (June 29, 1864)
The Crater (July 30, 1864)
Archer's Farm (August 18, 1864)
Davis' Farm (August 21, 1864)
Squirrel Level Road (September 30, 1864)
Jones' Farm (September 30, 1864)
Pegram's Farm (October 1, 1864)
Reams' Station (August 25, 1864)
Squirrel Level Road (October 8, 1864)
Burgess' Mill (October 27, 1864)
Hatcher's Run (February 5-7, 1865)
Fort Stedman (March 25, 1865)
Five Forks (April 1, 1865)

Petersburg Final Assault (April 2, 1865)
Appomattox Station (April 8, 1865)
Appomattox Court House (April 9, 1865)

136. VIRGINIA RICHMOND "DABNEY" ARTILLERY BATTERY

Nickname: Game Point Battery

Organization: Organized in early 1862. Enlisted for three years or the war on April 23, 1862. Intended to become part of Harris' Heavy Artillery Battalion, which failed to complete its organization. Became Company E, 20th Artillery Battalion, in late 1863 or early 1864.

First Commander: William J. Dabney (Captain)

Assignments: Unattached, Reserve Artillery, Army of Northern Virginia (June-July 1862)

Artillery, Department of North Carolina and Southern Virginia (September 1862-January 1863)

Unattached, French's Command, Department of North Carolina and Southern Virginia (January-February 1863)

Moseley's Artillery Battalion, French's Command, Department of North Carolina and Southern Virginia (February-April 1863)

Moseley's Artillery Battalion, Department of Southern Virginia (April-May 1863)

Moseley's Battalion, Artillery, Department of North Carolina (May-July 1863)

Moseley's Battalion, Artillery, Ransom's Division, Department of Richmond (July-September 1863)

Battles: Seven Days Battles (June 25-July 1, 1862)

Gaines' Mill (June 27, 1862)

New Bridge Road (June 28, 1862)

137. VIRGINIA RICHMOND "FAYETTE" ARTILLERY BATTERY

Organization: Organized by the conversion of Company F, 1st Artillery Regiment, to artillery service in early 1861. Served as Company I (AKA: H), 1st Artillery Regiment, until ca. July 1862. Armed with two 10-lb. Parrotts and four 6-lb. Smoothbores in August and September 1862. Armed with one 12-lb. Howitzer, three 6-lb. Smoothbores and two 10-lb. Parrotts on September 17, 1862. Became Company B, 38th Artillery Battalion, ca. June 1863.

First Commander: Henry Coalter Cabell (Captain)

Captain: Miles C. Macon

Assignments: Department of the Peninsula (January-April 1862)

Pryor's Brigade, Longstreet's Division, Department of Northern Virginia (April-May 1862)

Brown's Battalion, Reserve Artillery, Army of Northern Virginia (June-July 1862)

Artillery Battalion, McLaws' Division, 1st Corps, Army of Northern Virginia (September 1862)

Artillery Battalion, Pickett's Division, 1st Corps, Army of Northern Virginia (October 1862-February 1863)

Artillery Battalion, Pickett's Division, Department of North Carolina and Southern Virginia (February-April 1863)

Artillery Battalion, Pickett's Division, Department of Southern Virginia (April-May 1863)

Artillery Battalion, Pickett's Division, 1st Corps, Army of Northern Virginia (May-June 1863)

Battles: Yorktown Siege (April-May 1862)

Williamsburg (May 5, 1862)

Seven Days Battles (June 25-July 1, 1862)

Harpers Ferry (September 12-15, 1862)

Antietam (September 17, 1862)

Fredericksburg (December 13, 1862)

Suffolk Campaign (April-May 1863)

Further Reading: Chamberlayne, Edwin H., *War History and Roll of the Richmond Fayette Artillery, 38th Virginia Battalion Artillery, Confederate States Army, 1861-1865.*

138.   VIRGINIA RICHMOND "FAYETTE" ARTILLERY BATTERY, 2ND COMPANY

Organization: Organization attempted at Richmond in July and August 1861. Failed to complete its organization.

139.   VIRGINIA RICHMOND "FLYING" ARTILLERY BATTERY

See: VIRGINIA 24TH CAVALRY BATTALION, PARTISAN RANGERS

140.   VIRGINIA RICHMOND "GERMAN" LIGHT ARTILLERY BATTERY

Organization: Failed to complete its organization in early 1861.

First Commander: Louis von Buckholtz (Captain)

141.   VIRGINIA RICHMOND "HAMPDEN" ARTILLERY BATTERY

Organization: Organized in Richmond in April 1861. Mustered into state service for one year on May 11, 1861. Reorganized on April 21, 1862. Armed with three 6-lb. Smoothbores and one 10-lb. Parrott in August and September 1862. Richmond "Thomas" Artillery Battery merged into this battery on

October 4, 1862, per S.O. #209, Headquarters, Army of Northern Virginia. Became Company C, 38th Artillery Battalion, ca. June 1863.

First Commander: Lawrence Slaughter Marye (Captain)

Captain: William Henderson Caskie

Assignments: S. R. Anderson's brigade, Army of the Northwest (August-December 1861)

Gilham's Brigade, Army of the Northwest (December 1861)

Artillery, Army of the Northwest (January 1862)

Burks'-Campbell's Brigade, Valley District, Department of Northern Virginia (January-May 1862)

Artillery, Jackson's Division, Valley District, Department of Northern Virginia (May-June 1862)

Cunningham's-J. R. Jones' Brigade, Jackson's Division, 2nd Corps, Army of Northern Virginia (June-July 1862)

Artillery Battalion, Jackson's Division, 2nd Corps, Army of Northern Virginia (August 1862-February 1863)

Artillery Battalion, Pickett's Division, Department of Southern Virginia (April-May 1863)

Artillery Battalion, Pickett's Division, 1st Corps, Army of Northern Virginia (May-June 1863)

Battles: Kernstown (March 23, 1862)

Shenandoah Valley Campaign of 1862 (May-June 1862)

Cedar Mountain (August 9, 1862)

2nd Bull Run (August 28-30, 1862)

Harpers Ferry (September 12-15, 1862)

Antietam (September 17, 1862)

Fredericksburg (December 13, 1862)

Suffolk Campaign (April-May 1863)

142. VIRGINIA RICHMOND "HOME" ARTILLERY BATTERY

Organization: Organized in Richmond in early July 1861. Having failed to obtain guns, it was disbanded later the same month.

143. VIRGINIA RICHMOND HOWITZERS ARTILLERY BATTALION

Organization: Organized by the division of the prewar Howitzers Artillery Battery into three companies prior to May 11, 1861. A fourth company was briefly organized later. Batteries served separately.

First Commander: George Wythe Randolph (Major)

Further Reading: McCarthy, Carlton, *Contributions to a History of the Richmond Howitzers Battalion.* Daniel, Frederick S., *Richmond Howitzers in the War: Four Years Campaigning with the Army of Northern Virginia.*

144. VIRGINIA RICHMOND HOWITZERS ARTILLERY BATTALION, 1ST COMPANY

Organization: Organized at Richmond November 9, 1859. Enlisted on April 21, 1861. Reorganized in May 1862. Armed with two 10-lb. Parrotts and two 6-lb. Smoothbores in August and September 1862. Armed with two 3-inch Rifles and two 12-lb. Napoleons on July 1-3, 1863. One section armed with two 12-lb. Napoleons on May 10, 1864. ARmed with four 12-lb. Napoleons in December 1864. Captured as part of Walker's artillery column on April 8, 1865.

First Commander: John Camden Shields (Captain)

Captains: William P. Palmer

Edward S. McCarthy

Robert M. Anderson

Assignments: Bonham's Brigade, Army of the Potomac (July 1861)

Bonham's Brigade, 1st Corps, Army of the Potomac (July-August 1861)

Artillery, Forces at Dumfries (D. H. Hill's Command), Potomac District, Department of Northern Virginia (January-February 1862)

Griffith's Brigade, McLaws' Division, Magruder's Command, Department of Northern Virginia (April-May 1862)

Griffith's Brigade, Magruder's Division, Department of Northern Virginia (May 1862)

Griffith's Brigade, Magruder's Division, Magruder's Command, Army of Northern Virginia (June-July 1862)

Griffith's-Barksdale's Brigade, McLaws' Division, 1st Corps, Army of Northern Virginia (July-September 1862)

Artillery Battalion, McLaws' Division, 1st Corps, Army of Northern Virginia (September 1862-July 1863)

Cabell's Battalion, Artillery, 1st Corps, Army of Northern Virginia (July-September 1863)

Cabell's Battalion, Reserve Artillery, Army of Northern Virginia (September 1863-March 1864)

Cabell's Battalion, Artillery, 1st Corps, Army of Northern Virginia (March 1864-April 1865)

Battles: Blackburn's Ford (July 18, 1861)

1st Bull Run (July 21, 1861)

Yorktown Siege (April-May 1862)

Williamsburg skirmish (May 4, 1862)

Seven Days Battles (June 25-July 1, 1862)

South Mountain (September 14, 1862)
Antietam (September 17, 1862)
Fredericksburg (December 13, 1862)
Chancellorsville (May 1-4, 1863)
Gettysburg (July 1-3, 1863)
Bristoe Campaign (October 1863)
Morton's Ford (February 7, 1864)
The Wilderness (May 5-6, 1864)
Spotsylvania Court House (May 8-21, 1864)
North Anna (May 23-26, 1864)
Cold Harbor (June 1-3, 1864)
Petersburg Siege (June 1864-April 1865)
Appomattox Campaign (March-April 1865)

Further Reading: McCarthy, Carlton, *Contributions to a History of the Richmond Howitzers Battalion.* Daniel, Frederick S., *Richmond Howitzers in the War: Four Years Campaigning with the Army of Northern Virginia.*

145. VIRGINIA RICHMOND HOWITZERS ARTILLERY BATTALION, 2ND COMPANY

Organization: Organized prior to May 11, 1861. Served in the 1st Artillery Regiment (as Companies A, I and K) until it became independent ca. September 2, 1864. Armed with two 10-lb. Parrotts, one 2.6-inch Hotchkiss Rifle and one 12-lb. Dahlgren Howitzer from September 17, 1862, to October 17, 1862. Armed with four 10-lb. Parrotts on July 1-3, 1863. Armed with two 10-lb. Parrotts and two 12-lb. Napoleons on December 28, 1864. Surrendered at Appomattox Court House, Virginia, on April 9, 1865.

First Commander: Lorraine Farquhar Jones (Captain)

Assignments: Artillery, Department of the Peninsula (June-October 1861)
Artillery, Forces at Leesburg (D. H. Hill's Command), Potomac District, Department of Northern Virginia (January-March 1862)
Reserve Artillery, Army of Northern Virginia (April-June 1862)
Brown's Battalion, Reserve Artillery, Army of Northern Virginia (June 1862-February 1863)
Brown's Battalion, Reserve Artillery, 2nd Corps, Army of Northern Virginia (February-July 1863)
Brown's-Hardaway's Battalion, Artillery, 2nd Corps, Army of Northern Virginia (July 1863-June 1864)
Cutshaw's Battalion, Artillery, Valley District, Department of Northern Virginia (September 1864-March 1865)
Cutshaw's Battalion, Artillery, 2nd Corps, Army of Northern Virginia (March-April 1865)

Battles: Big Bethel (June 10, 1861)
Yorktown Siege (April-May 1862)
Seven Pines (May 31-June 1, 1862)
Seven Days Battles (June 25-July 1, 1862)
Antietam (September 17, 1862)
Fredericksburg (December 13, 1862)
Chancellorsville (May 1-4, 1863)
Gettysburg (July 1-3, 1863)
Bristoe Campaign (October 1863)
Mine Run Campaign (November-December 1863)
The Wilderness (May 5-6, 1864)
Spotsylvania Court House (May 8-21, 1864)
North Anna (May 23-26, 1864)
Cold Harbor (June 1-3, 1864)
Cedar Creek (October 19, 1864)
Waynesborough (March 2, 1865)
Petersburg Siege (June 1864-April 1865)
Appomattox Court House (April 9, 1865)
Further Reading: McCarthy, Carlton, *Detailed Minutie of Soldier Life in the Army of Northern Virginia, 1861-1865.* McCarthy, Carlton, *Contributions to a History of the Richmond Howitzers Battalion.*

146. VIRGINIA RICHMOND HOWITZERS ARTILLERY BATTALION, 3RD COMPANY

Organization: Organized prior to May 11, 1861. Served as part of the 1st Artillery Regiment and later the 1st Artillery Battalion until the latter was disbanded on January 18, 1865, per S.O. #14, Adjutant and Inspector General's Office, and this company became independent. Armed with four 3-inch Rifles on July 1-3, 1863. Armed with two 3-inch Rifles and two 12-lb. Napoleons on May 10, 1864. Reduced to a section armed with two 3-inch Rifles on May 11, 1864. Armed with four 12-lb. Napoleons on December 28, 1864. Surrendered at Appomattox Court House, Virginia, on April 9, 1865.
First Commander: Benjamin H. Smith (Captain)
Assignments: Artillery, Department of the Peninsula (June-October 1861)
Artillery, Forces at Leesburg (D. H. Hill's Command), Potomac District, Department of Northern Virginia (January-March 1862)
Reserve Artillery, Army of Northern Virginia (April-June 1862)
Brown's Battalion, Reserve Artillery, Army of Northern Virginia (June 1862-February 1863)
Brown's Battalion, Reserve Artillery, 2nd Corps, Army of Northern Virginia (February-July 1863)

Brown's-Hardaway's Battalion, Artillery, 2nd Corps, Army of Northern Virginia (July 1863-June 1864)

Hardaway's Battalion, Artillery, 1st Corps, Army of Northern Virginia (June 1864-March 1865)

Hardaway's Battalion, Artillery, 2nd Corps, Army of Northern Virginia (March-April 1865)

Battles: Big Bethel (June 10, 1861)
near Newport News (July 5, 1861)
Yorktown Siege (April-May 1862)
Seven Days Battles (June 25-July 1, 1862)
Antietam (September 17, 1862)
Charlestown, West Virginia (October 16, 1862)
Fredericksburg (December 13, 1862)
Chancellorsville (May 1-4, 1863)
Gettysburg (July 1-3, 1863)
The Wilderness (May 5-6, 1864)
Spotsylvania Court House (May 8-21, 1864)
North Anna (May 23-26, 1864)
Cold Harbor (June 1-3, 1864)
Petersburg Siege (June 1864-April 1865)
3rd New Market Heights (September 29, 1864)
Chaffin's Farm (September 29, 1864)
Fort Gilmer (September 29-30, 1864)
Appomattox Court House (April 9, 1865)

Further Reading: McCarthy, Carlton, *Contributions to a History of the Richmond Howitzers Battalion*. Daniel, Frederick S., *Richmond Howitzers in the War: Four Years Campaigning with the Army of Northern Virginia*.

147. VIRGINIA RICHMOND HOWITZERS ARTILLERY BATTALION, 4TH COMPANY

Organization: Organized on July 18, 1861. Disbanded by order of Governor John Letcher on August 29, 1861.

First Commander: Napoleon B. Binford (Captain)

Further Reading: McCarthy, Carlton, *Contributions to a History of the Richmond Howitzers Battalion*. Daniel, Frederick S., *Richmond Howitzers in the War: Four Years Campaigning with the Army of Northern Virginia*.

148. VIRGINIA RICHMOND "JOHNSON" ARTILLERY BATTERY

Nickname: Jackson's Flying Artillery

Organization: Organized at Richmond ca. March 18, 1862. Armed with two 3-inch Rifles and two 12-lb. Howitzers on September 17-20, 1862. Armed with two 3-inch Rifles and two 12-lb. Napoleons from July 1, 1863, to December 28, 1864. Surrendered at Appomattox Court House, Virginia, on April 9, 1865.

First Commander: Marmaduke Johnson (Captain)

Captain: Valentine J. Clutter

Assignments: Artillery Battalion, A. P. Hill's Division, Army of Northern Virginia (June 1862)

Artillery Battalion, A. P. Hill's Division, 1st Corps, Army of Northern Virginia (June-July 1862)

Branch's Brigade, A. P. Hills' Division, 1st Corps, Army of Northern Virginia (July 1862)

Artillery Battalion, A. P. Hill's Division, 2nd Corps, Army of Northern Virginia (July 1862-February 1863)

Hardaway's-McIntosh's Battalion, Reserve Artillery, 2nd Corps, Army of Northern Virginia (February-June 1863)

McIntosh's Battalion, Reserve Artillery, 3rd Corps, Army of Northern Virginia (June-July 1863)

McIntosh's Battalion, Artillery, 3rd Corps, Army of Northern Virginia (July 1863-September 1864)

Johnson's Battalion, Artillery, 1st Corps, Army of Northern Virginia (September 1864-March 1865)

Johnson's Battalion, Artillery, 2nd Corps, Army of Northern Virginia (March-April 1865)

Battles: Seven Days Battles (June 25-July 1, 1862)

Mechanicsville (June 26, 1862)

Gaines' Mill (June 27, 1862)

Shepherdstown Ford (September 20, 1862)

Fredericksburg (section) (December 13, 1862)

Gettysburg (July 1-3, 1863)

Bristoe Campaign (October 1863)

Mine Run Campaign (November-December 1863)

The Wilderness (May 5-6, 1864)

Spotsylvania Court House (May 8-21, 1864)

North Anna (May 23-26, 1864)

Cold Harbor (June 1-3, 1864)

Petersburg Siege (June 1864-April 1865)

Appomattox Court House (April 9, 1865)

149. VIRGINIA RICHMOND "LETCHER" ARTILLERY BATTERY, PROVISIONAL ARMY

Organization: Organized in Richmond on February 17, 1862. Armed from June 26 to July 1, 1862, with two 3-inch Rifles, two 6-lb. Smoothbores, and two

12-lb. Howitzers. From July 1-3, 1863, armed with two 12-lb. Napoleons and two 10-lb. Parrotts. On December 28, 1864, the armament comprised four 12-lb. Napoleons. Surrendered at Appomattox Court House, Virginia, on April 9, 1865.

First Commander: Greenlee Davidson (Captain)

Captain: Thomas A. Brander

Assignments: Artillery Battalion, A. P. Hill's Division, Army of Northern Virginia (June 1862)

Artillery Battalion, A. P. Hill's Division, 1st Corps, Army of Northern Virginia (June-July 1862)

Gregg's Brigade, A. P. Hill's Division, 1st Corps, Army of Northern Virginia (July 1862)

Artillery Battalion, A. P. Hill's Division, 2nd Corps, Army of Northern Virginia (August 1862-May 1863)

Pegram's Battalion, Reserve Artillery, 3rd Corps, Army of Northern Virginia (May-July 1863)

Pegram's Battalion, Artillery, 3rd Corps, Army of Northern Virginia (July 1863-April 1865)

Battles: Seven Days Battles (June 25-July 1, 1862)

Gaines' Mill (June 27, 1862)

Frayser's Farm (June 30, 1862)

Malvern Hill (July 1, 1862)

Cedar Mountain (August 9, 1862)

Warrenton Springs (August 23, 1862)

2nd Bull Run (August 28-30, 1862)

Chantilly (September 1, 1862)

Harpers Ferry (September 12-15, 1862)

Antietam (September 17, 1862)

Shepherdstown Ford (September 20, 1862)

Fredericksburg (December 13, 1862)

Chancellorsville (May 1-4, 1863)

Gettysburg (July 1-3, 1863)

Bristoe Campaign (October 1863)

Bristoe Station (October 14, 1863)

Mine Run Campaign (November-December 1863)

The Wilderness (May 5-6, 1864)

Spotsylvania Court House (May 8-21, 1864)

North Anna (May 22-26, 1864)

Cold Harbor (June 1-3, 1864)

Petersburg Siege (June 1864-April 1865)

Reams' Station (June 29, 1864)

The Crater (July 30, 1864)
Weldon Railroad (August 18-21, 1864)
Reams' Station (August 25, 1864)
Squirrel Level Road (September 30, 1864)
Jones' Farm (September 30, 1864)
Pegram's Farm (October 1, 1864)
Squirrel Level Road (October 8, 1864)
Burgess' Mill (October 27, 1864)
Hatcher's Run (February 5-7, 1865)
Fort Stedman (March 25, 1865)
Five Forks (April 1, 1865)
Petersburg Final Assault (April 2, 1865)
Appomattox Station (April 8, 1865)
Appomattox Court House (April 9, 1865)

150. VIRGINIA RICHMOND "MARTIN" ARTILLERY BATTERY

Organization: Organized for the war at Richmond on April 23, 1862. Composed of Virginians and North Carolinians. Served as Company B, 12th Light Artillery Battalion. The North Carolinians were transferred to Company D, 12th Light Artillery Battalion, on October 13, 1863, per S.O. #243, Adjutant and Inspector General's Office. Armed with four guns on June 30, 1864. Armed with three 12-lb. Napoleons and one 12-lb. Howitzer on December 28, 1864. Surrendered at Appomattox Court House, Virginia, on April 9, 1865.

First Commander: S. Taylor Martin (Captain)

Assignments: Pryor's Brigade, French's Command, Department of North Carolina and Southern Virginia (January-February 1863)

Artillery Battalion, Department of Southern Virginia (April-May 1863)

Bogg's Battalion, Artillery, Department of North Carolina (June-July 1863)

Bogg's Battalion, Artillery, Ransom's Division, Department of Richmond (July-September 1863)

Bogg's Battalion, Artillery, Department of North Carolina (October 1863-January 1864)

Bogg's Battalion, Light Artillery, District of the Cape Fear (January-February 1864)

1st Military District, Department of North Carolina and Southern Virginia (May-June 1864)

Bogg's Battalion, Artillery, Department of North Carolina and Southern Virginia (June-October 1864)

Bogg's-Sturdivant's Battalion, Artillery, 4th Corps, Army of Northern Virginia (October 1864-April 1865)

Battles: Kelly's Store (January 30, 1863)

Suffolk Campaign (April-May 1863)
Petersburg Siege (June 1864-April 1865)
Appomattox Campaign (March-April 1865)

151. VIRGINIA RICHMOND "ORANGE" LIGHT ARTILLERY BATTERY

Organization: Organized in Richmond in May 1861. This company was variously styled as Companies F and D, 1st (Fitzgerald's) Confederate Light Artillery Regiment, which did not complete its organization in early 1862. Reorganized on March 20, 1862. Armed with one 3-inch Rifle, one 12-lb. Howitzer and three 6-lb. Smoothbores on September 17, 1862. Goochland Artillery Battery and Campbell "Long Island" Artillery Battery disbanded and men assigned to this company on October 4, 1862, per S.O. #209, Headquarters, Army of Northern Virginia. Battery reorganized again on October 9, 1862. Armed with two 3-inch Rifles and two 10-lb. Parrotts on July 1-3, 1863. Armed with two 12-lb. Howitzers on December 26, 1864. Surrendered at Appomattox Court House, Virginia, on April 9, 1865.

First Commander: Thomas Jefferson Peyton (Captain)

Captain: Charles W. Fry

Assignments: Artillery, Department of the Peninsula (October-December 1861)

McLaws' Division, Department of the Peninsula (January-April 1862)

Reserve Artillery, Army of Northern Virginia (April-June 1862)

Jones' Battalion, Army of Northern Virginia (June-September 1862)

Artillery Battalion, D. H. Hill's-Rodes' Division, 2nd Corps, Army of Northern Virginia (September 1862-July 1863)

Carter's-Page's Battalion, Artillery, 2nd Corps, Army of Northern Virginia (July 1863-June 1864)

Page's Battalion, Artillery, Valley District, Department of Northern Virginia (September-November 1864)

Cutshaw's Battalion, Artillery, Valley District, Department of Northern Virginia (November 1864-March 1865)

Cutshaw's Battalion, Artillery, 2nd Corps, Army of Northern Virginia (March-April 1865)

Battles: Seven Days Battles (June 25-July 1, 1862)

White Oak Swamp (June 30, 1862)

Antietam (September 17, 1862)

Fredericksburg (December 13, 1862)

Chancellorsville (May 1-4, 1863)

Gettysburg (July 1-3, 1863)

Bristoe Campaign (October 1863)

Mine Run Campaign (November-December 1863)
The Wilderness (May 5-6, 1864)
Spotsylvania Court House (May 8-21, 1864)
North Anna (May 23-26, 1864)
Cold Harbor (June 1-3, 1864)
Cedar Creek (October 19, 1864)
Waynesborough (March 2, 1865)
Petersburg Siege (June 1864-April 1865)
Appomattox Court House (April 9, 1865)

152. VIRGINIA RICHMOND "OTEY" ARTILLERY BATTERY

Organization: Organized for the war on March 14, 1862. Mustered into Confederate service for the war on March 22, 1862. Became Company A, 13th Light Artillery Battalion, in late 1863.

First Commander: George Gaston Otey (Captain)

Field Officer: David Norvell Walker

Assignments: Artillery Battalion, District of Lewisburg ("Army of New River"), Department of Southwestern Virginia (May 1862)

King's Artillery Battalion, Army of the Kahawha, Department of Southwestern Virginia (September 1862)

Artillery Battalion, Department of Western Virginia (February-March 1863)

Unattached, Department of Western Virginia (April-May 1863)

King's-Owen's Artillery Battalion, Department of Western Virginia (May-October 1863)

King's Artillery Battalion, Ransom's Division, Department of Southwestern Virginia and East Tennessee (October-December 1863)

Battles: Giles Court House, West Virginia (May 10, 1862)

Kanawha Campaign (September 1862)

Fayetteville, West Virginia (September 10, 1862)

Charleston, West Virginia (September 13, 1862)

153. VIRGINIA RICHMOND "PARKER" ARTILLERY BATTERY

Organization: Organized for three years or the war at Richmond in early 1862. Mustered into Confederate service on March 14, 1862. Intended to form part of the 1st (Fitzgerald's) Confederate Artillery Regiment, which never completed its organization. Subsequently intended to form part of the 4th Artillery Regiment, which also failed to complete its organization. Armed with two 3-inch Rifles and two 12-lb. Howitzers in August and September 1862. Armed with three 3-inch Rifles and one 10-lb. Parrott on July 1-3, 1863. Armed with four 3-inch Rifles on December 28, 1864. Surrendered at Appomattox Court House, Virginia, on April 9, 1865.

First Commander: William Watts Parker (Captain)

Assignments: Lee's-Alexander's Battalion, Reserve Artillery, 1st Corps, Army of Northern Virginia (August 1862-July 1863)

Alexander's Battalion, Artillery, 1st Corps, Army of Northern Virginia (July-September 1863)

Alexander's Artillery Battalion, Longstreet's Corps, Army of Tennessee (September-November 1863)

Alexander's Artillery Battalion, Department of East Tennessee (November 1863-April 1864)

Alexander's-Huger's Battalion, Artillery, 1st Corps, Army of Northern Virginia (April 1864-April 1865)

Battles: 2nd Bull Run (August 28-30, 1862)

Antietam (September 17, 1862)

Fredericksburg (December 13, 1862)

Chancellorsville (May 1-4, 1863)

Gettysburg (July 1-3, 1863)

Chattanooga Siege (September-November 1863)

Knoxville Siege (November 1863)

Bean's Station (December 14, 1863)

The Wilderness (May 5-6, 1864)

Spotsylvania Court House (May 8-21, 1864)

North Anna (May 23-26, 1864)

Cold Harbor (June 1-3, 1864)

Petersburg Siege (June 1864-April 1865)

Appomattox Court House (April 9, 1865)

Further Reading: Krick, Robert K., *Parker's Virginia Battery, C.S.A.* Figg, Royal W., *"Where Men Only Dare to Go!" Or, The Story of a Boy Company (C.S.A.), By an Ex-Boy.*

154.   VIRGINIA RICHMOND "PURCELL" ARTILLERY BATTERY

Organization: Organized for one year on April 20, 1861. Early in the war mustered as a company in the 4th Artillery Regiment, which failed to complete its organization. From May 31, 1861, through July 21, 1861, battery was armed with four 6-lb. Rifles. Per S.O. #209, Adjutant and Inspector General's Office, dated October 4, 1862, the Monroe "Dixie" Artillery Battery disbanded and the men and horses were assigned to this battery as were 34 men from the Bedford Artillery. Armed with four 12-lb. Napoleons between July 1, 1863, and December 28, 1864. Surrendered at Appomattox Court House, Virginia, on April 9, 1865.

First Commander: R. Lindsay Walker (Captain)

Captains: William J. Pegram

Joseph McGraw

George M. Cayce

Assignments: District of the Aquia, Department of Fredericksburg (July 1861)

Reserve Brigade, Army of the Potomac (July 1861)

Reserve Brigade, 1st Corps, Army of the Potomac (July 1861)

District of the Aquia, Department of Fredericksburg (July-September 1861)

Walker's Brigade, District of the Aquia, Department of Fredericksburg (September-October 1861)

Walker's Brigade, Aquia District, Department of Northern Virginia (October 1861-March 1862)

Artillery Battalion, A. P. Hill's Division, Army of Northern Virginia (June 1862)

Artillery Battalion, A. P. Hill's Division, 1st Corps, Army of Northern Virginia (June-July 1862)

Field's Brigade, A. P. Hill's Division, 1st Corps, Army of Northern Virginia (July 1862)

Artillery Battalion, A. P. Hill's Division, 2nd Corps, Army of Northern Virginia (July 1862-May 1863)

Pegram's Battalion, Reserve Artillery, 3rd Corps, Army of Northern Virginia (May-July 1863)

Pegram's Battalion, Artillery, 3rd Corps, Army of Northern Virginia (July 1863-April 1865)

Battles: Aquia Creek (May 31-June 1, 1861)

1st Bull Run (July 21, 1861)

Mouth of the Potomac Creek (section) (August 23, 1861)

Seven Days Battles (June 25-July 1, 1862)

Beaver Dam Creek (June 26, 1862)

Gaines' Mill (June 27, 1862)

Frayser's Farm (June 30, 1862)

Malvern Hill (July 1, 1862)

Cedar Mountain (August 9, 1862)

Warrenton Springs (August 23, 1862)

2nd Bull Run (August 28-30, 1862)

Chantilly (September 1, 1862)

Harpers Ferry (September 12-15, 1862)

Antietam (September 17, 1862)

Shepherdstown Ford (September 20, 1862)

Castleman's Ferry (November 3, 1862)

Fredericksburg (December 13, 1862)

Chancellorsville (May 1-4, 1863)

Gettysburg (July 1-3, 1863)
Bristoe Campaign (October 1863)
Bristoe Station (October 14, 1863)
Mine Run Campaign (November-December 1863)
The Wilderness (May 5-6, 1864)
Spotsylvania Court House (May 8-21, 1864)
North Anna (May 22-26, 1864)
Cold Harbor (June 1-3, 1864)
Petersburg Siege (June 1864-April 1865)
Reams' Station (June 29, 1864)
The Crater (July 30, 1864)
Weldon Railroad (August 18-21, 1864)
Reams' Station (August 25, 1864)
Squirrel Level Road (September 30, 1864)
Jones' Farm (September 30, 1864)
Pegram's Farm (October 1, 1864)
Squirrel Level Road (October 8, 1864)
Burgess' Mill (October 27, 1864)
Hatcher's Run (February 5-7, 1865)
Fort Stedman (March 25, 1865)
Five Forks (April 1, 1865)
Petersburg Final Assault (April 2, 1865)
Appomattox Station (April 8, 1865)
Appomattox Court House (April 9, 1865)
Further Reading: Dawson, Francis W., *Reminiscences of Confederate Service*,
1861-1865.

155. Virginia Richmond "Thomas" Artillery Battery

Organization: Organized for one year at Richmond on May 10, 1861. Battery
was intended to form part of the 4th Artillery Regiment. Armed with four 6-lb.
Smoothbores on July 21, 1861. Battery disbanded and men assigned to the
Richmond "Hampden" Artillery on October 4, 1862, per S.O. #209, Headquar-
ters, Army of Northern Virginia.
First Commander: Philip Beverly Standard
Captain: Edwin J. Anderson
Assignments: Unattached, Army of the Shenandoah (July 1861)
Unattached, 2nd Corps, Army of the Potomac (July 1861)
Wilcox's Brigade, Longstreet's Division, Army of Northern Virginia (June
    1862)
Wilcox's Brigade, Longstreet's Division, 1st Corps, Army of Northern Virginia
    (June-August 1862)

Wilcox's Brigade, Wilcox's Division, 1st Corps, Army of Northern Virginia
    (August-September 1862)
Unattached, Reserve Artillery, Army of Northern Virginia (September-October
    1862)
Battles: 1st Bull Run (July 21, 1861)
Seven Days Battles (June 25-July 1, 1862)
Gaines' Mill (June 26, 1862)
Frayser's Farm (June 30, 1862)
Kelly's Ford skirmish (August 21, 1862)

156. VIRGINIA RINGGOLD ARTILLERY BATTERY
See: VIRGINIA DANVILLE "RINGGOLD" ARTILLERY BATTERY

157. VIRGINIA ROANOKE ARTILLERY BATTERY
Organization: Organized as horse artillery on October 8, 1863. Apparently
included in General Robert E. Lee's surrender at Appomattox Court House on
April 9, 1865. May have escaped the actual surrender with Rosser's Cavalry
Division.
First Commander: Warren S. Lurty (Captain)
Assignments: W. L. Jackson's Cavalry Brigade, Department of Western Vir-
    ginia and East Tennessee (December 1863-January 1864)
W. L. Jackson's Cavalry Brigade, Department of Western Virginia (January-
    February 1864)
Artillery, Department of Western Virginia (February-April 1864)
W. L. Jackson's Cavalry Brigade, Department of Western Virginia (April-June
    1864)
Horse Artillery Battalion, Ransom's-Lomax's Cavalry Division, Valley District,
    Department of Northern Virginia (June 1864-March 1865)
Thomson's Battalion, Horse Artillery, Cavalry Corps, Army of Northern
    Virginia (March-April 1865)
Battles: Lynchburg Campaign (June 1864)
Petersburg Siege (June 1864-April 1865)
Appomattox Campaign (March-April 1865)

158. VIRGINIA ROBERTSON'S HEAVY ARTILLERY BATTALION
Organization: Failed to complete its organization in June 1862.
First Commander: James E. Robertson (Captain)

159. VIRGINIA ROCKBRIDGE, 1ST ARTILLERY BATTERY
Organization: Organized in Rockbridge County on April 12, 1861. Mustered
into state service at Staunton, Rockbridge County, on April 29, 1861. Mustered

into Confederate service on May 11, 1861. Armed with three 6-lb. Smooth-bores and one 12-lb. Howitzer on June 30, 1861. Armed with three 6-lb. Smoothbores, one 12-lb. Howitzer and two 10-lb. Parrotts in April 1862. Reorganized on April 22, 1862. Armed with two 6-lb. Smoothbores, two 12-lb. Howitzers and two 10-lb. Parrotts in May and June 1862. Armed with two 20-lb. and two 10-lb. Parrotts from August to October 17, 1862. Armed with four 20-lb. Parrotts on June 1-3, 1863. Armed with two 3-inch Rifles and two 10-lb. Parrotts on December 28, 1864. Battery was attached to the 1st Artillery Regiment and later to the 1st Artillery Battalion. Surrendered at Appomattox Court House, Virginia, on April 9, 1865.

First Commander: John A. McCausland (Captain)

Captains: William N. Pendleton
William McLaughlin
William T. Poague
Archibald Graham

Assignments: 1st Brigade, Army of the Shenandoah (June-July 1861)
1st Brigade, 2nd Corps, Army of the Potomac (July-October 1861)
Stonewall Brigade, Valley District, Department of Northern Virginia (November 1861-May 1862)
Artillery Battalion, Jackson's Division, Valley District, Department of Northern Virginia (May-June 1862)
Stonewall Brigade, Jackson's Division, 2nd Corps, Army of Northern Virginia (June-July 1862)
Artillery Battalion, Jackson's Division, 2nd Corps, Army of Northern Virginia (August-September 1862)
Brown's Battalion, Reserve Artillery, Army of Northern Virginia (October 1862-February 1863)
Brown's Battalion, Reserve Artillery, 2nd Corps, Army of Northern Virginia (February-July 1863)
Brown's-Hardaway's Battalion, Artillery, 2nd Corps, Army of Northern Virginia (July 1863-June 1864)
Hardaway's Battalion, Artillery, 1st Corps, Army of Northern Virginia (June 1864-March 1865)
Hardaway's Battalion, Artillery, 2nd Corps, Army of Northern Virginia (March-April 1865)

Battles: Falling Waters (detachment) (July 2, 1861)
1st Bull Run (July 21, 1861)
Romney Campaign (January 1862)
Kernstown (March 23, 1862)
Cedar Creek (March 24, 1862)
Shenandoah Valley Campaign of 1862 (May-June 1862)

Middletown (May 24, 1862)
1st Winchester (May 25, 1862)
Port Republic (June 9, 1862)
Seven Days Battles (June 25-July 1, 1862)
White Oak Swamp (June 30, 1862)
Malvern Hill (July 1, 1862)
Cedar Mountain (August 9, 1862)
Cunningham's Ford (August 21, 1862)
Manasass Junction (August 28, 1862)
2nd Bull Run (August 28-30, 1862)
Chantilly (September 1, 1962)
Harpers Ferry (September 12-15, 1862)
Antietam (September 17, 1862)
Fredericksburg (December 13, 1862)
Chancellorsville (May 1-4, 1863)
Gettysburg (July 1-3, 1863)
Bristoe Campaign (October 1863)
Mine Run Campaign (November-December 1863)
The Wilderness (May 5-6, 1864)
Spotsylvania Court House (May 8-21, 1864)
North Anna (May 23-26, 1864)
Cold Harbor (June 1-3, 1864)
Petersburg Siege (June 1864-April 1865)
3rd New Market Heights (September 29, 1864)
Appomattox Court House (April 9, 1865)

Further Reading: Driver, Robert J., Jr., *The 1st and 2nd Rockbridge Artillery*. Cockrell, Monroe F., ed., *Gunner with Stonewall: Reminiscences of William Thomas Poague.* Moore, Edward A., *The Story of a Cannoneer Under Stonewall Jackson, in Which Is Told the Part Taken by the Rockbridge Artillery in the Army of Northern Virginia.*

160. VIRGINIA ROCKBRIDGE, 2ND ARTILLERY BATTERY

Organization: Organized by the conversion of 1st Company B, 52nd Infantry Regiment, to artillery service on September 28, 1861, per S.O. #165, Adjutant and Inspector General's Office. Reorganized on May 1, 1862. Armed with two 6-lb. Smoothbores, one 3-inch Rifle and one 10-lb. Parrott in August and September 1862. Armed with four 3-inch Rifles on July 1-3, 1863. Armed with three 24-lb. Howitzers on December 28, 1864. Surrendered at Appomattox Court House, Virginia, on April 9, 1865.
First Commander: John Miller (Captain)
Captains: John A. M. Lusk

William K. Donald

Assignments: E. Johnson's Brigade, Army of the Northwest (November 1861-December 1861)

Artillery, Army of the Northwest (March-May 1862)

Artillery Battalion, Ewell's Division, Valley District, Department of Northern Virginia (May-June 1862)

Artillery Battalion, Jackson's Division, 2nd Corps, Army of Northern Virginia (September 1862-February 1863)

Hardaway's-McIntosh's Battalion, Reserve Artillery, 2nd Corps, Army of Northern Virginia (February-June 1863)

McIntosh's Battalion, Reserve Artillery, 3rd Corps, Army of Northern Virginia (June-July 1863)

McIntosh's Battalion, Artillery, 3rd Corps, Army of Northern Virginia (July 1863-April 1865)

Battles: Camp Alleghany, West Virginia (December 13, 1861)

Shenandoah Valley Campaign of 1862 (May-June 1862)

Strasburg (June 1, 1862)

Cross Keys (June 8, 1862)

Fredericksburg (December 13, 1862)

Chancellorsville (May 1-4, 1863)

Gettysburg (July 1-3, 1863)

Bristoe Campaign (October 1863)

Bristoe Station (October 14, 1863)

Mine Run Campaign (November-December 1863)

The Wilderness (May 5-6, 1864)

Spotsylvania Court House (May 8-21, 1864)

North Anna (May 23-26, 1864)

Cold Harbor (June 1-3, 1864)

Petersburg Siege (June 1864-April 1865)

The Crater (July 30, 1864)

Petersburg Final Assault (April 2, 1865)

Appomattox Court House (April 9, 1865)

Further Reading: Driver, Robert J., Jr., *The 1st and 2nd Rockbridge Artillery.*

161. VIRGINIA SALEM FLYING ARTILLERY BATTERY

Organization: Organized by the conversion of 1st Company A, 9th Infantry regiment, to artillery service upon its reorganization on May 8, 1862. At that time attached to the 1st Artillery Regiment and later to the 1st Artillery Battalion. Armed with two 12-lb. Howitzers and two 6-lb. Smoothbores from August to October 17, 1862. Armed with two 3-inch Rifles and two 12-lb.

Napoleons on July 1-3, 1863. Surrendered at Appomattox Court House, Virginia, on April 9, 1865.

First Commander: Abraham Hupp (Captain)

Captain: Charles Beale Griffin

Assignments: Brown's Battalion, Reserve Artillery, Army of Northern Virginia (July 1862-February 1863)

Brown's Battalion, Reserve Artillery, 2nd Corps, Army of Northern Virginia (February-July 1863)

Brown's-Hardaway's Battalion, Artillery, 2nd Corps, Army of Northern Virginia (July 1863-June 1864)

Hardaway's Battalion, Artillery, 1st Corps, Army of Northern Virginia (June 1864-March 1865)

Hardaway's Battalion, Artillery, 2nd Corps, Army of Northern Virginia (March-April 1865)

Battles: Antietam (September 17, 1862)

Fredericksburg (December 13, 1862)

Chancellorsville (May 1-4, 1863)

2nd Winchester (June 14-15, 1863)

Gettysburg (July 1-3, 1863)

Bristoe Campaign (October 1863)

Mine Run Campaign (November-December 1863)

The Wilderness (May 5-6, 1864)

Spotsylvania Court House (May 8-21, 1864)

North Anna (May 23-26, 1864)

Cold Harbor (June 1-3, 1864)

Petersburg Siege (June 1864-April 1865)

Chaffin's Farm (September 29, 1864)

Fort Gilmer (September 29-30, 1864)

Appomattox Court House (April 9, 1865)

162. VIRGINIA SHOCKHOE ARTILLERY BATTERY

Organization: Organization attempted in Richmond during August and September 1861. Failed to complete its organization.

163. VIRGINIA SONS OF FLUVANNA ARTILLERY BATTERY

See: VIRGINIA FLUVANNA ARTILLERY BATTERY, NO. 1

164. VIRGINIA SOUTHSIDE HEAVY ARTILLERY BATTERY

Organization: Organized in Chesterfield County on January 7, 1862. Known as Company C, 2nd Artillery Regiment, in early 1862. Reorganized for the war on June 3, 1862. Surrendered at Appomattox Court House, Virginia, on April 9, 1865.

First Commander: Augustus Henry Drewry (Captain)

Captains: James B. Jones

John W. Drewry

Assignments: Drewry's Bluff, Department of Richmond (July 1863-May 1864)

Drewry's Bluff, Department of North Carolina and Southern Virginia (May-October 1864)

Drewry's Bluff, Department of Richmond (October 1864-March 1865)

Smith's Battalion, Artillery, 4th Corps, Army of Northern Virginia (March-April 1865)

Battles: Drewry's Bluff (May 16, 1864)

Petersburg Siege (June 1864-April 1865)

Appomattox Court House (April 9, 1865)

165. VIRGINIA STAFFORD LIGHT ARTILLERY BATTERY

Organization: Organized for one year in Stafford County on August 5, 1861. Intended to become part of the 4th Artillery Regiment, which failed to complete its organization. Armed with three 12-lb. Howitzers, two 3-inch Rifles and one 10-lb. Parrott from June 25, 1862, to July 1, 1862. Armed with three 10-lb. Parrotts and three 12-lb. Howitzers in August and September 1862. Armed with two 10-lb. Parrotts on December 28, 1864. Surrendered at Appomattox Court House, Virginia, on April 9, 1865.

First Commander: John Rogers Cooke (Captain)

Captains: Thomas B. French

Raleigh L. Cooper

Assignments: Walker's Brigade, Aquia District, Department of Northern Virginia (November 1861-March 1862)

Walker's Brigade, Department of North Carolina (April-June 1862)

Artillery Battalion, Holmes' Division, Army of Northern Virginia (June-July 1862)

Artillery Battalion, Department of North Carolina (July-August 1862)

Walker's-Cooke's Brigade, Walker's-Ransom's Division, 1st Corps, Army of Northern Virginia (August 1862-January 1863)

Cooke's Brigade, French's Command, Department of North Carolina (January-February 1863)

Cooke's Brigade, Department of North Carolina (June-July 1863)

Cooke's Brigade, Department of Richmond (July-August 1863)

Department of Richmond (August-December 1863)

Kemper's Brigade, Department of Richmond (December 1863-January 1864)

Maryland Line, Department of Richmond (February-April 1864)

Braxton's Battalion, Artillery, 2nd Corps, Army of Northern Virginia (April-June 1864)

Braxton's Battalion, Artillery, Valley District, Department of Northern Virginia (June 1864-March 1865)

Braxton's Battalion, Artillery, 2nd Corps, Army of Northern Virginia (March-April 1865)

Battles: Seven Days Battles (June 25-July 1, 1862)
Harpers Ferry (September 12-15, 1862)
Antietam (September 17, 1862)
Fredericksburg (December 13, 1862)
The Wilderness (May 5-6, 1864)
Spotsylvania Court House (May 8-21, 1864)
North Anna (May 23-26, 1864)
Cold Harbor (June 1-3, 1864)
Lynchburg Campaign (June 1864)
Monocacy (July 9, 1864)
3rd Winchester (September 19, 1864)
Fisher's Hill (September 22, 1864)
Cedar Creek (October 19, 1864)
Petersburg Siege (June 1864-April 1865)
Appomattox Court House (April 9, 1865)

166. VIRGINIA STAUNTON ARTILLERY BATTERY

Organization: Organized in Augusta County in November 1859. Enlisted for one year on April 17, 1861. Armed with four 6-lb. Smoothbores on July 21, 1861. Reorganized on April 22, 1862. Armed with two 6-lb. Smoothbores in August and September 1862. Armed with four 12-lb. Napoleons on July 1-3, 1863. Armed with two 3-inch Rifles on December 28, 1864. Surrendered at Appomattox Court House, Virginia, on April 9, 1865.

First Commander: John D. Imboden (Captain)

Captains: William L. Balthis
Asher Waterman Garber

Assignments: Bee's Brigade, Army of the Shenandoah (July 1861)

Bee's-Whiting's Brigade, 2nd Corps, Army of the Potomac (July-October 1861)

Whiting's Brigade, Forces near Dumfries (Whiting), 2nd Corps, Potomac District, Department of Northern Virginia (October 1861-January 1862)

Whiting's Brigade, Forces near Dumfries (Whiting), Potomac District, Department of Northern Virginia (January-March 1862)

Whiting's Brigade, Whiting's-G. W. Smith's Division, Army of Northern Virginia (March-June 1862)

Artillery Battalion, Whiting's Division, Valley District, Department of Northern Virginia (June 1862)

Artillery Battalion, Whiting's Division, 2nd Corps, Army of Northern Virginia (June-July 1862)

Artillery Battalion, Whiting's Division, Army of Northern Virginia (July 1862)

Artillery Battalion, Whiting's Division, 1st Corps, Army of Northern Virginia (July 1862)

Texas Brigade, Whiting's Division, 1st Corps, Army of Northern Virginia (July-August 1862)

Artillery Battalion, Ewell's-Early's Division, 2nd Corps, Army of Northern Virginia (August 1862-July 1863)

Jones'-Cutshaw's Battalion, Artillery, 2nd Corps, Army of Northern Virginia (July 1863-May 1864)

Cutshaw's Battalion, Artillery, Valley District, Department of Northern Virginia (October 1864-March 1865)

Cutshaw's Battalion, Artillery, 2nd Corps, Army of Northern Virginia (March-April 1865)

Battles: 1st Bull Run (July 21, 1861)

Yorktown Siege (April-May 1862)

Seven Days Battles (June 25-July 1, 1862)

Bristoe and Manassas Junction (August 26-27, 1862)

2nd Bull Run (August 28-30, 1862)

Harpers Ferry (September 12-15, 1862)

Fredericksburg (December 13, 1862)

Chancellorsville (May 1-4, 1863)

2nd Winchester (June 14-15, 1863)

Gettysburg (July 1-3, 1863)

Bristoe Campaign (October 1863)

Mine Run Campaign (November-December 1863)

The Wilderness (May 5-6, 1864)

Spotsylvania Court House (May 8-21, 1864)

North Anna (May 23-26, 1864)

Cold Harbor (June 1-3, 1864)

Cedar Creek (October 19, 1864)

Waynesborough (March 2, 1865)

Petersburg Siege (from December 1864) (June 1864-April 1865)

Appomattox Court House (April 9, 1865)

167.   Virginia Staunton Hill Artillery Battery
See: Virginia Charlotte "Staunton Hill" Artillery Battery

168. VIRGINIA STAUNTON HORSE ARTILLERY BATTERY

Organization: Organized by the conversion of 1st Company A, 62nd Infantry Regiment (Mounted), in February 1863. Armed with six guns from July 1863 to May 1864. Apparently disbanded in April 1865.

First Commander: John H. McClanahan (Captain)

Assignments: Northwestern Virginia Brigade, Department of Northern Virginia (March-July 1863)

Valley District, Department of Northern Virginia (July-December 1863)

Northwest Virginia Brigade, Valley District, Department of Northern Virginia (December-June 1864)

Horse Artillery, Cavalry, Valley District, Department of Northern Virginia (June-July 1864)

Horse Artillery Battalion, Lomax's Cavalry Division, Valley District, Department of Northern Virginia (August 1864-March 1865)

McGregor's Battalion, Horse Artillery, Cavalry Corps, Army of Northern Virginia (March-April 1865)

Battles: Jones' and Imboden's West Virginia Raid (April 1863)

Gettysburg (July 1-3, 1863)

Williamsport (July 5, 1863)

New Market (May 15, 1864)

Lynchburg Campaign (June 1864)

3rd Winchester (September 19, 1864)

Fisher's Hill (September 22, 1864)

Cedar Creek (October 19, 1864)

Waynesborough (March 2, 1865)

Further Reading: Driver, Robert J., *The Staunton Artillery—McClanahan's Battery.*

169. VIRGINIA STUART HORSE ARTILLERY BATTERY, 1ST COMPANY

Organization: Organized as the Newtown Artillery in 1861. Converted to horse artillery in November 1861. Armed with four 3-inch Rifles on July 1-3, 1863. Surrendered at Appomattox Court House, Virginia, on April 9, 1865.

First Commander: John Pelham (Captain)

Captains: James Breathed

Philip Preston Johnston

Daniel Shanks

Assignments: Cavalry Brigade, Potomac District, Department of Northern Virginia (November 1861-March 1862)

Cavalry Brigade, Army of Northern Virginia (March-July 1862)

Horse Artillery Battalion, Cavalry Division, Army of Northern Virginia (July 1862-September 1863)

Horse Artillery Battalion, Cavalry Corps, Army of Northern Virginia (September 1863-May 1864)

Horse Artillery Battalion, Rosser's Cavalry Division, Valley District, Department of Northern Virginia (October 1864-March 1865)

Horse Artillery Battalion, Lomax's Cavalry Division, Valley District, Department of Northern Virginia (March 1865)

Breathed's Battalion, Horse Artillery, Cavalry Corps, Army of Northern Virginia (March-April 1865)

Battles: Stuart's 1st Ride Around McClellan (section) (June 13-15, 1862)
Seven Days Battles (June 25-July 1, 1862)
Gaines' Mill (June 27, 1862)
Operations against Union shipping on the James River (July 5-7, 1862)
2nd Bull Run (August 28-30, 1862)
Antietam (September 17, 1862)
Union (November 2, 1862)
Fredericksburg (December 13, 1862)
Raid on Dumfries and Fairfax Station (December 27-29, 1862)
Kelly's Ford (March 17, 1863)
Chancellorsville (May 1-4, 1863)
Brandy Station (June 9, 1863)
Aldie (June 17, 1863)
Hanover, Pennsylvania (June 30, 1863)
Carlisle (July 1, 1863)
Gettysburg (July 1-3, 1863)
Funkstown and Boonesborough (July 6-10, 1863)
Bristoe Campaign (October 1863)
near Brandy Station (October 11-12, 1863)
Mine Run Campaign (November-December 1863)
Stanardsville, Virginia (February 29, 1864)
Shady Grove (May 8, 1864)
Cold Harbor (June 1-3, 1864)
Trevilian Station (June 11-12, 1864)
Petersburg Siege (June 1864-April 1865)
Tom's Brook (October 9, 1864)
Cedar Creek (October 19, 1864)
Appomattox Court House (April 9, 1865)

170. VIRGINIA STUART HORSE ARTILLERY BATTERY, 2ND COMPANY

Organization: Organized by the division of the 1st Company on August 9, 1862. Armed with two 3-inch Rifles and two 12-lb. Napoleons on July 1-3,

1863. Armed with four 3-inch Rifles on December 28, 1864. Surrendered at Appomattox Court House, Virginia, on April 9, 1865.

First Commander: Mathias Winston Henry (Captain)

Captains: William M. McGregor

G. Wilmer Brown

Assignments: Horse Artillery Battalion, Cavalry Division, Army of Northern Virginia (August 1862-September 1863)

Horse Artillery Battalion, Cavalry Corps, Army of Northern Virginia (September 1863-March 1865)

McGregor's Battalion, Horse Artillery, Cavalry Corps, Army of Northern Virginia (March 1865)

Thomson's Battalion, Horse Artillery, Cavalry Corps, Army of Northern Virginia (March-April 1865)

Battles: Fredericksburg (December 13, 1862)

Raid on Dumfries and Fairfax Station (December 27-29, 1862)

Chancellorsville (May 1-4, 1863)

Brandy Station (June 9, 1863)

Hanover, Pennsylvania (June 30, 1863)

Gettysburg (July 1-3, 1863)

Funkstown and Boonesborough (July 6-10, 1863)

Bristoe Campaign (October 1863)

Mine Run Campaign (November-December 1863)

Stanardsville, Virginia (February 29, 1864)

Petersburg Siege (June 1864-April 1865)

Appomattox Court House (April 9, 1865)

171. VIRGINIA SURRY LIGHT ARTILLERY BATTERY

Organization: Organized by the conversion of 1st Company I, 3rd Infantry Regiment, to artillery service in the spring of 1862. Surrendered at Appomattox Court House, Virginia, on April 9, 1865.

First Commander: Thomas W. Ruffin (Captain)

Captain: James DeWitt Hankins

Assignments: Artillery Battalion, Department of North Carolina (July 1862)

Lightfoot's Light Artillery Battalion, Richmond Defenses, Department of Richmond (July 1863-April 1865)

Lightfoot's Battalion, Artillery, 2nd Corps, Army of Northern Virginia (April 1865)

Battles: Port Walthall Junction (May 7, 1864)

Swift Creek (May 9, 1864)

Petersburg Siege (June 1864-April 1865)

Appomattox Court House (April 9, 1865)

Further Reading: Jones, Benjamin Washington, *Under the Stars and Bars.*

172. VIRGINIA THOMAS ARTILLERY BATTERY

See: VIRGINIA RICHMOND "THOMAS" ARTILLERY BATTERY

173. VIRGINIA TURNER ARTILLERY BATTERY

Organization: Organized for one year in Goochland County in the summer of 1861. Mustered in for one year from August 29, 1861. Reorganized on May 12, 1862. Disbanded and the men transferred to the King William Artillery Battery on October 4, 1862, per S.O. #209, Headquarters, Army of Northern Virginia.

First Commander: Walter Daniel Leake (Captain)

Assignments: Department of South Carolina, Georgia and Florida (December 1861-July 1862)

Drayton's Brigade, D. R. Jones' Division, 1st Corps, Army of Northern Virginia (August-September 1862)

Artillery Battalion, D. R. Jones' Division, 1st Corps, Army of Northern Virginia (September-October 1862)

Battles: Port Royal Ferry, South Carolina (January 1, 1862)

2nd Bull Run (August 28-30, 1862)

174. VIRGINIA UNITED ARTILLERY BATTERY

Organization: Organized by the conversion of 1st Company E, 41st Infantry Regiment, to heavy artillery service on April 19, 1862, per S.O. #90, Adjutant and Inspector General's Office. Assigned as 1st Company C, 19th Heavy Artillery Battalion, on June 21, 1862, per S.O. #143, Adjutant and Inspector General's Office. Again became an independent company on October 1, 1862, per S.O. #92, Headquarters, Richmond Defences. Surrendered at Appomattox Court House, Virginia, on April 9, 1865.

First Commander: Thomas Kevill (Captain)

Assignments: Department of Norfolk (March-April 1862)

Mahone's Brigade, Huger's Division, Department of Northern Virginia (April-June 1862)

Drewry's Bluff, Department of Richmond (July 1863-May 1864)

Drewry's Bluff, Department of North Carolina and Southern Virginia (May-October 1864)

Drewry's Bluff, Department of Richmond (October 1864-March 1865)

Smith's Battalion, Artillery, 4th Corps, Army of Northern Virginia (March-April 1865)

Battles: Aboard the CSS *Virginia* at Hampton Roads (detachment) (March 8-9, 1862)

Drewry's Bluff (May 16, 1864)
Petersburg Siege (June 1864-April 1865)
Appomattox Court House (April 9, 1865)

175. VIRGINIA WARRENTON ARTILLERY BATTERY

Organization: Organized for three years or the war in Fauquier County on March 10, 1862. Reorganized on April 16, 1862. Assigned as 1st Company A, 12th Artillery Battalion, on May 15, 1862, per S.O. #112, Adjutant and Inspector General's Office. However, it soon became an independent battery again. Armed with one 12-lb. Howitzer, one 12-lb. Napoleon and two 6-lb. Smoothbores in August and September 1862. Armed with two 12-lb. Howitzers and two 12-lb. Napoleons on July 1-3, 1863. Armed with two 12-lb. Napoleons on December 28, 1864. Surrendered at Appomattox Court House, Virignia, on April 9, 1865.

First Commander: James Vass Brooke (Captain)

Captain: Addison W. Utterback

Assignments: Brown's Battalion, Reserve Artillery, Army of Northern Virginia (September 1862-February 1863)

Brown's Battalion, Reserve Artillery, 2nd Corps, Army of Northern Virginia (February-June 1863)

Poague's Battalion, Artillery, 3rd Corps, Army of Northern Virginia (July 1863-April 1865)

Battles: Fredericksburg (December 13, 1862)

Chancellorsville (May 1-4, 1863)

Gettysburg (July 1-3, 1863)

Falling Waters (July 14, 1863)

Bristoe Campaign (October 1863)

Mine Run Campaign (November-December 1863)

The Wilderness (May 5-6, 1864)

Spotsylvania Court House (May 8-21, 1864)

North Anna (May 23-26, 1864)

Cold Harbor (June 1-3, 1864)

Petersburg Siege (June 1864-April 1865)

Appomattox Court House (April 9, 1865)

176. VIRGINIA WASHINGTON ARTILLERY BATTERY

Also Known As: Hampton Artillery Battery

Organization: Organized by the conversion of 1st Company K, 32nd Infantry Regiment, to artillery service ca. September 1861. Served as Company A, 1st Artillery Regiment. Disbanded in the summer of 1862.

First Commander: Charles L. Smith (Captain)

Captain: William W. Fraser
Assignments: Artillery, Department of the Peninsula (September 1861-April 1862)
Brown's Regiment, Reserve Artillery, Army of Northern Virginia (July 1862)
Battle: Yorktown Siege (April-May 1862)

177. VIRGINIA WEST AUGUSTA ARTILLERY BATTERY

Nickname: West Augusta Guards
Organization: Organized by the conversion of Company L, 5th Infantry Regiment, to artillery service in November 1861. Reorganized as infantry and redesignated as Company L, 5th Infantry Regiment, in April 1862.
First Commander: James Hurley Waters (Captain)
Assignments: Artillery, Valley District, Department of Northern Virginia (November 1861-January 1862)
Stonewall Brigade, Valley District, Department of Northern Virginia (March-April 1862)
Battle: Kernstown (March 23, 1862)

178. VIRGINIA WILLIAMSBURG ARTILLERY BATTERY

Nickname: Lee Artillery
Organization: Organized for one year in James City County on May 13, 1861. Served as Company F, 1st Artillery Regiment. Reorganized on May 10, 1862. Disbanded and the men transferred to the other companies of the regiment on October 4, 1862, per S.O. #209, Headquarters, Army of Northern Virginia.
First Commander: William Robertson Garrett (Captain)
Captain: John Archer Coke
Assignments: Artillery, Department of the Peninsula (October 1861-January 1862)
McLaws' Division, Department of the Peninsula (January-April 1862)
McLaws' Brigade, McLaws' Division, Magruder's Command, Department of Northern Virginia (April 1862)
McLaws' Brigade, Magruder's Division, Department of Northern Virginia (May-June 1862)
Brown's Battalion, Reserve Artillery, Army of Northern Virginia (June-October 1862)
Battles: Yorktown Siege (April-May 1862)
Williamsburg (May 5, 1862)
Seven Days Battles (June 25-July 1, 1862)
Antietam (September 17, 1862)

179. VIRGINIA WINCHESTER ARTILLERY BATTERY

Nickname: Jackson Artillery

Organization: Organized for the war at Winchester on March 10, 1862. Armed with four Rifles in May and June 1862. Consolidated with the Alleghany Artillery Battery on September 23, 1862.

First Commander: Wilfred Emory Cutshaw (Captain)

Assignments: Artillery Battalion, Jackson's Division, Valley District, Department of Northern Virginia (May-June 1862)

Artillery Battalion, Jackson's Division, 2nd Corps, Army of Northern Virginia (June-September 1862)

Unattached, Reserve Artillery, Army of Northern Virginia (September 1862)

Battles: Shenandoah Valley Campaign of 1862 (May-June 1862)

2nd Bull Run (August 28-30, 1862)

Antietam (September 17, 1862)

180.   VIRGINIA WISE ARTILLERY BATTERY

Organization: Organized for one year on April 19, 1861. Assigned to the 1st (Pendleton's) Artillery Regiment, which failed to complete its organization. Armed with four 6-lb. Smoothbores on July 21, 1861. Reorganized on April 26, 1862. Armed with two 12-lb. Howitzers and two 6-lb. Smoothbores in June and July 1862. Disbanded, with most of the men assigned to the Bath Artillery, on October 4, 1862, per S.O. #209, Headquarters, Army of Northern Virginia.

First Commander: Ephraim G. Alburtis (Captain)

Captain: James S. Brown

Assignments: Bartow's Brigade, Army of the Shenandoah (July 1861)

Bartow's-S. Jones' Brigade, 2nd Corps, Army of the Potomac (July-October 1861)

S. Jones' Brigade, 2nd Corps, Potomac District, Department of Northern Virginia (October 1861-January 1862)

S. Jones' Brigade, G. W. Smith's Division, Potomac District, Department of Northern Virginia (January-April 1862)

Anderson's Brigade, Magruder's Division, Army of Northern Virginia (June 1862)

Artillery Battalion, D. R. Jones' Division, Magruder's Command, Army of Northern Virginia (June-July 1862)

D. R. Jones'-Semmes'-G. T. Anderson's Brigade, D. R. Jones' Division, 1st Corps, Army of Northern Virginia (July-September 1862)

Artillery Battalion, D. R. Jones' Division, 1st Corps, Army of Northern Virginia (September-October 1862)

Battles: 1st Bull Run (July 21, 1861)

Seven Days Battles (June 25-July 1, 1862)

2nd Bull Run (August 28-30, 1862)

Harpers Ferry (September 12-15, 1862)

Antietam (September 17, 1862)

181. VIRGINIA WISE LEGION ARTILLERY BATTALION

Organization: Organized with four companies on July 23, 1861. Broken up in early 1862.
First Commander: Wade Hampton Gibbes (Major)

182. VIRGINIA WISE LEGION ARTILLERY BATTALION, COMPANY A

Organization: Organized for six months on June 21, 1861. Mustered into state service for six months on June 21, 1861. Mustered out on December 21, 1861, per S.O. #272, Adjutant and Inspector General's Office.
First Commander: James Kirby (Captain)
Captain: George Hart
Assignment: Troops in Kanawha Valley (July-September 1861)

183. VIRGINIA WISE LEGION ARTILLERY BATTALION, COMPANY B

Nickname: Pearlsburg Reserves
Organization: Organized for one year on May 26, 1861. Mustered in on June 30, 1861. Reorganized and became the Giles Light Artillery on May 1, 1862.
First Commander: William W. McComas (Captain)
Captain: David Alexander French
Assignment: Troops in Kanawha Valley (July-August 1861)
Battles: Elizabeth City, North Carolina (February 10, 1862)
South Mills (April 19, 1862)

184. VIRGINIA WISE LEGION ARTILLERY BATTALION, COMPANY C

Nickname: Centreville Rifles
Organization: Mustered in Prince William County on June 8, 1861. Mustered in on July 2, 1861. Reorganized as an independent company on May 15, 1862.
First Commander: William M. Lowry (Captain)
Assigments: Troops in Kanawha Valley (July-August 1861)
Artillery Battalion, District of Lewisburg (March-May 1862)
Artillery Battalion, District of Lewisburg ("Army of New River"), Department of Southwestern Virginia (May 1862)
Battle: Giles Court House, West Virginia (May 10, 1862)
Further Reading: Scott, J. L., *Lowry's, Bryan's, and Chapman's Batteries of Virginia Artillery.*

185. VIRGINIA WISE LEGION ARTILLERY BATTALION, COMPANY D

Nickname: Goochland Artillery

Organization: Organized for one year on July 20, 1861. Mustered in on August 3, 1861. Reorganized as the Goochland Artillery Battery in March or April 1862.

First Commander: Bernard Roemer (Captain)

Assignments: Troops in Kanawha Valley (July-August 1861)

Army of the Kanawha (August-October 1861)

Army of the Kanawha, Department of Northern Virginia (October 1861-January 1862)

186. VIRGINIA YORKTOWN ARTILLERY BATTERY

See: VIRGINIA HALIFAX LIGHT ARTILLERY BATTERY

187. VIRGINIA YORKTOWN "MAGRUDER" LIGHT ARTILLERY BATTERY

Organization: Organized for two years or the war in Richmond on March 31, 1862. Armed with one 3-inch Rifle and one 6-lb. Smoothbore from June 24 to July 1, 1862. Disbanded and the men were transferred to the Bedford Light Artillery Battery on October 4, 1862, per S.O. #209, Headquarters, Army of Northern Virginia.

First Commander: Thomas Jefferson Page, Jr. (Captain)

Assignments: Cobb's Brigade, Magruder's Division, Department of Northern Virginia (May 1862)

Toombs' Brigade, Magruder's Division, Army of Northern Virginia (June 1862)

Artillery Battalion, Magruder's Command, Army of Northern Virginia (June-July 1862)

Unattached, Reserve Artillery, Army of Northern Virginia (July-October 1862)

Battles: Yorktown Siege (April-May 1862)

Seven Days Battles (June 25-July 1, 1862)

Antietam (September 17, 1862)

CAVALRY

188. VIRGINIA 1ST CAVALRY BATTALION, LOCAL DEFENSE TROOPS

Organization: Organized with three companies at Richmond in July and August 1863. Apparently disbanded upon the fall of Richmond on April 2, 1865.

First Commander: William M. Browne (Colonel)

Assignment: Unattached, Department of Richmond (August 1863-June 1864)

Battle: Petersburg Siege (June 1864-April 1865)

189. VIRGINIA 1ST (FUNSTEN'S) CAVALRY BATTALION

See: VIRGINIA 17TH CAVALRY BATTALION

190. VIRGINIA 1ST (JOHNSON'S) CAVALRY BATTALION

Nickname: Virginia Lee's Legion Cavalry Battalion

Organization: Organized with eight companies ca. November 1, 1861. Consolidated with Lee's Cavalry Squadron and designated as the 9th Cavalry Regiment on January 18, 1862, per S.O. #6, Headquarters, Aquia District, Department of Northern Virginia.

First Commander: John E. Johnson (Lieutenant Colonel)

Field Officer: Richard L. T. Beale (Major)

Assignment: Unattached, Aquia District, Department of Northern Virginia (November 1861-January 1862)

191. VIRGINIA 1ST CAVALRY REGIMENT

Organization: Organization for one year with 12 companies completed on July 16, 1861. Company N, a Mississippi company, assigned on August 31, 1861. 1st Companies D and K became Companies D and C, 6th Cavalry Regiment, respectively, on September 12, 1861, per S.O. #276, Adjutant and Inspector

General's Office. Company O, an Alabama company, assigned on October 19, 1861. Companies N and O became Companies A and D, 2nd Mississippi Cavalry Battalion, respectively, on October 24, 1861, per S.O. #188, Adjutant and Inspector General's Office. Regiment reorganized on April 23, 1862. A cavalry company unofficially attached to the 26th Infantry Regiment became 2nd Company L at this time. 2nd Company L became A, 5th Cavalry Regiment, on June 25, 1862, per S.O. # 146, Adjutant and Inspector General's Office. Surrendered at Appomattox Court House, Virginia, on April 9, 1865.

First Commander: James Ewell Brown "Jeb" Stuart (Colonel)

Field Officers: Luke T. Brien (Lieutenant Colonel)
R. Welby Carter (Major, Lieutenant Colonel, Colonel)
James H. Drake (Major, Lieutenant Colonel, Colonel)
Charles R. Irving (Major)
William E. "Grumble" Jones (Colonel)
Fitzhugh Lee (Lieutenant Colonel, Colonel)
William A. Morgan (Major, Lieutenant Colonel, Colonel)
Robert Swan (Major)

Assignments: Cavalry, Army of the Shenandoah (July-July 1861)
Cavalry, 2nd Corps, Army of the Potomac (July-September 1861)
Cavalry Brigade, Army of the Potomac (September-November 1861)
Cavalry Brigade, Potomac District, Department of Northern Virginia (November 1861-March 1862)
Cavalry Brigade, Army of Northern Virginia (March-July 1862)
Fitz. Lee's Brigade, Cavalry Division, Army of Northern Virginia (July 1862-September 1863)
Wickham's Brigade, Fitz. Lee's Division, Cavalry Corps, Army of Northern Virginia (September 1863-July 1864)
Wickham's Brigade, Fitz. Lee's-Rosser's Cavalry Division, Valley District, Department of Northern Virginia (August 1864-January 1865)
Wickham's-Munford's Brigade, Fitz. Lee's Division, Cavalry Corps, Army of Northern Virginia (February-April 1865)

Battles: Falling Waters (July 2, 1861)
1st Bull Run (July 21, 1861)
Bailey's Crossroads (August 27, 1861)
Lewinsville, Virginia (one company) (September 11, 1861)
Fall's Church Road (detachment) (November 18, 1861)
Williamsburg (May 5, 1862)
Ellison's Mill, New Bridge, and Mechanicsville (detachment) (May 23-24, 1862)
Stuart's 1st Ride Around McClellan (June 13-15, 1862)
Seven Days Battles (June 25-July 1, 1862)
Gaines' Mill (June 27, 1862)

Verdon, Virginia (one squadron) (July 22, 1862)
Stuart's Expedition from Hanover Court House to near Fredericksburg (August 2-8, 1862)
2nd Bull Run (August 28-30, 1862)
Antietam (September 17, 1862)
Corbin's Crossroads, near Amissville, Virginia (November 10, 1862)
Fredericksburg (December 13, 1862)
Raid on Dumfries and Fairfax Station (December 27-29, 1862)
Hartwood Church (February 25, 1863)
Kelly's Ford (March 17, 1863)
Chancellorsville (May 1-4, 1863)
Brandy Station (June 9, 1863)
Aldie (June 17, 1863)
Middleburg (June 19, 1863)
Gettysburg (July 1-3, 1863)
Shepherdstown (July 16, 1863)
Bristoe Campaign (October 1863)
Mine Run Campaign (November-December 1863)
Upperville (December 17, 1863)
The Wilderness (May 5-6, 1864)
Spotsylvania Court House (May 8-21, 1864)
North Anna (May 22-26, 1864)
Haw's Shop (May 28, 1864)
Cold Harbor (June 1-3, 1864)
Trevilian Station (June 11-12, 1864)
Petersburg Siege (June 1864-April 1865)
3rd Winchester (September 19, 1864)
Tom's Brook (October 9, 1864)
Cedar Creek (October 19, 1864)
Appomattox Court House (April 9, 1865)

192. VIRGINIA 1ST CAVALRY REGIMENT, PARTISAN RANGERS
See: VIRGINIA 62ND MOUNTED INFANTRY REGIMENT

193. VIRGINIA 1ST CAVALRY REGIMENT, WISE LEGION
See: VIRGINIA 10TH CAVALRY REGIMENT

194. VIRGINIA 2ND CAVALRY BATTALION
Organization: Organized with six companies ca. May 1862. Increased to a regiment and designated as the 5th Cavalry regiment on June 25, 1862, per S.O. #146, Adjutant and Inspector General's Office.

First Commander: Henry C. Pate (Lieutenant Colonel)

195. VIRGINIA 2ND CAVALRY REGIMENT

Organization: Organized in state service for one year as the 30th Regiment at Lynchburg from May 11, 1861, to June 8, 1861. Field officers had been appointed on May 8, 1861. Transferred to Confederate service on July 1, 1861. Designated as the 2nd Cavalry Regiment ca. October 31, 1861. Reorganized on April 24, 1862. Disbanded at Lynchburg on April 10, 1865.

First Commander: Richard C. W. Radford (Colonel)

Field Officers: Cary Breckinridge (Major, Lieutenant Colonel)
William F. Graves (Major)
John S. Langhorne (Major)
Thomas T. Munford (Lieutenant Colonel, Colonel)
James W. Watts (Lieutenant Colonel)

Assignments: Cavalry, Army of the Potomac (July 1861)
Cavalry, 1st Corps, Army of the Potomac (July-September 1861)
Cavalry Brigade, Army of the Potomac (September-November 1861)
Cavalry Brigade, Potomac District, Department of Northern Virginia (November 1861-March 1862)
Cavalry, Forces at Leesburg (D. H. Hill's Command), Potomac District, Department of Northern Virginia (four companies) (January 1862)
Cavalry, Ewell's Division, Department of Northern Virginia (March-May 1862)
Cavalry, Ewell's Division, Valley District, Department of Northern Virginia (May-June 1862)
Cavalry Brigade, Valley District, Department of Northern Virginia (June 1862)
Cavalry, 2nd Corps, Army of Northern Virginia (June 1862)
Robertson's Brigade, Cavalry Division, Army of Northern Virginia (August-November 1862)
Fitz. Lee's Brigade, Cavalry Division, Army of Northern Virginia (November 1862-September 1863)
Wickham's Brigade, Fitz. Lee's Division, Cavalry Corps, Army of Northern Virginia (September 1863-July 1864)
Wickham's Brigade, Fitz. Lee's-Rosser's Cavalry Division, Valley District, Department of Northern Virginia (August 1864-January 1865)
Wickham's-Munford's Brigade, Fitz. Lee's Division, Cavalry Corps, Army of Northern Virginia (February-April 1865)

Battles: Blackburn's Ford (detachment) (July 17, 1861)
1st Bull Run (July 21, 1861)
Dranesville (detachment) (December 20, 1861)
Shenandoah Valley Campaign of 1862 (May 1862-June 1862)

Linden, Virginia (May 15, 1862)
Seven Days Battles (June 25-July 1, 1862)
Lewis' Ford (August 30, 1862)
2nd Bull Run (August 28-30, 1862)
Leesburg, Virginia (September 2, 1862)
Poolesville, Maryland (September 8, 1862)
South Mountain (September 14, 1862)
Antietam (September 17, 1862)
Charleston, West Virginia (detachment) (October 16, 1862)
Fredericksburg (December 13, 1862)
Raid on Dumfries and Fairfax Station, December 27-29, 1862)
Hartwood Church (February 25, 1863)
Kelly's Ford (March 17, 1863)
Chancellorsville (May 1-4, 1863)
Brandy Station (June 9, 1863)
Aldie (June 17, 1863)
Middleburg (June 19, 1863)
Gettysburg (July 1-3, 1863)
Bristoe Campaign (October 1863)
Mine Run Campaign (November-December 1863)
The Wilderness (May 5-6, 1864)
Spotsylvania Court House (May 8-21, 1864)
North Anna (May 22-26, 1864)
Haw's Shop (May 28, 1864)
Cold Harbor (June 1-3, 1864)
Trevilian Station (June 11-12, 1864)
Petersburg Siege (June 1864-April 1865)
3rd Winchester (September 19, 1864)
Tom's Brook (October 9, 1864)
Cedar Creek (October 19, 1864)
Appomattox Court House (April 9, 1865)

196. VIRGINIA 3RD CAVALRY REGIMENT

Organization: Organized with 11 companies in state service for one year as
the 2nd Cavalry Regiment in May and June 1862. Transferred to Confederate
service on July 1, 1861. Designated as the 3rd Cavalry Regiment ca. October
31, 1861. Reorganized on April 26, 1862. 1st Company I became Company H,
5th Cavalry Regiment, on June 25, 1862, per S.O. #146, Adjutant and Inspector
General's Office. Regiment surrendered at Appomattox Court House, Virginia,
on April 9, 1865.

First Commander: Robert Johnston (Colonel)

Field Officers: Henry Carrington (Major)

William R. Carter (Major, Lieutenant Colonel)

William M. Field (Lieutenant Colonel)

Thomas F. Goode (Major, Lieutenant Colonel, Colonel)

Thomas H. Owen (Lieutenant Colonel, Colonel)

Jefferson C. Phillips (Major)

John T. Thornton (Lieutenant Colonel)

Assignments: Department of the Peninsula (September-October 1861)

Cavalry, Department of the Peninsula (October 1861-April 1862)

McLaws' Division, Department of the Peninsula (January-February 1862)

Cavalry Brigade, Army of Northern Virginia (April-July 1862)

Fitz. Lee's Brigade, Cavalry Division, Army of Northern Virginia (July 1862-
September 1863)

Wickham's Brigade, Fitz. Lee's Division, Cavalry Corps, Army of Northern
Virginia (September 1863-July 1864)

Wickham's Brigade, Fitz. Lee's-Rosser's Cavalry Division, Valley District, Department of Northern Virginia (August 1864-January 1865)

Wickham's-Munford's Brigade, Fitz. Lee's Division, Cavalry Corps, Army of
Northern Virginia (February-April 1865)

Battles: near New Market Bridge (detachment) (July 19, 1861)

Back River Road (detachment) (July 19, 1861)

Back River (squadron) (July 24, 1861)

near New Market Bridge (November 11, 1861)

Yorktown Siege (April-May 1862)

Williamsburg (May 5, 1862)

Seven Days Battles (June 25-July 1, 1862)

Scout in King William, King and Queen and Gloucester counties (detachment)
(July 22-30, 1862)

Stuart's Expedition from Hanover Court House to near Fredericksburg (August
2-8, 1862)

2nd Bull Run (August 28-30, 1862)

Antietam (September 17, 1862)

Mountville, Virginia (October 31, 1862)

Corbin's Crossroads, near Amissville, Virginia (November 10, 1862)

Fredericksburg (December 13, 1862)

Raid on Dumfries and Fairfax Station (December 27-29, 1862)

Hartwood Church (February 25, 1863)

Kelly's Ford (March 17, 1863)

Chancellorsville (May 1-4, 1863)

Brandy Station (June 9, 1863)

Aldie (June 17, 1863)

Middleburg (July 19, 1863)
Gettysburg (July 1-3, 1863)
Bristoe Campaign (October 1863)
Mine Run Campaign (November-December 1863)
The Wilderness (May 5-6, 1864)
Spotsylvania Court House (May 8-21, 1864)
North Anna (May 22-26, 1864)
Haw's Shop (May 28, 1864)
Cold Harbor (June 1-3, 1864)
Trevilian Station (June 11-12, 1864)
Petersburg Siege (June 1864-April 1865)
Reams' Station (June 29, 1864)
3rd Winchester (September 19, 1864)
Tom's Brook (October 9, 1864)
Cedar Creek (October 19, 1864)
Appomattox Court House (April 9, 1865)

197. VIRGINIA 4TH CAVALRY REGIMENT

Organization: Organized with six companies for one year at Sangster's Crossroads on September 19, 1861, per S.O. #248, Headquarters Virginia Forces, Richmond, dated September 4, 1861. Companies F, G and I assigned in September 1861. Reorganized on April 25, 1862. Company K assigned on May 23, 1862, per S.O. #118, Adjutant and Inspector General's Office. Surrendered at Appomattox Court House, Virginia, on April 9, 1865.
First Commander: Beverly H. Robertson (Colonel)
Field Officers: Alexander M. Hobson (Major)
Stephen D. Lee (Colonel)
Charles Old (Major)
William H. F. Payne (Major, Lieutenant Colonel, Colonel)
Robert Randolph (Major, Lieutenant Colonel)
Robert E. Utterback (Major)
Williams C. Wickham (Lieutenant Colonel, Colonel)
William B. Wooldridge (Major, Lieutenant Colonel, Colonel)
Assignments: Cavalry Brigade, Army of the Potomac (September-November 1861)
Cavalry Brigade, Potomac District, Department of Northern Virginia (November 1861-March 1862)
Cavalry Brigade, Army of Northern Virginia (March-July 1862)
Fitz. Lee's Brigade, Cavalry Division, Army of Northern Virginia (July 1862-September 1863)

Wickham's Brigade, Fitz. Lee's Division, Cavalry Corps, Army of Northern
    Virginia (September 1863-July 1864)
Wickham's Brigade, Fitz. Lee's-Rosser's Cavalry Division, Valley District, De-
    partment of Northern Virginia (August 1864-January 1865)
Wickham's-Munford's Brigade, Fitz. Lee's Division, Cavalry Corps, Army of
    Northern Virginia (February-April 1865)
Battles: Yorktown Siege (April-May 1862)
Williamsburg (May 5, 1862)
Ellison's Mill, New Bridge and Mechanicsville (detachment) (May 23-24,
    1862)
Hanover Court House (detachment) (May 27, 1862)
Stuart's 1st Ride Around McClellan (June 13-15, 1862)
Seven Days Battles (June 25-July 1, 1862)
Scout in King William, King and Queen and Gloucester counties (detachment)
    (July 22-30, 1862)
2nd Bull Run (August 28-30, 1862)
South Mountain (September 14, 1862)
Antietam (September 17, 1862)
Mountville, Virginia (October 31, 1862)
Corbin's Crossroads, near Amissville, Virginia (November 10, 1862)
Fredericksburg (December 13, 1862)
Raid on Dumfries and Fairfax Station (December 27-29, 1862)
Kelly's Ford (March 17, 1863)
Chancellorsville (May 1-4, 1863)
Brandy Station (June 9, 1863)
Aldie (June 17, 1863)
Middleburg (June 19, 1863)
Westminster, Maryland (June 29, 1863)
Gettysburg (July 1-3, 1863)
Bristoe Campaign (October 1863)
Mine Run Campaign (November-December 1863)
Thoroughfare Mountain (January 27, 1864)
near Greenwich (two men) (April 11, 1864)
near Catlett's Station (three men) (April 16, 1864)
The Wilderness (May 5-6, 1864)
Spotsylvania Court House (May 8-21, 1864)
North Anna (May 22-26, 1864)
Haw's Shop (May 28, 1864)
Cold Harbor (June 1-3, 1864)
Trevilian Station (June 11-12, 1864)
Petersburg Siege (June 1864-April 1865)

Reams' Station (June 29, 1864)
3rd Winchester (September 19, 1864)
Tom's Brook (October 9, 1864)
Cedar Creek (October 19, 1864)
Five Forks (April 1, 1865)
Appomattox Court House (April 9, 1865)
Further Reading: Stiles, Kenneth L., *4th Virginia Cavalry.* Hackley, Woodford
B., *The Little Fork Rangers: A Sketch of Company "D" Fourth Virginia Cavalry.*

198. VIRGINIA 5TH CAVALRY REGIMENT

Organization: Organized by the addition of companies to the 2nd Cavalry
Battalion on June 25, 1862, per S.O. #146, Adjutant and Inspector General's
Office. Consolidated with the 15th Cavalry Regiment and designated as the
5th Consolidated Cavalry Regiment on November 8, 1864.
First Commander: Thomas L. Rosser (Colonel)
Field Officers: James H. Allen (Lieutenant Colonel)
Reuben B. Boston (Colonel)
Beverly B. Douglas (Major)
John Eells (Major)
Cyrus Harding, Jr. (Major)
H. Clay Pate (Lieutenant Colonel, Colonel)
John W. Puller (Major)
Assignments: Cavalry Brigade, Army of Northern Virginia (June-July 1862)
Fitz. Lee's Brigade, Cavalry Division, Army of Northern Virginia (July 1862-
    September 1863)
Lomax's-Payne's Brigade, Fitz. Lee's Division, Cavalry Corps, Army of North-
    ern Virginia (September 1863-September 1864)
Payne's Brigade, Fitz. Lee's-Rosser's Cavalry Division, Valley District, Depart-
    ment of Northern Virginia (September-November 1864)
Battles: Seven Days Battles (June 25-July 1, 1862)
Scout in King William, King and queen and Gloucester counties (detachment)
    (July 22-30, 1862)
2nd Bull Run (August 28-30, 1862)
Antietam (September 17, 1862)
Fredericksburg (December 13, 1862)
Raid on Dumfries and Fairfax Station (December 27-29, 1862)
Kelly's Ford (March 17, 1863)
Stoneman's Raid (April-May 1863)
Aldie (June 17, 1863)
Middleburg (June 19, 1863)
Upperville (June 21, 1863)

Gettysburg (July 1-3, 1863)
Bristoe Campaign (October 1863)
Mine Run Campaign (November-December 1863)
Raid on Eastern Shore of Virginia (detachment) (March 5, 1864)
The Wilderness (May 5-6, 1864)
Spotsylvania Court House (May 8-21, 1864)
North Anna (May 22-26, 1864)
Cold Harbor (June 1-3, 1864)
Petersburg Siege (June 1864-April 1865)
3rd Winchester (September 19, 1864)
Cedar Creek (October 19, 1864)
New Creek (November 28, 1864)

199. VIRGINIA 5TH CAVALRY REGIMENT, PROVISIONAL ARMY

Organization: Organized with nine companies for one year at or near Norfolk ca. July 1861. Company K enlisted on March 9, 1862, for three years. Companies A, B and I became Companies C, A and B, 14th Cavalry Battalion, respectively, on May 1, 1862. Companies C, D, E, F, G, H and K assigned to the 16th Cavalry Battalion on June 26, 1862. Note: This regiment was never fully organized.
First Commander: John Mullins (Major)
Field Officer: Benjamin Allston (Major)

200. VIRGINIA 5TH CONSOLIDATED CAVALRY REGIMENT

Organization: Organized by the consolidation of the 5th and 15th Cavalry Regiments on November 8, 1861. Companies A through F came from the 5th Cavalry Regiment and companies G through K came from the 15th Cavalry Regiment. Surrendered at Appomattox Court House, Virginia, on April 9, 1865.
First Commander: Reuben B. Boston (Colonel)
Field Officers: James H. Allen (Lieutenant Colonel)
Cyrus Harding, Jr. (Major)
Assignments: Payne's Brigade, Fitz. Lee's-Rosser's Cavalry Division, Valley District, Department of Northern Virginia (November 1864-February 1865)
Payne's Brigade, Fitz. Lee's Division, Cavalry Corps, Army of Northern Virginia (February-April 1865)
Battles: Petersburg Siege (from February 1865) (June 1864-April 1865)
Five Forks (April 1, 1865)
near Fair Haven, Chesapeake, Maryland (Company F) (April 4, 1865)
High Bridge (April 7, 1865)
Appomattox Court House (April 9, 1865)

201. VIRGINIA 6TH CAVALRY REGIMENT

Organization: Organized with seven companies on September 12, 1861, per S.O. #276, Adjutant and Inspector General's Office. Company C assigned on September 31, 1861. 1st Company E, a Georgia company, assigned in October 1861. Company I assigned in November 1861. 1st Company E transferred to the Jeff Davis (Miss.) Cavalry Legion on December 7, 1861, per S.O. #260, Adjutant and Inspector General's Office. 2nd Company E assigned on March 26, 1862, per S.O. #69, Adjutant and Inspector General's Office. Surrendered at Appomattox Court House, Virginia, on April 9, 1865.

First Commander: Charles W. Field (Colonel)

Field Officers: John G. Cabell (Major, Lieutenant Colonel)
Cabell E. Flournoy (Major)
Thomas S. Flournoy (Major)
John S. Green (Major, Lieutenant Colonel)
Daniel A. Grimsley (Major)
Julian Harrison (Lieutenant Colonel, Colonel)
Daniel T. Richards (Lieutenant Colonel)

Assignments: Cavalry Brigade, Army of the Potomac (September-November 1861)

Cavalry Brigade, Potomac District, Department of Northern Virginia (November 1861-March 1862)

Cavalry, Ewell's Division, Department of Northern Virginia (March-May 1862)

Cavalry, Ewell's Division, Valley District, Department of Northern Virginia (May-June 1862)

Cavalry Brigade, Valley District, Department of Northern Virginia (June-July 1862)

Robertson's-Jones' Brigade, Cavalry Division, Army of Northern Virginia (August-December 1862)

Jones' Cavalry Brigade, Valley District, Department of Northern Virginia (December 1862-May 1863)

Jones' Brigade, Cavalry Division, Army of Northern Virginia (May-September 1863)

Jones' Brigade, Hampton's Division, Cavalry Corps, Army of Northern Virginia (September 1863)

Lomax's Brigade, Fitz. Lee's Division, Cavalry Corps, Army of Northern Virginia (September 1863-July 1864)

Lomax's-Payne's Brigade, Fitz. Lee's-Rosser's Cavalry Division, Valley District, Department of Northern Virginia (August 1864-February 1865)

Payne's Brigade, Fitz. Lee's Division, Cavalry Corps, Army of Northern Virginia (February-April 1865)

Battles: Burke's Station (December 4, 1861)
Shenandoah Valley Campaign of 1862 (May-June 1862)
Front Royal (May 23, 1862)
1st Winchester (May 25, 1862)
Cross Keys (June 8, 1862)
Port Republic (June 9, 1862)
Stuart's 1st Ride Around McClellan (Company D) (June 12-15, 1862)
Seven Days Battles (two companies) (June 25-July 1, 1862)
Gaines' Mill (two companies) (June 27, 1862)
Cedar Mountain (August 9, 1862)
Catlett's Station (August 22, 1862)
Warrenton Springs (August 23, 1862)
2nd Bull Run (August 28-30, 1862)
South Mountain (September 14, 1862)
Charleston, West Virginia (October 16, 1862)
Expedition to Moorefield and Petersburg, West Virginia (January 2-5, 1863)
Jones' and Imboden's West Virginia Raid (April 20-May 21, 1863)
Greenland Gap, West Virginia (April 25, 1863)
Fairmont, West Virginia (April 29, 1863)
Brandy Station (June 9, 1863)
Millville (June 21, 1863)
Hanover, Pennsylvania (June 30, 1863)
Gettysburg (July 1-3, 1863)
Funkstown, Maryland (July 7, 1863)
Williamsport (July 1863)
White Post (August 11, 1863)
Bristoe Campaign (October 1863)
Auburn (August 13, 1863)
Mine Run Campaign (November-December 1863)
The Wilderness (May 5-6, 1864)
Spotsylvania Court House (May 8-21, 1864)
Yellow Tavern (May 11, 1864)
North Anna (May 22-26, 1864)
Cold Harbor (June 1-3, 1864)
Trevilian Station (June 11-12, 1864)
Petersburg Siege (June 1864-April 1865)
Reams' Station (August 25, 1864)
3rd Winchester (September 19, 1864)
Weyer's Cave (September 26-27, 1864)
Cedar Creek (October 19, 1864)
New Creek (October 28, 1864)

Five Forks (April 1, 1865)
High Bridge (April 7, 1865)
Appomattox Court House (April 9, 1865)
Further Reading: Opie, John Newton, A *Rebel Cavalryman with Lee, Stuart and Jackson.*

202. VIRGINIA 7TH CAVALRY REGIMENT

Organization: Organized in the spring of 1861 for one year in state service and eventually comprised 29 companies. Transferred to Confederate service on July 1, 1861. Ten companies became the 12th Cavalry Regiment on June 21, 1862. Seven companies became the 17th Cavalry Battalion on June 21, 1862. One company was ordered to report to Major General William W. Loring on June 25, 1862, per S.O. #146, Adjutant and Inspector General's Office, and finally became Company G, 14th Cavalry Regiment, per S.O. #208, Adjutant and Inspector General's Office, dated September 5, 1862. One company became the Ashby Horse Artillery in June 19862. Surrendered at Appomattox Court House, Virginia, on April 9, 1865.
First Commander: Angus W. McDonald (Colonel)
Field Officers: Turner Ashby (Lieutenant Colonel, Colonel)
Richard H. Dulany (Lieutenant Colonel, Colonel)
Oliver R. Funsten, Jr. (Major)
Daniel C. Hatcher (Major)
William E. "Grumble" Jones (Colonel)
Thomas Marshall (Major, Lieutenant Colonel)
Samuel B. Myers (Major)
Assignments: Winchester (September 1861-October 1862)
Cavalry, Valley District, Department of Northern Virginia (October-May 1862)
Cavalry, Jackson's Division, Valley District, Department of Northern Virginia (May-June 1862)
Cavalry Brigade, Valley District, Department of Northern Virginia (June-July 1862)
Robertson's Cavalry Brigade, 2nd Corps, Army of Northern Virginia (August 1862)
Robertson's-Jones' Brigade, Cavalry Division, Army of Northern Virginia (August-November 1862)
Jones' Cavalry Brigade, Valley District, Department of Northern Virginia (December 1862-May 1863)
Jones' Brigade, Cavalry Division, Army of Northern Virginia (May-September 1863)
Jones'-Rosser's Brigade, Hampton's-Butler's Division, Cavalry Corps, Army of Northern Virginia (September 1863-September 1864)
Rosser's Brigade, Fitz. Lee's-Rosser's Cavalry Division, Valley District, Department of Northern Virginia (September 1864-March 1865)

Dearing's Brigade, Rosser's (new) Division, Cavalry Corps, Army of Northern
   Virginia (March-April 1865)
Battles: Hanging Rock Pass, West Virginia (September 23, 1861)
Romney (September 24-25, 1861)
Bolivar Heights (four companies) (October 16, 1861)
Kernstown (March 23, 1862)
Shenandoah Valley Campaign of 1862 (May-June 1862)
Orange Court House (August 2, 1862)
Cedar Mountain (August 9, 1862)
2nd Bull Run (August 28-30, 1862)
Lewis' Ford (August 30, 1862)
Poolesville, Maryland (September 8, 1862)
Antietam (September 17, 1862)
Charleston, West Virginia (October 16, 1862)
Expedition to Moorefield and Petersburg, West Virginia (January 2-5, 1863)
Jones' and Imboden's West Virginia Raid (April 20-May 21, 1863)
Greenland Gap, West Virginia (April 25, 1863)
Brandy Station (June 9, 1863)
Middleburg (June 19, 1863)
Upperville (June 21, 1863)
Gettysburg (July 1-3, 1863)
Funkstown, Maryland (July 7, 1863)
Utz's Ford (October 7, 1863)
Bristoe Campaign (October 1863)
Mine Run Campaign (November-December 1863)
The Wilderness (May 5-6, 1864)
Spotsylvania Court House (May 8-21, 1864)
North Anna (May 22-26, 1864)
Haw's Shop (May 28, 1864)
Cold Harbor (June 1-3, 1864)
Petersburg Siege (June 1864-April 1865)
Hampton-Rosser Cattle Raid (September 16, 1864)
3rd Winchester (September 19, 1864)
Cedar Creek (October 19, 1864)
New Creek (November 28, 1864)
Appomattox Court House (April 9, 1865)

203. VIRGINIA 8TH CAVALRY BATTALION

Organization: Organized with seven companies from part of the 1st Cavalry
Regiment, Wise Legion, on March 29, 1862, per S.O. #72, Adjutant and

Inspector General's Office. Increased to a regiment on September 24, 1862, and designated as the 10th Cavalry Regiment.

First Commander: J. Lucius Davis (Lieutenant Colonel)
Field Officers: Charles B. Duffield (Major)
Joseph T. Rosser (Major)
Assignments: Department of the Peninsula (March-April 1862)
Cavalry Brigade, Army of Northern Virginia (May-July 1862)
Hampton's Brigade, Cavalry Division, Army of Northern Virginia (July-September 1862)
Battles: Yorktown Siege (April-May 1862)
Williamsburg (May 5, 1862)
Seven Days Battles (June 25-July 1, 1862)
White Oak Swamp Bridge (August 5, 1862)
Antietam (September 17, 1862)

204.   VIRGINIA 8TH CAVALRY REGIMENT

Organization: Organized for one year with nine companies in late 1861 or January 1862. Reorganized on May 15, 1862. Surrendered at Appomattox Court House, Virginia, on April 9, 1865.
First Commander: Walter J. Jenifer (Colonel)
Field Officers: Thomas B. Bowen (Major)
Alphonso F. Cook (Lieutenant Colonel)
James M. Corns (Colonel)
Patrick M. Edmonston (Lieutenant Colonel)
Henry Fitzhugh, Jr. (Major, Lieutenant Colonel)
Albert G. Jenkins (Lieutenant Colonel)
Assignments: Army of the Kanawha (September-December 1861)
District of Lewisburg (March-May 1862)
District of Lewisburg, Department of Southwestern Virginia (May-November 1862)
Cavalry, Department of Western Virginia (November 1862)
Cavalry Brigade, Department of Western Virginia (February-May 1863)
Jenkins' Brigade, Cavalry Division, Army of Northern Virginia (May-August 1863)
Jones' Cavalry Brigade, Ransom's Division, Department of Western Virginia and East Tennessee (October-November 1863)
Jones' Cavalry Brigade, Ransom's Division, Department of East Tennessee (November-December 1863)
Jones' Cavalry Brigade, Ransom's Division, Department of Western Virginia and East Tennessee (December 1863-February 1864)
Jones' Brigade, Cavalry, Department of East Tennessee (February-March 1864)
Jones' Brigade, Jones' Division, Cavalry Corps, Department of East Tennessee (March-April 1864)

Jones' Brigade, Cavalry, Department of East Tennessee (April-May 1864)

Jones'-B. T. Johnson's Cavalry Brigade, Department of Southwestern Virginia (May-June 1864)

B. T. Johnson's Brigade, Ransom's-Lomax's Cavalry Division, Valley District, Department of Northern Virginia (July-November 1864)

Payne's Brigade, Fitz. Lee's-Rosser's Cavalry Division, Valley District, Department of Northern Virginia (November 1864-January 1865)

Payne's Brigade, Fitz. Lee's Division, Cavalry Corps, Army of Northern Virginia (February-April 1865)

Battles: Camp Creek, Stone River Valley, West Virginia (May 1, 1862)

Giles Court House, West Virginia (May 10, 1862)

Lewisburg, West Virginia (May 23, 1862)

Jenkins' Expedition into West Virginia and Ohio (seven companies) (August 22-September 19, 1862)

Buckhannon, West Virginia (seven companies) (August 30, 1862)

Weston, West Virginia (seven companies) (August 31, 1862)

Glenville, West Virginia (seven companies) (September 1, 1862)

Spencer Court House, West Virginia (seven companies) (September 2, 1862)

White Sulphur Springs, West Virginia (August 26-27, 1863)

Knoxville Siege (November-December 1863)

Rogersville, Tennessee (November 6, 1863)

Jonesville, Virginia (January 3, 1864)

Gibson's and Wyerman's Mills, Indian Creek, Virginia (February 22, 1864)

Piedmont (June 5, 1864)

Lynchburg Campaign (June 1864)

Monocacy (July 9, 1864)

Chambersburg (July 30, 1864)

Moorefield, West Virginia (August 7, 1864)

3rd Winchester (September 19, 1864)

Fisher's Hill (September 22, 1864)

Cedar Creek (October 19, 1864)

New Creek (November 28, 1864)

Petersburg Siege (from February 1865) (June 1864-April 1865)

High Bridge (April 7, 1865)

Appomattox Court House (April 9, 1865)

Further Reading: Dickinson, Jack L., *8th Virginia Cavalry.*

205. VIRGINIA 9TH CAVALRY REGIMENT

Organization: Organized by the addition of two companies, known unofficially as Lee's Squadron, to the 1st (Johnson's) Cavalry Battalion on January 18, 1862, per S.O. #6, Headquarters, Aquia District, Department of Northern

Virginia. Reorganized ca. April 18, 1862. Surrendered at Appomattox Court House, Virginia, on April 9, 1865.

First Commander: John E. Johnson (Colonel)

Field Officers: Richard L. T. Beale (Major, Lieutenant Colonel)
William H. F. Lee (Lieutenant Colonel, Colonel)
Meriwether Lewis (Major, Lieutenant Colonel)
Samuel A. Swann (Major)
Thomas C. Waller (Major, Lieutenant Colonel, Colonel)

Assignments: Cavalry, Aquia District, Department of Northern Virginia (January-April 1862)
Cavalry Brigade, Army of Northern Virginia (June-July 1862)
Fitz. Lee's Brigade, Cavalry Division, Army of Northern Virginia (July-November 1862)
W. H. F. Lee's Brigade, Cavalry Division, Army of Northern Virginia (November 1862-September 1863)
W. H. F. Lee's Brigade, Fitz. Lee's Division, Cavalry Corps, Army of Northern Virginia (September 1863-May 1864)
Chambliss'-Beale's Brigade, W. H. F. Lee's Division, Cavalry Corps, Army of Northern Virginia (May 1864-April 1865)

Battles: US Occupation of Fredericksburg (April 19, 1862)
Stuart's 1st Ride Around McClellan (June 13-15, 1862)
Seven Days Battles (June 25-July 1, 1862)
Scout in King William, King and Queen and Gloucester counties (detachment) (July 22-30, 1862)
Stuart's Expedition from Hanover Court House to near Fredericksburg (August 2-8, 1862)
2nd Bull Run (August 28-30, 1862)
Antietam (September 17, 1862)
Mountville, Virginia (October 31, 1862)
Leeds' Ferry (December 2, 1862)
Fredericksburg (December 13, 1862)
Raid on Dumfries and Fairfax Station (December 27-29, 1862)
Rappahannock Bridge, Kelly's Ford, Welford's Ford and Beverly Ford (April 14-15, 1863)
Stoneman's Raid (April-May 1863)
Brandy Station (June 9, 1863)
Middleburg (June 19, 1863)
Hanover, Pennsylvania (June 30, 1863)
Gettysburg (July 1-3, 1863)
Bristoe Campaign (October 1863)
Mine Run Campaign (November-December 1863)

The Wilderness (May 5-6, 1864)
Spotsylvania Court House (May 8-21, 1864)
North Anna (May 22-26, 1864)
Haw's Shop (May 28, 1864)
Cold Harbor (June 1-3, 1864)
Petersburg Siege (June 1864-April 1865)
Jones' Farm (September 30, 1864)
Vaughan Road (October 2, 1864)
Appomattox Court House (April 9, 1865)
Further Reading: Krick, Robert K., *9th Virginia Cavalry*.

206.   VIRGINIA 10TH CAVALRY BATTALION

See: KENTUCKY 1ST CAVALRY BATTALION, MOUNTED RIFLES

207.   VIRGINIA 10TH CAVALRY REGIMENT

Organization: Organized by the increase of the 8th Cavalry Battalion to a regiment on September 24, 1862. Surrendered at Appomattox Court House, Virginia, on April 9, 1865.

First Commander: J. Lucius Davis (Colonel)

Field Officers: Robert A. Caskie (Major, Lieutenant Colonel, Colonel)
William B. Clement (Major, Lieutenant Colonel)
Zachariah D. McGruder (Lieutenant Colonel)
Joseph T. Rosser (Major)

Assignments: Hampton's Brigade, Cavalry Division, Army of Northern Virginia (September-November 1862)
W. H. F. Lee's Brigade, Cavalry Division, Army of Northern Virginia (November 1862-September 1863)
W. H. F. Lee's Brigade, Fitz. Lee's Division, Cavalry Corps, Army of Northern Virginia (September 1863-April 1864)
Chambliss'-Beale's Brigade, W. H. F. Lee's Division, Cavalry Corps, Army of Northern Virginia (April 1864-April 1865)

Battles: Stuart's 2nd Ride Around McClellan (detachment) (October 9-12, 1862)
Fredericksburg (December 13, 1862)
Raid on Dumfries and Fairfax Station (December 27-29, 1862)
Stoneman's Raid (April-May 1863)
Brandy Station (June 9, 1863)
Middleburg (June 19, 1863)
Hanover, Pennsylvania (June 30, 1863)
Gettysburg (July 1-3, 1863)
Hagerstown, Maryland (July 5, 1863)

Bristoe Campaign (October 1863)
Mine Run Campaign (November-December 1863)
The Wilderness (May 5-6, 1864)
Spotsylvania Court House (May 8-21, 1864)
North Anna (May 22-26, 1864)
Haw's Shop (May 28, 1864)
Cold Harbor (June 1-3, 1864)
Petersburg Siege (June 1864-April 1865)
Jones' Farm (October 1, 1864)
Vaughan Road (October 2, 1864)
Appomattox Court House (April 9, 1865)

208. VIRGINIA 11TH CAVALRY BATTALION
See: KENTUCKY 1ST CAVALRY BATTALION, MOUNTED RIFLES

209. VIRGINIA 11TH CAVALRY REGIMENT
Organization: Organized by the assignment of two companies from the 5th Cavalry Regiment to the eight companies of the 17th Cavalry Battalion on February 5, 1863, per S.O. #36, Headquarters Army of Northern Virginia. Surrendered at Appomattox Court House, Virginia, on April 9, 1865.
First Commander: Lunsford L. Lomax (Colonel)
Field Officers: Mottsom D. Ball (Major, Lieutenant Colonel)
Oliver R. Funsten, Jr. (Lieutenant Colonel, Colonel)
William H. Harness (Major)
Edward H. McDonald (Major)
Assignments: Jones' Cavalry Brigade, Valley District, Department of Northern Virginia (February-May 1863)
Jones' Brigade, Cavalry Division, Army of Northern Virginia (May-September 1863)
Lomax's Brigade, Fitz. Lee's Division, Cavalry Corps, Army of Northern Virginia (September 1863)
Jones'-Rosser's Brigade, Hampton's-Butler's Division, Cavalry Corps, Army of Northern Virginia (September 1863-September 1864)
Rosser's Brigade, Fitz. Lee's-Rosser's Cavalry Division, Valley District, Department of Northern Virginia (September 1864-March 1865)
Dearing's Brigade, Rosser's (new) Division, Cavalry Corps, Army of Northern Virginia (March-April 1865)
Battles: Jones' and Imboden's West Virginia Raid (April 20-May 21, 1863)
Bridgeport, West Virginia (April 30, 1863)
Brandy Station (June 9, 1863)
Upperville (June 21, 1863)

near Woodstock (June 26, 1863)
Gettysburg (June 1-3, 1863)
Hagerstown, Maryland (July 5, 1863)
Rixey's Ford, Virginia (September 2, 1863)
Bristoe Campaign (October 1863)
Mine Run Campaign (November-December 1863)
The Wilderness (May 5-6, 1864)
Spotsylvania Court House (May 8-21, 1864)
North Anna (May 22-26, 1864)
Haw's Shop (May 28, 1864)
Cold Harbor (June 1-3, 1864)
Petersburg Siege (June 1864-April 1865)
Hampton-Rosser Cattle Raid (September 16, 1864)
3rd Winchester (September 19, 1864)
Tom's Brook (October 9, 1864)
Cedar Creek (October 19, 1864)
New Creek (November 28, 1864)
Appomattox Court House (April 9, 1865)
Further Reading: Armstrong, Richard L., *11th Virginia Cavalry.*

210.   VIRGINIA 12TH CAVALRY REGIMENT

Organization: Organized by the assignment of 10 companies from the 7th Cavalry Regiment on June 21, 1862. Surrendered at Appomattox Court House, Virginia, on April 9, 1865.

First Commander: Asher W. Harman (Colonel)

Field Officers: Richard H. Burks (Lieutenant Colonel)
John L. Knott (Major)
Thomas B. Massie (Major, Lieutenant Colonel)

Assignments: Cavalry Brigade, Valley District, Department of Northern Virginia (June-July 1862)

Cavalry Brigade, 2nd Corps, Army of Northern Virginia (August 1862)

Robertson's-Jones' Brigade, Cavalry Division, Army of Northern Virginia (August-November 1862)

Jones' Cavalry Brigade, Valley District, Department of Northern Virginia (December 1862-May 1863)

Jones' Brigade, Cavalry Division, Army of Northern Virginia (May-September 1863)

Jones'-Rosser's Brigade, Hampton's-Butler's Division, Cavalry Corps, Army of Northern Virginia (September 1863-September 1864)

Rosser's Brigade, Fitz. Lee's Cavalry Division, Valley District, Department of Northern Virginia (September 1864-March 1865)

Dearing's Brigade, Rosser's (new) Division, Cavalry Corps, Army of Northern
   Virginia (March-April 1865)
Battles: 2nd Bull Run (August 28-30, 1862)
Lewis' Ford (August 30, 1862)
Poolesville, Maryland (September 8, 1862)
South Mountain (September 14, 1862)
Antietam (September 17, 1862)
Charlestown, West Virginia (October 16, 1862)
Berryville (November 29, 1862)
Expedition to Moorefield and Petersburg, West Virginia (January 2-5, 1863)
Jones' and Imboden's West Virginia Raid (April 20-May 21, 1863)
Greenland Gap, West Virginia (April 25, 1863)
Fairmont, West Virginia (April 29, 1863)
Brandy Station (June 9, 1863)
Upperville (June 21, 1863)
Falling Waters (detachment) (July 4, 1863)
Bristoe Campaign (October 1863)
Mine Run Campaign (November-December 1863)
The Wilderness (May 5-6, 1864)
Spotsylvania Court House (May 8-21, 1864)
North Anna (May 22-26, 1864)
Haw's Shop (May 28, 1864)
Cold Harbor (June 1-3, 1864)
Petersburg Siege (June 1864-April 1865)
Hampton-Rosser Cattle Raid (September 16, 1864)
3rd Winchester (September 19, 1864)
Tom's Brook (October 9, 1864)
Cedar Creek (October 19, 1864)
New Creek (November 28, 1864)
High Bridge (April 7, 1865)
Appomattox Court House (April 9, 1865)
Further Reading: Frye, Dennis E., *12th Virginia Cavalry*.

211. VIRGINIA 13TH CAVALRY REGIMENT

Organization: Organized by the increase of the 16th Cavalry Battalion to a
regiment on July 29, 1862, per S.O. #175, Adjutant and Inspector General's
Office. Company K organized from the other companies ca. August 13, 1862.
Surrendered at Appomattox Court House, Virginia, on April 9, 1865.
First Commander: John R. Chambliss, Jr. (Colonel)
Field Officers: Benjamin W. Belsches (Major)
Joseph E. Gillette (Major)

Jefferson C. Phillips (Lieutenant Colonel, Colonel)
Alexander Savage (Lieutenant Colonel)
Thomas E. Upshaw (Major, Lieutenant Colonel)
Benjamin F. Winfield (Major)
Assignments: Unattached, Department of North Carolina (July-September 1862)
Chambliss' Command, Department of North Carolina and Southern Virginia (September-November 1862)
W. H. F. Lee's Brigade, Cavalry Division, Army of Northern Virginia (December 1862-September 1863)
W. H. F. Lee's Brigade, Fitz. Lee's Division, Cavalry Corps, Army of Northern Virginia (September 1863-April 1864)
Chambliss'-Beale's Brigade, W. H. F Lee's Division, Cavalry Corps, Army of Northern Virginia (April 1864-April 1865)
Battles: Fredericksburg (December 13, 1862)
Raid on Dumfries and Fairfax Station (December 27-29, 1862)
Rappahannock Bridge, Kelly's Ford, Welford's Ford and Beverly Ford (April 14-15, 1863)
Stoneman's Raid (April-May 1863)
Brandy Station (June 9, 1863)
Middleburg (June 19, 1863)
Hanover, Pennsylvania (June 30, 1863)
Gettysburg (July 1-3, 1863)
Bristoe Campaign (October 1863)
Brandy Station (October 11, 1863)
Mine Run Campaign (November-December 1863)
The Wilderness (May 5-6, 1864)
Spotsylvania Court House (May 8-21, 1864)
North Anna (May 22-26, 1864)
Haw's Shop (May 28, 1864)
Cold Harbor (June 1-3, 1864)
Petersburg Siege (June 1864-April 1865)
Jones' Farm (October 1, 1864)
Vaughan Road (October 2, 1864)
Appomattox Court House (April 9, 1865)
Further Reading: Balfour, Daniel T., *13th Virginia Cavalry.*

212. VIRGINIA 14TH CAVALRY BATTALION

Nickname: Chesapeake Battalion
Organization: Organized with four companies ca. May 1, 1862. Consolidated with the 15th Cavalry Battalion and designated as the 15th Cavalry Regiment

on September 11, 1862, per S.O. #213, Adjutant and Inspector General's Office.

First Commander: Edgar Burroughs (Major)

Assignments: Daniel's Brigade, Department of North Carolina (June-July 1862)

Ransom's Brigade, Department of North Carolina (July-September 1862)

Battles: Seven Days Battles (June 25-July 1, 1862)

Malvern Cliff (June 30, 1862)

213. VIRGINIA 14TH CAVALRY REGIMENT

Organization: Organized with nine companies in part from Jackson's Cavalry Squadron on September 5, 1862, per S.O. #208, Adjutant and Inspector General's Office. Tenth Company formed later from the other companies. Regiment furloughed for two months in January 1865. Surrendered at Appomattox Court House, Virginia, on April 9, 1865.

First Commander: Charles E. Thoburn (Colonel)

Field Officers: Robert A. Bailey (Lieutenant Colonel, Colonel)

James Cochran (Colonel)

Benjamin F. Eakle (Major)

John A. Gibson (Lieutenant Colonel)

George Jackson (Major)

Assignments: Cavalry Brigade, Department of Western Virginia (February-May 1863)

Jenkins' Brigade, Cavalry Division, Army of Northern Virginia (May-August 1863)

Jenkins' Cavalry Brigade, Department of Western Virginia (August-September 1863)

Jenkins' Cavalry Brigade, Department of Western Virginia and East Tennessee (September-October 1863)

Jenkins' Brigade, Ransom's Cavalry Division, Department of Western Virginia and East Tennessee (October-December 1863)

Jenkins' Cavalry Brigade, Department of Western Virginia and East Tennessee (December 1863-January 1864)

Jenkins' Cavalry Brigade, Department of Western Virginia (January-June 1864)

McCausland's Brigade, Cavalry Division, Valley District, Department of Northern Virginia (June-July 1864)

McCausland's Brigade, Cavalry Division, Valley District, Department of Northern Virginia (September 1864-January 1865)

McCausland's Brigade, Lomax's Cavalry Division, Valley District, Department of Northern Virginia (March-April 1865)

Battles: Fayetteville, West Virginia (September 10, 1862)
Cotton Hill (September 11, 1862)
Montgomery's Ferry (September 12, 1862)
Charleston, West Virginia (September 13, 1862)
Buffalo (September 27, 1862)
Charlestown (October 6, 1862)
Bullstown (October 9, 1862)
Charleston (October 16, 1862)
Kanawha Falls (October 31, 1862)
Middletown (June 11, 1863)
2nd Winchester (June 14-15, 1863)
White Post (June 14, 1863)
Bunker Hill (June 15, 1863)
Martinsburg, West Virginia (June 15, 1863)
Greencastle (June 20, 1864)
Chambersburg (June 20, 1863)
Monterey, Pennsylvania (Company D) (June 22, 1863)
Greencastle, Pennsylvania (Company I) (June 22, 1863)
Harrisburg, Pennsylvania (June 28-29, 1863)
Carlisle (June 29, 1863)
Gettysburg (July 1-3, 1863)
Monterey Gap (July 5, 1863)
Hagerstown, Maryland (July 6, 1864)
Boonsboro (July 7-8, 1863)
Williamsport (July 14, 1863)
Shepherdstown (July 16, 1863)
Chester Gap (July 21, 1863)
Brandy Station (August 1, 1863)
Kelly's Ford (August 2-3, 1864)
Little Washington (August 24, 1863)
Droop Mountain (November 6, 1863)
Greenbrier River (December 12, 1863)
Cloyd's Mountain (May 9, 1864)
Lynchburg Campaign (June 1864)
White Sulphur Springs (June 1, 1864)
Covington (June 2, 1864)
Panther Gap (June 4, 1864)
Goshen (June 6, 1864)
Buffalo Gap (June 7, 1864)
Staunton Road (June 8, 1864)
Arbor Hill (June 10, 1864)

Newport (June 10, 1864)
Middlebrook (June 10, 1864)
Brownsburg (June 10, 1864)
Lexington (June 11, 1864)
Broad Creek (June 13, 1864)
Buchanan (June 13, 1864)
Peaks Gap (June 14, 1864)
Fancy Farm (June 15, 1864)
Otter River (June 16, 1864)
New London (June 16, 1864)
Lynchburg (June 17-18, 1864)
Forest Depot (June 18, 1864)
Liberty (June 20, 1864)
Salem (June 21, 1864)
Leetown, West Virginia (July 3, 1864)
North Mountain (July 4, 1864)
Hagerstown, Maryland (July 7, 1864)
Fredericksburg, Maryland (July 8, 1864)
Monocacy (July 9, 1864)
Urbanna (July 10, 1864)
Rockville (July 10, 1864)
Fort Stevens (July 11, 1864)
Rockville (July 13, 1864)
Edwards Ferry (July 14, 1864)
Snicker's Gap (July 17, 1864)
Ashby's Gap (July 18, 1864)
Berry's Ferry (July 19, 1864)
Darkesville, West Virginia (July 19, 1864)
Winchester (July 20, 1864)
Stephenson's Depot (July 20, 1864)
Kernstown (July 23, 1864)
Winchester (July 24, 1864)
Martinsburg, West Virginia (July 25, 1864)
Clear Spring, Maryland (July 29, 1864)
Mercersburg, Pennsylvania (July 29, 1864)
Chambersburg (July 30, 1864)
McConnellsburg (July 30, 1864)
Cumberland, Maryland (August 1, 1864)
Old Town (August 2, 1864)
Green Springs (August 2, 1864)
Hancock, Maryland (August 2, 1864)

New Creek, West Virginia (August 4, 1864)
Moorefield, West Virginia (August 7, 1864)
Fisher's Hill (August 13, 1864)
Fisher's Hill (August 15, 1864)
Kernstown (August 17, 1864)
Winchester (August 17, 1864)
Opequon (August 19-20, 1864)
Charlestown (August 21, 1864)
Summit Point (August 21, 1864)
Halltown (August 22, 1864)
Charlestown, West Virginia (August 23, 1864)
Kearneyville (August 25, 1864)
Leetown, West Virginia (August 26, 1864)
Smithfield (August 28, 1864)
Opequon (August 29, 1864)
Brucetown (August 30, 1864)
Opequon (September 1, 1864)
Bunker Hill (September 3, 1864)
Stephenson's Depot (September 5, 1864)
Big Spring, West Virginia (September 10, 1864)
Darkesville, West Virginia (September 10, 1864)
Darkesville, West Virginia (September 12, 1864)
3rd Winchester (September 19, 1864)
Front Royal Pike (September 21, 1864)
Milford (September 22, 1864)
Luray (September 24, 1864)
Port Republic (September 26, 1864)
Waynesborough (September 29, 1864)
Brown's Gap (October 4, 1864)
Strasburg (October 9, 1864)
Fisher's Hill (October 9, 1864)
Woodstock (October 10, 1864)
Cedar Creek (October 11, 1864)
Cedar Creek (October 19, 1864)
Stony Point (October 19, 1864)
Bentonville (October 23, 1864)
Milford (October 25-26, 1864)
Nineveh, Virginia (November 12, 1864)
Front Royal (November 22, 1864)
Berry's Ford (December 17, 1864)
Madison Court House (December 20, 1864)

Liberty Mills (December 22, 1864)
Jack's Shop (December 23, 1864)
Gordonsville (December 24, 1864)
Petersburg Siege (from March 1865) (June 1864-April 1865)
Quaker Road (March 29, 1865)
White Oak Road (March 31, 1865)
Five Forks (April 1, 1865)
Avery's Church Road (April 4, 1865)
Amelia Springs (April 5, 1865)
Jetersville (April 6, 1865)
Deatonsville (April 6, 1865)
High Bridge (April 7, 1865)
Farmville (April 7, 1865)
Appomattox Court House (April 9, 1865)
Further Reading: Driver, Robert J., *14th Virginia Cavalry.*

214. VIRGINIA 15TH CAVALRY BATTALION

Nickname: Northern Neck Rangers
Organization: Organized for the war with four companies in the spring of 1862. Consolidated with the 14th Cavalry Battalion and two independent companies and designated as the 15th Cavalry Regiment on September 15, 1862, per S.O. #213, Adjutant and Inspector General's Office.
First Commander: John Critcher (Major)
Assignments: Cavalry Brigade, Army of Northern Virginia (July-July 1862) Department of North Carolina (July-September 1862)
Battle: Seven Days Battles (June 25-July 1, 1862)

215. VIRGINIA 15TH CAVALRY REGIMENT

Organization: Organized by the consolidation of the 14th and 15th Cavalry Battalions and two independent companies on September 15, 1862, per S.O. #213, Adjutant and Inspector General's Office. Consolidated with the 5th Cavalry Regiment and designated as the 5th Consolidated Cavalry Regiment on November 8, 1864.
First Commander: William B. Ball (Colonel)
Field Officers: Edgar Burroughs (Major)
Charles R. Collins (Major, Colonel)
John Critcher (Lieutenant Colonel)
Assignments: Unattached, Department of North Carolina and Southern Virginia (October 1862)
Chambliss' Command, Unattached, Department of North Carolina and Southern Virginia (October-November 1862)

W. H. F. Lee's Brigade, Cavalry Division, Army of Northern Virginia (November 1862-September 1863)

Lomax's Brigade, Fitz. Lee's Division, Cavalry Corps, Army of Northern Virginia (September 1863-August 1864)

Lomax's-Payne's Brigade, Fitz. Lee's-Rosser's Cavalry Division, Valley District, Department of Northern Virginia (August-November 1864)

Fredericksburg (December 13, 1862)

Raid on Dumfries and Fairfax Station (December 27-29, 1862)

Chancellorsville (May 1-4, 1863)

Middleburg (June 19, 1863)

Gettysburg (July 1-3, 1863)

Bristoe Campaign (October 1863)

Mine Run Campaign (November-December 1863)

The Wilderness (May 5-6, 1864)

Todd's Tavern (May 5, 1864)

Spotsylvania Court House (May 8-21, 1864)

North Anna (May 22-26, 1864)

Cold Harbor (June 1-3, 1864)

Petersburg Siege (June 1864-April 1865)

3rd Winchester (September 19, 1864)

Cedar Creek (October 19, 1864)

216. VIRGINIA 16TH CAVALRY BATTALION

Organization: Organized with eight companies (seven from the 5th Cavalry Regiment, Provisional Army) on June 26, 1862, per S.O. #147, Adjutant and Inspector General's Office. Increased to a regiment and designated as the 13th Cavalry Regiment on July 29, 1862, per S.O. #175, Adjutant and Inspector General's Office.

First Commander: Benjamin W. Belsches (Major)

Assignment: Unattached, Department of North Carolina (June-July 1862)

217. VIRGINIA 16TH CAVALRY REGIMENT

Organization: Organized by the consolidation of Ferguson's (six companies) and Caldwell's (four companies) Cavalry Battalions on January 15, 1863. Surrendered at Appomattox Court House, Virginia, on April 9, 1865.

First Commander: Milton J. Ferguson (Colonel)

Field Officers: William L. Graham (Lieutenant Colonel) James H. Nounnan (Major)

Assignments: Cavalry Brigade, Department of Western Virginia (January-May 1863)

Jenkins' Brigade, Cavalry Division, Army of Northern Virginia (May-August 1863)

Jenkins' Cavalry Brigade, Ransom's Division, Department of Western Virginia and East Tennessee (August-November 1863)

Jenkins' Cavalry Brigade, Ransom's Division, Department of East Tennessee (November-December 1863)

Jenkins'-McCausland's Cavalry Brigade, Department of Western Virginia and East Tennessee (December 1863-June 1864)

McCausland's Cavalry Brigade, Ransom's-Lomax's Cavalry Division, Valley District, Department of Northern Virginia (June 1864-January 1865)

McCausland's Brigade, Rosser's Division, Cavalry Corps, Army of Northern Virginia (March-April 1865)

Battles: 2nd Winchester (June 14-15, 1863)
Harrisburg, Pennsylvania (June 28-29, 1863)
Gettysburg (July 1-3, 1863)
Droop Mountain (November 6, 1863)
Knoxville Siege (November-December 1863)
Capture of the USS *Levi* on the Kanawha River, West Virginia (February 3, 1864)
Lynchburg Campaign (June 1864)
Monocacy (July 9, 1864)
Chambersburg (July 30, 1864)
3rd Winchester (September 19, 1864)
Fisher's Hill (September 22, 1864)
Cedar Creek (October 19, 1864)
Petersburg Siege (from March 1865) (June 1864-April 1865)
Appomattox Court House (April 9, 1865)

218.   VIRGINIA 17TH CAVALRY BATTALION

Also Known As: Virginia 1st (Funsten's) Cavalry Battalion
Organization: Organized by the assignment of seven excess companies of the 7th Cavalry Regiment on June 20, 1862. Sometimes unofficially referred to as the 1st Cavalry Battalion. Company C, 24th Cavalry Battalion, assigned as Company H ca. January 5, 1863. Consolidated with two companies of the 5th Cavalry Regiment and designated as the 11th Cavalry Regiment on February 5, 1863, per S.O. #36, Army of Northern Virginia.
First Commander: Oliver R. Funsten, Sr. (Lieutenant Colonel)
Field Officer: William Patrick (Major)
Assignments: Cavalry Brigade, Valley District, Department of Northern Virginia (July-July 1862)

Cavalry Brigade, Jackson's Command, Army of Northern Virginia (August 1862)

Robertson's-Jones' Brigade, Cavalry Division, Army of Northern Virginia (August-November 1862)

Jones' Cavalry Brigade, Valley District, Department of Northern Virginia (December 1862-February 1863)

Battles: Cedar Mountain (August 9, 1862)

2nd Bull Run (August 28-30, 1862)

Antietam (September 17, 1862)

Expedition to Moorefield and Petersburg, West Virginia (January 2-5, 1863)

219. VIRGINIA 17TH CAVALRY REGIMENT

Organization: Organized by the addition of three companies to the 33rd Cavalry Battalion on January 28, 1863. Surrendered at Appomattox Court House, Virginia, on April 9, 1865.

First Commander: William H. French (Colonel)

Field Officers: Frederick F. Smith (Major)

William C. Tavenner (Lieutenant Colonel)

Assignments: Cavalry Brigade, Department of Western Virginia (January-May 1863)

Jenkins' Brigade, Cavalry Division, Army of Northern Virginia (May-August 1863)

Jenkins' Cavalry Brigade, Ransom's Division, Department of Western Virginia and East Tennessee (August-November 1863)

Jenkins' Cavalry Brigade, Ransom's Division, Department of East Tennessee (November-December 1863)

Jenkins'-McCausland's Cavalry Brigade, Department of Western Virginia and East Tennessee (December-June 1864)

McCausland's Brigade, Ransom's-Lomax's Cavalry Division, Valley District, Department of Northern Virginia (June 1864-January 1865)

McCausland's Brigade, Rosser's Division, Cavalry Corps, Army of Northern Virginia (March-April 1865)

Battles: Gettysburg (June 26, 1863)

Gettysburg (July 1-3, 1863)

Knoxville Siege (November-December 1863)

Cloyd's Mountain (May 9, 1864)

Lynchburg Campaign (June 1864)

Monocacy (July 9, 1864)

Chambersburg (July 30, 1864)

3rd Winchester (September 19, 1864)

Fisher's Hill (September 22, 1864)

Cedar Creek (October 19, 1864)

Petersburg Siege (from March 1865) (June 1864-April 1865)

Appomattox Court House (April 9, 1865)

220. Virginia 18th Cavalry Regiment

Organization: Organized by the assignment of the cavalry companies of the 1st Cavalry Regiment, Partisan Rangers, ca. December 15, 1862. Apparently disbanded in April 1865.

First Commander: George W. Imboden (Colonel)

Field Officers: David E. Beall (Lieutenant Colonel)

Alexander Monroe (Major)

Assignments: Northwestern Virginia Brigade, Department of Northern Virginia (December 1862-July 1863)

Valley District, Department of Northern Virginia (July-December 1863)

Imboden's Command, Valley District, Department of Northern Virginia (December 1863-January 1864)

Northwestern Virginia Brigade, Department of Northern Virginia (February-June 1864)

Imboden's Brigade, Ransom's-Lomax's Cavalry Division, Valley District, Department of Northern Virginia (June 1864-April 1865)

Battles: Jones' and Imboden's West Virginia Raid (April 20-May 21, 1863)

Gettysburg (July 1-3, 1863)

Waynesboro, Pennsylvania (July 5, 1863)

Williamsport (July 5, 1863)

New Market (May 15, 1864)

Lynchburg Campaign (June 1864)

Monocacy (July 9, 1864)

3rd Winchester (September 19, 1864)

Fisher's Hill (September 22, 1864)

Cedar Creek (October 19, 1864)

Further Reading: Delauter, Roger U., *18th Virginia Cavalry.*

221. Virginia 19th Cavalry Regiment

Organization: Organized principally from the 3rd Infantry Regiment, State Line, on April 11, 1863. Disbanded on April 15, 1865.

First Commander: William L. Jackson (Colonel)

Field Officers: George Downs (Major)

William P. Thompson (Lieutenant Colonel)

Assignments: Jenkins' Cavalry Brigade, Department of Western Virginia (April-May 1863)

Jenkins' Brigade, Cavalry Division, Army of Northern Virginia (May-July 1863)

Jackson's Cavalry Brigade, Department of Western Virginia and East Tennessee (December 1863-June 1864)

Jackson's Cavalry Brigade, Department of Western Virginia and East Tennessee (December 1863-June 1864)

Jackson's-Davidson's-Jackson's Brigade, Ransom's-Lomax's Cavalry Division, Valley District, Department of Northern Virginia (June 1864-April 1865)

Battles: Jones' and Imboden's West Virginia Raid (April 20-May 21, 1863)

Expedition to Beverly, West Virginia (June 29-July 4, 1863)

Droop Mountain (November 6, 1863)

Marling's Bottom, West Virginia (April 19, 1864)

Lynchburg Campaign (June 1864)

Monocacy (July 9, 1864)

3rd Winchester (September 19, 1864)

Fisher's Hill (September 22, 1864)

Cedar Creek (October 19, 1864)

222.   VIRGINIA 20TH CAVALRY REGIMENT

Organization: Organized on August 14, 1863. Disbanded on April 15, 1865.

First Commander: William W. Arnett (Colonel)

Field Officers: Dudley Evans (Lieutenant Colonel)

Elihu Hutton (Major)

John B. Lady (Major, Lieutenant Colonel)

Assignments: Jackson's Cavalry Brigade, Department of Western Virginia and East Tennessee (December 1863-June 1864)

Jackson's-Davidson's-Jackson's Brigade, Ransom's- Lomax's Cavalry Division, Valley District, Department of Northern Virginia (June 1864-April 1865)

Battles: Droop Mountain (November 6, 1863)

Lynchburg Campaign (June 1864)

Monocacy (July 9, 1864)

3rd Winchester (September 19, 1864)

Fisher's Hill (September 22, 1864)

Cedar Creek (October 19, 1864)

223.   VIRGINIA 21ST CAVALRY REGIMENT

Organization: Organized from the Virginia State Line on August 27, 1863. Surrendered at Appomattox Court House, Virginia, on April 9, 1865.

First Commander: William E. Peters (Colonel)

Field Officers: David Edmundson (Lieutenant Colonel)

Stephen P. Halsey (Colonel)

Assignments: Jones' Cavalry Brigade, Ransom's Division, Department of Western Virginia and East Tennessee (August 1863-January 1864)

Jones' Cavalry Brigade, Department of Southwestern Virginia and East Tennessee (January 1864)

Jones' Cavalry Brigade, Ransom's Division, Department of Western Virginia (January-February 1864)

Jones' Brigade, Cavalry, Department of East Tennessee (February-March 1864)

Jones' Brigade, Jones' Division, Cavalry Corps, Department of East Tennessee (March-April 1864)

Jones' Brigade, Cavalry, Department of East Tennessee (April-May 1864)

Jones'-B. T. Johnson's Brigade, Department of Western Virginia (May-June 1864)

B. T. Johnson's Brigade, Ransom's-Lomax's Cavalry Division, Valley District, Department of Northern Virginia (July-November 1864)

McCausland's Brigade, Lomax's Cavalry Division, Valley District, Department of Northern Virginia (November 1864-March 1865)

McCausland's Brigade, Rosser's Division, Cavalry Corps, Army of Northern Virginia (March-April 1865)

Battles: Knoxville Siege (November-December 1863)

Rogersville, Tennessee (November 6, 1863)

Gibson's and Wyerman's Mills, Indian Creek, Virginia (February 22, 1864)

Cloyd's Mountain (May 9, 1864)

Piedmont (June 5, 1864)

Lynchburg Campaign (June 1864)

Monocacy (July 9, 1864)

Chambersburg (July 30, 1864)

Moorefield, West Virginia (August 7, 1864)

3rd Winchester (September 19, 1864)

Fisher's Hill (September 22, 1864)

Cedar Creek (October 19, 1864)

Appomattox Court House (April 9, 1865)

224. VIRGINIA 22ND CAVALRY REGIMENT

Nickname: Bowen's Regiment Virginia Mounted Riflemen

Organization: Organized by the consolidation of Baldwin's Cavalry Squadron Partisan Rangers and eight new companies on October 27, 1863. Surrendered at Appomattox Court House, Virginia, on April 9, 1865.

First Commander: Henry S. Bowen (Colonel)

Field Officers: Henry F. Kendrick (Major)

John T. Radford (Lieutenant Colonel)

Assignments: Unattached, Department of Western Virginia and East Tennessee (November 1863-April 1864)

Jenkins' Cavalry Brigade, Department of Western Virginia (April-May 1864)

Jones'-B. T. Johnson's Brigade, Ransom's-Lomax's Cavalry Division, Valley District, Department of Northern Virginia (June-October 1864)

McCausland's Brigade, Lomax's Cavalry Division, Valley District, Department of Northern Virginia (October 1864)

B. T. Johnson's Brigade, Lomax's Cavalry Division, Valley District, Department of Northern Virginia (October-November 1864)

McCausland's Brigade, Lomax's Cavalry Division, Valley District, Department of Northern Virginia (November-March 1865)

McCausland's Brigade, Rosser's Division, Cavalry Corps, Army of Northern Virginia (March-April 1865)

Battles: Lynchburg Campaign (June 1864)

Monocacy (July 9, 1864)

Chambersburg (July 30, 1864)

3rd Winchester (September 19, 1864)

Fisher's Hill (September 22, 1864)

Cedar Creek (October 19, 1864)

Cedarville (November 12, 1864)

Appomattox Court House (April 9, 1865)

225.   VIRGINIA 23RD CAVALRY REGIMENT

Organization: Organized by consolidation of the 41st Cavalry Battalion (seven companies), two companies of O'Ferrall's Cavalry Battalion and one independent company on April 28, 1864 per S.O. #99, Adjutant and Inspector General's Office. Apparently disbanded in April 1865.

First Commander: Robert White (Colonel)

Field Officers: Fielding H. Calmes (Major)

Charles T. O'Ferrall (Lieutenant Colonel)

Assignments: Northwestern Virginia Brigade, Department of Northern Virginia (April-June 1864)

Imboden's Brigade, Ransom's-Lomax's Cavalry Division, Valley District, Department of Northern Virginia (June 1864-April 1865)

Battles: Middletown (April 24, 1864)

New Market (May 15, 1864)

Lynchburg Campaign (June 1864)

Monocacy (July 9, 1864)

3rd Winchester (September 19, 1864)

Fisher's Hill (September 22, 1864)

Cedar Creek (October 19, 1864)

226. VIRGINIA 24TH CAVALRY BATTALION, PARTISAN RANGERS

Organization: Organized with three cavalry companies and one artillery company by September 12, 1862. Artillery company disbanded in June 1863 per orders of June 5, 1863, from the Adjutant and Inspector General's Office. Battalion disbanded as rowdy and useless per S.O. #3, Adjutant and Inspector General's Office, dated January 5, 1863.

First Commander: John Scott (Major)

227. VIRGINIA 24TH CAVALRY REGIMENT

Organization: Organized by the addition of two companies from the 8th (Dearing's) Confederate Cavalry Regiment to the 42nd Cavalry Battalion on June 8, 1864, per S.O. #133, Adjutant and Inspector General's Office. Surrendered at Appomattox Court House, Virginia, on April 9, 1865.

First Commander: William T. Robins (Colonel)

Field Officers: Theophilus G. Barham (Lieutenant Colonel)
John R. Robertson (Major)

Assignments: Gary's Cavalry Brigade, Department of Richmond (June 1864-January 1865)
Gary's Brigade, Fitz. Lee's Division, Cavalry Corps, Army of Northern Virginia (January-April 1865)

Battles: Petersburg Siege (June 1864-April 1865)
3rd New Market Heights (September 29, 1864)
Roper's Farm (September 30, 1864)
Sayler's Creek (April 6, 1865)
Appomattox Court House (April 9, 1865)

228. VIRGINIA 25TH CAVALRY REGIMENT

Organization: Organized by the addition of one company to the 27th Partisan Rangers Battalion on July 8, 1864, per S.O. #159, Adjutant and Inspector General's Office. Apparently disbanded in April 1865.

First Commander: Warren M. Hopkins (Colonel)

Field Officers: Henry A. Edmundson (Lieutenant Colonel)
Sylvester P. McConnell (Major)

Assignments: McCausland's Brigade, Ransom's-Lomax's Division, Valley District, Department of Northern Virginia (July-November 1864)
Imboden's Brigade, Lomax's Cavalry Division, Valley District, Department of Northern Virginia (November 1864-April 1865)

Battles: Monocacy (July 9, 1864)
Chambersburg (July 30, 1864)
Moorefield, West Virginia (August 7, 1864)

3rd Winchester (September 19, 1864)
Fisher's Hill (September 22, 1864)
Cedar Creek (October 19, 1864)

229. VIRGINIA 26TH CAVALRY REGIMENT

Organization: Organized officially by the Richmond authorities by the consolidation of the 46th (six companies) and 47th (four companies) Cavalry Battalions on February 9, 1865, per S.O. #33, Adjutant and Inspector General's Office. There had been an informal field consolidation since July 1864. Consolidated into a regiment in the field on November 2, 1864, per S.O. #101, Headquarters Valley District, Department of Northern Virginia. Disbanded on April 15, 1865.
First Commander: Joseph R. Kessler (Lieutenant Colonel)
Field Officer: Henry D. Ruffner (Major, Lieutenant Colonel)
Assignment: Davidson's-Jackson's Brigade, Lomax's Cavalry Division, Valley District, Department of Northern Virginia (February-April 1865)

230. VIRGINIA 27TH CAVALRY BATTALION, PARTISAN RANGERS

Nicknames: Virginia 27th Mounted Rifles Battalion
Virginia Trigg's Cavalry Battalion, Partisan Rangers
Organization: Organized with six companies ca. September 1, 1862. Company G organized on September 27, 1862. Company H organized on October 3, 1863. Company I organized on April 18, 1863. Tenth company added and the battalion redesignated as the 25th Cavalry Regiment on July 8, 1864, per S.O. #159, Adjutant and Inspector General's Office.
First Commander: Henry A. Edmundson (Lieutenant Colonel)
Field Officer: Sylvester P. McConnell (Major)
Assignments: Unattached, Elzey's Command, Department of North Carolina and Southern Virginia (December 1862)
Colston's Brigade, Elzey's Command, Department of North Carolina and Southern Virginia (December 1862)
District of Abingdon, Department of East Tennessee (February-March 1863)
Marshall's-Preston's Brigade, Department of East Tennessee (April-July 1863)
Preston's Brigade, Army of East Tennessee, Department of Tennessee (July-August 1863)
Jones' Cavalry Brigade, Department of Western Virginia and East Tennessee (October-November 1863)
Jones' Cavalry Brigade, Ransom's Division, Department of East Tennessee (November 1863-January 1864)
Jones' Brigade, Cavalry, Department of East Tennessee (January-March 1864)

Jones' Brigade, Jones' Division, Cavalry Corps, Department of East Tennessee (March-April 1864)

Jones' Brigade, Cavalry, Department of East Tennessee (April-May 1864)

Jones' Cavalry Brigade, Department of Southwestern Virginia (May-June 1864)

———— Brigade, Ransom's Cavalry Division, Valley District, Department of Northern Virginia (June-July 1864)

Battles: Wheeler's and Roddey's Raid (September 30-October 17, 1863)

Knoxville Siege (November-December 1863)

Rogersville, Tennessee (November 6, 1863)

Jonesville, Virginia (January 3, 1864)

Gibson's and Wyerman's Mills, Indian Creek, Virginia (February 22, 1864)

Piedmont (June 5, 1864)

Lynchburg Campaign (June 1864)

231. VIRGINIA 30TH CAVALRY REGIMENT

See: VIRGINIA 2ND CAVALRY REGIMENT

232. VIRGINIA 31ST CAVALRY BATTALION

Organization: Organized with two companies on March 19, 1862. Increased to six companies and designated as the 40th Cavalry Battalion ca. July 16, 1863.

First Commander: John F. Wren (Major)

233. VIRGINIA 32ND CAVALRY BATTALION

Organization: Organized with two companies on November 25, 1862. Consolidated with the 40th Cavalry Battalion and designated as the 42nd Cavalry Battalion on September 24, 1863, per S.O. #277, Adjutant and Inspector General's Office.

First Commander: John R. Robertson (Major)

Assignments: Wise's Brigade, Elzey's Command, Department of Virginia and North Carolina (March-April 1863)

Wise's Brigade, Department of Richmond (April-September 1863)

Battle: Lamb's Ferry, Chickahominy River, Virginia (August 25, 1863)

234. VIRGINIA 33RD CAVALRY BATTALION

Organization: Organized with seven companies on December 27, 1862. Increased to a regiment and designated as the 17th Cavalry Regiment on January 28, 1863.

First Commander: William H. French (Lieutenant Colonel)

235. VIRGINIA 34TH CAVALRY BATTALION

Nickname: Virginia 1st Mounted Rifles Battalion

Organization: Organized with three companies initially on June 1, 1862. Company D organized on September 1, 1863. Company E organized on October 3, 1862. Regiment organization completed on December 1, 1862. Company F organized on July 18, 1863. Company G organized on October 31, 1864. McFarlane's Cavalry Squadron became Companies H and I in May 1864. Company K organized on April 1, 1864.

First Commander: Vincent A. Witcher (Major, Lieutenant Colonel)

Field Officers: John A. McFarlane (Major)

William Straton (Major)

Assignments: District of Abingdon, Department of East Tennessee (February 1863)

Cavalry Brigade, Department of Western Virginia (February-May 1863)

Jenkins' Brigade, Cavalry Division, Army of Northern Virginia (May-August 1863)

Jones' Cavalry Brigade, Ransom's Division, Department of Western Virginia and East Tennessee (October-November 1863)

Jones' Brigade, Jones' Cavalry Division, Department of East Tennessee (November-December 1863)

Jones' Cavalry Brigade, Ransom's Division, Department of Western Virginia and East Tennessee (December-January 1864)

Jones' Cavalry Brigade, Department of Southwestern Virginia and East Tennessee (January 1864)

Jones' Cavalry Brigade, Department of East Tennessee (January-March 1864)

Jones' Brigade, Jones' Division, Cavalry Corps, Department of East Tennessee (March-April 1864)

Jones' Brigade, Cavalry, Department of East Tennessee (April-May 1864)

Jones'-B. T. Johnson's Cavalry Brigade, Department of Southwestern Virginia and East Tennessee (May-June 1864)

B. T. Johnson's Brigade, Ransom's-Lomax's Cavalry Division, Valley District, Department of Northern Virginia (June-November 1864)

Witcher's Cavalry Command, Department of Western Virginia and East Tennessee (November 1864-April 1865)

Battles: Harrisburg, Pennsylvania (June 28-29, 1863)

Gettysburg (July 1-3, 1863)

Blue Springs (October 10, 1864)

Knoxville Siege (November-December 1863)

Gibson's and Wyerman's Mills, Indian Creek, Virginia (February 22, 1864)

Piedmont (June 5, 1864)

Lynchburg Campaign (June 1864)

Monocacy (July 9, 1864)
Chambersburg (July 30, 1864)
3rd Winchester (September 19, 1864)
Fisher's Hill (September 22, 1864)
Buckhannon, West Virginia (September 27-28, 1864)
Cedar Creek (October 19, 1864)
Capture of the *Barnum* and *Fawn* on the Big Sandy River, West Virginia
(November 5, 1864)

236. VIRGINIA 35TH CAVALRY BATTALION

Nickname: White's Cavalry Battalion (prior to its official organization)
Organization: Organized unofficially in the fall of 1862. Battalion officially
organized and designated as the 35th Cavalry Battalion on February 4, 1863,
per Adjutant and Inspector General's Office. Finally composed of six compa-
nies. Surrendered at Appomattox Court House on April 9, 1865.
First Commander: Elijah V. White (Major, Lieutenant Colonel)
Field Officers: George M. Ferneyhough (Major)
Franklin M. Myers (Major)
Assignments: Jones' Brigade, Cavalry Division, Army of Northern Virginia
(November 1862)
Jones' Cavalry Brigade, Valley District, Department of Northern Virginia
(December 1862-May 1863)
Jones' Brigade, Cavalry Division, Army of Northern Virginia (May-September
1863)
Jones'-Rosser's Brigade, Hampton's-Butler's Division, Cavalry Corps, Army of
Northern Virginia (September 1863-September 1864)
Rosser's Brigade, Fitz. Lee's-Rosser's Cavalry Division, Valley District, Depart-
ment of Northern Virginia (September 1864-March 1865)
Dearing's Brigade, Rosser's (new) Division, Cavalry Corps, Army of Northern
Virginia (March-April 1865)
Battles: Philomont, Virginia (November 10, 1862)
Poolesville, Maryland (Company B) (November 25, 1862)
Berryville (November 29, 1862)
Poolesville, Maryland (December 24, 1862)
Brandy Station (June 9, 1863)
Gettysburg (June 22, 1863)
Gettysburg (June 26, 1863)
Edwards' Ferry, Maryland (August 27, 1863)
Barbee's Crossroads, Virginia (September 1, 1863)
Lewinsville, Virginia (October 1, 1863)
Bristoe Campaign (October 1863)

Mine Run Campaign (November-December 1863)
The Wilderness (May 5-6, 1864)
Spotsylvania Court House (May 8-21, 1864)
North Anna (May 22-26, 1864)
Haw's Shop (May 28, 1864)
Cold Harbor (June 1-3, 1864)
Petersburg Siege (June 1864-April 1865)
Hampton-Rosser Cattle Raid (September 16, 1864)
3rd Winchester (September 19, 1864)
Tom's Brook (October 9, 1864)
Cedar Creek (October 19, 1864)
New Creek (November 28, 1864)
Appomattox Court House (April 9, 1865)
Further Reading: Divene, John E., *35th Battalion Virginia Cavalry.*

237. VIRGINIA 36TH CAVALRY BATTALION

Organization: Organized with four companies on February 5, 1863. 1st Company F, 14th Cavalry Regiment, assigned as Company E between May and August 1863. Disbanded in April 1865.

First Commander: James W. Sweeney (Major)

Assignments: Cavalry Brigade, Department of Western Virginia (February-May 1863)

Jenkins' Brigade, Cavalry Division, Army of Northern Virginia (May-August 1863)

Jones' Cavalry Brigade, Ransom's Division, Department of Western Virginia and East Tennessee (October-November 1863)

Jones' Cavalry Brigade, Ransom's Division, Department of East Tennessee (November-December 1863)

Jones' Cavalry Brigade, Ransom's Division, Department of Southwestern Virginia and East Tennessee (December 1863-January 1864)

Jones' Cavalry Brigade, Department of Southwestern Virginia and East Tennessee (January 1864)

Jones' Cavalry Brigade, Department of East Tennessee (January-February 1864)

Jones' Brigade, Cavalry, Department of East Tennessee (February-March 1864)

Jones' Brigade, Jones' Division, Cavalry Corps, Department of East Tennessee (March-April 1864)

Jones' Brigade, Cavalry, Department of East Tennessee (April-May 1864)

Jones'-B. T. Johnson's Cavalry Brigade, Department of Southwestern Virginia and East Tennessee (May-June 1864)

B. T. Johnson's Brigade, Ransom's-Lomax's Cavalry Division, Valley District, Department of Northern Virginia (June-November 1864)

Payne's Brigade, Rosser's Cavalry Division, Valley District, Department of Northern Virginia (November-December 1864)
Witcher's Command, Department of Western Virginia and East Tennessee (February-April 1865)
Battles: Harrisburg, Pennsylvania (June 28-29, 1863)
Gettysburg (July 1-3, 1863)
Knoxville Siege (November-December 1863)
Rogersville, Tennessee (November 6, 1863)
Gibson's and Wyerman's Mills, Indian Creek, Virginia (February 22, 1864)
Piedmont (June 5, 1864)
Lynchburg Campaign (June 1864)
Monocacy (July 9, 1864)
Chambersburg (July 30, 1864)
Moorefield, West Virginia (August 7, 1864)
3rd Winchester (September 19, 1864)
Fisher's Hill (September 22, 1864)
Cedar Creek (October 19, 1864)
Further Reading: Scott, J. L., *36th and 37th Battalions Virginia Cavalry.*

238. VIRGINIA 37TH CAVALRY BATTALION

Organization: Organized with four companies as Dunn's Partisan Rangers Battalion on August 2, 1862. Company E organized on October 1, 1862. Company F, a North Carolina company, organized on October 26, 1862. Converted to regular cavalry and officially designated as the 37th Cavalry Battalion in November 1862. Company H organized on January 8, 1863. Company G organized on February 6, 1863. Company I organized on April 1, 1863. Company K transferred from the 21st Cavalry Regiment prior to June 5, 1864. Apparently disbanded in April 1865.
First Commander: Ambrose C. Dunn (Lieutenant Colonel)
Field Officer: James R. Claiborne (Major)
Assignments: Cavalry Brigade, Department of Western Virginia (February-May 1863)
Jenkins' Brigade, Cavalry Division, Army of Northern Virginia (May-July 1863)
Jones' Cavalry Brigade, Ransom's Division, Department of Western Virginia and East Tennessee (October 1863-January 1864)
Jones' Cavalry Brigade, Department of Southwestern Virginia and East Tennessee (January 1864)
Jones' Cavalry Brigade, Department of East Tennessee (January-February 1864)
Unattached, Department of Western Virginia (Company H) (February-April 1864)
Jones' Brigade, Cavalry, Department of East Tennessee (February-March 1864)

Jones' Brigade, Jones' Division, Cavalry Corps, Department of East Tennessee
(March-April 1864)

Jones' Brigade, Cavalry, Department of East Tennessee (April-May 1864)

Cavalry Brigade, Department of Southwestern Virginia and East Tennessee
(May-June 1864)

McCausland's Brigade, Ransom's-Lomax's Cavalry Division, Valley District,
Department of Northern Virginia (June-October 1864)

B. T. Johnson's Brigade, Lomax's Cavalry Division, Valley District, Department
of Northern Virginia (October 1864)

McCausland's Brigade, Lomax's Cavalry Division, Valley District, Department
of Northern Virginia (October-November 1864)

Jackson's-Davidson's-Jackson's Brigade, Lomax's Cavalry Division, Valley District, Department of Northern Virginia (November 1864-April 1865)

Battles: Jones' and Imboden's West Virginia Raid (April 20-May 21, 1863)
Expedition to Beverly, West Virginia (June 29-July 4, 1863)
White Sulpher Springs West Virginia (August 26-27, 1863)
Knoxville Siege (November 1863)
Rogersville, Tennessee (November 6, 1863)
Jonesville, Virginia (January 3, 1864)
Gibson's and Wyerman's Mills, Indian Creek, Virginia (February 22, 1864)
Piedmont (June 5, 1864)
Lynchburg Campaign (June 1864)
Monocacy (July 9, 1864)
Chambersburg (July 30, 1864)
3rd Winchester (September 19, 1864)
Fisher's Hill (September 22, 1864)
Cedar Creek (October 19, 1864)

Further Reading: Scott, J. L., *36th and 37th Battalions Virginia Cavalry.*

239. VIRGINIA 39TH CAVALRY BATTALION

Organization: Organized with four companies on September 24, 1864. First
known as the 13th Cavalry Battalion. Surrendered at Appomattox Court
House, Virginia, on April 9, 1865.

First Commander: John H. Richarson (Major)

Assignments: Provost Guard, Army of Northern Virginia (December 1863-
April 1865)

Department of Henrico (Company D) (March 1864)

Battle: Petersburg Siege (June 1864-April 1865)

240. VIRGINIA 40TH CAVALRY BATTALION

Organization: Organized by the addition of four companies to the 31st Cavalry Battalion (two companies) ca. July 16, 1863. Consolidated with the 32nd Cavalry Battalion and designated as the 42nd Cavalry Battalion on September 24, 1863, per S.O. #227, Adjutant and Inspector General's Office.
First Commander: John F. Wren (Major)
Field Officer: William T. Robins (Lieutenant Colonel)
Assignments: Godwin's Command, Department of Richmond (July-August 1863)
Cavalry, Wise's Brigade, Department of Richmond (August 1863-September 1864)

241. VIRGINIA 41ST CAVALRY BATTALION

Organization: Organized with four companies on September 18, 1863, per S.O. #222, Adjutant and Inspector General's Office. Three additional companies organized later. Consolidated with O'Ferrall's Cavalry Battalion and one independent company and designated as the 23rd Cavalry Regiment on April 28, 1864, per S.O. #99, Adjutant and Inspector General's Office.
First Commander: Robert White (Major, Lieutenant Colonel)
Assignment: Northwestern Virginia Brigade, Department of Northern Virginia (September 1863-April 1864)
Battles: Jones' and Imboden's West Virginia Raid (April 20-May 21, 1863) Greenland Gap, Pennsylvania (April 25, 1863)

242. VIRGINIA 42ND CAVALRY BATTALION

Organization: Organized by consolidation of 32nd (two companies) and 40th (six companies) Cavalry Battalions on September 24, 1863, per S.O. #227, Adjutant and Inspector General's Office. Consolidated with two companies from the 8th (Dearing's) Confederate Cavalry Regiment and designated as the 24th Cavalry Regiment on June 14, 1864, per S.O. #133, Adjutant and Inspector General's Office, dated June 8, 1864.
First Commander: William T. Robins (Lieutenant Colonel)
Field Officer: John R. Robertson (Major)
Assignments: Cavalry, Department of Richmond (September 1863-January 1864)
Hunton's Brigade, Department of Richmond (February-May 1864)
Unattached, Department of Richmond (May-June 1864)

243. VIRGINIA 43RD CAVALRY BATTALION, PARTISAN RANGERS

Nickname: Virginia 43rd Cavalry Battalion

Organization: Organization begun March 26, 1863. Company organized at Rector's Crossroads on June 10, 1863. Company B formed from a part of Company A at Scuffleburg on October 1, 1863. Company C organized at Rectortown on December 15, 1863. Company D organized at Paris on March 28, 1864. Company E organized at Upperville on July 28, 1864. Artillery Company organized in the summer of 1864. Company F organized at Piedmont on September 13, 1864. Artillery Company disbanded on November 27, 1864, per S.O. #261, Adjutant and Inspector General's Office, dated November 2, 1864. Company G organized from the Artillery Company on November 28, 1864. Increased to a regiment and designated as Mosby's Partisan Rangers Regiment on December 7, 1864.

First Commander: John S. Mosby (Major, Lieutenant Colonel)

Field Officer: William Henry Chapman (Major)

Assignments: Unattached, Cavalry Division, Army of Northern Virginia (March-September 1863)

Unattached, Cavalry Corps, Army of Northern Virginia (September 1863-May 1864)

Unattached, Department of Northern Virginia (May-December 1864)

Battles: Seneca Mills, Maryland (June 11, 1863)

Ewell's Chapel (June 22, 1863)

Rectortown and Salem (July 20, 1863)

Mt. Zion Church (July 30, 1863)

Padgett's near Alexandria (August 1863)

Fairfax Court House (August 6, 1863)

Annandale (August 11, 1863)

Billy Gooding's Tavern on Little River Turnpike 10 miles from Alexandria (August 24, 1864)

Carter Run (September 6, 1863)

Fayetteville, West Virginia (September 16, 1863)

Stuart's, near Chantilly (October 16, 1863)

Old Ox Road (October 16, 1863)

near Little River Turnpike 3 miles from Fairfax Court House (October 22, 1863)

near Warrenton (October 26, 1863)

near Warrenton (November 6, 1863)

near Bealeton Station (November 21, 1863)

Brandy Station (November 26, 1863)

Five Points (January 1, 1864)

Lee's Ridge (January 6, 1864)

Berryville (February 5, 1864)

near Upperville (February 20, 1864)

Anker's Shop near Dranesville (February 22, 1864)
near Greenwich (March 8, 1864)
Kabletown (March 10, 1864)
near Bunker Hill (March 27, 1864)
Hunter's Mill (April 22, 1864)
near Loughbourough's (April 19, 1864)
near Winchester (May 9, 1864)
near Strasburg (May 9, 1864)
near Belle Plain (May 9, 1864)
near Front Royal (ca. May 10, 1864)
Waterford (May 17, 1864)
Guard Hill (May 21, 1864)
near Chantilly and Centerville (June 24, 1864)
Charlestown, West Virginia (June 29, 1864)
Duffield Depot (June 29, 1864)
near Point of Rocks (July 4, 1864)
Skinner's House, near Mt. Zion (July 6, 1864)
near Snickersville (July 18, 1864)
Ashby's Gap (July 18, 1864)
Cheek's Ford (July 30, 1864)
near Burke's Station (August 8, 1864)
Old Braddock Road, near Alexandria (August 8, 1864)
Fairfax Station (August 8, 1864)
near Berryville (August 13, 1864)
between Charlestown and Berryville (August 15, 1864)
near Castleman's Ferry (August 15, 1864)
Sheppard's Mill Road (August 19, 1864)
Annandale (August 24, 1864)
near Berryville (September 3, 1864)
Myer's Ford (September 4, 1864)
Snicker's Gap (September 15, 1864)
near Chester Gap (September 23, 1864)
on the Valley Turnpike (September 25, 1864)
near Gainesville (October 4, 1864)
Salem (October 5, 1864)
near Rectortown (October 5, 1864)
Salem (October 6, 1864)
Rectortown (October 6, 1864)
Rectortown and Salem (October 7, 1864)
Ashby's Gap (October 9, 1864)
Port Tobacco, Maryland (October 9, 1864)

Sandy Springs, near Rockville, Maryland (October 9, 1864)
near The Plains (October 10, 1864)
"Glen Welby," near Salem (October 10, 1864)
near The Plains (October 11, 1864)
near Newton (October 11, 1864)
Brown's Crossing, near Kearneysville (October 12, 1864)
Duffield (October 14, 1864)
Adamstown (October 14, 1864)
Falls Church (October 17, 1864)
Capture of General Duffie (October 24, 1864)
near Upperville (October 29, 1864)
near Winchester (November 16, 1864)
near Berry's Ferry (November 16, 1864)
near Myerstown (November 16, 1864)
near Charlestown (November 22, 1864)
near White Post (November 24, 1864)
near Goresville (November 27, 1864)

Further Reading: Mosby, John Singleton, *Memoirs.* Williamson, James J., *Mosby's Rangers: A Record of the Operations of the Forty-third Battalion Virginia Cavalry.*

244.   VIRGINIA 46TH CAVALRY BATTALION

Organization: Organized with six companies on February 26, 1864. Consolidated with the 47th Cavalry Battalion and designated as the 26th Cavalry Regiment on February 9, 1865, per S.O. #33, Adjutant and Inspector General's Office.

First Commander: Joseph R. Kessler (Lieutenant Colonel)

Field Officer: Henry D. Ruffner (Major)

Assignments: Jackson's Cavalry Brigade, Department of Western Virginia (February-June 1864)

Jackson's-Davidson's-Jackson's Brigade, Lomax's Cavalry Division, Valley District, Department of Northern Virginia (February-June 1864)

Battles: Lynchburg Campaign (June 1864)

Monocacy (July 9, 1864)

3rd Winchester (September 19, 1864)

Fisher's Hill (September 22, 1864)

Cedar Creek (October 19, 1864)

245.   VIRGINIA 47TH CAVALRY BATTALION

Organization: Organized with four companies on April 1, 1864. Consolidated with the 46th Cavalry Battalion and designated as the 26th Cavalry Regiment on February 9, 1865, per S.O. #33, Adjutant and Inspector General's Office.

First Commander: William N. Harman (Major)

Assignments: Jackson's Cavalry Brigade, Department of Southwestern Virginia (April-June 1864)

Jackson's-Davidson's-Jackson's Brigade, Ransom's-Lomax's Cavalry Division, Valley District, Department of Northern Virginia (June 1864-February 1865)

Battles: Lynchburg Campaign (June 1864)

Monocacy (July 9, 1864)

3rd Winchester (September 19, 1864)

Fisher's Hill (September 22, 1864)

Cedar Creek (October 19, 1864)

246. VIRGINIA 62ND CAVALRY REGIMENT

See: VIRGINIA 62ND MOUNTED INFANTRY REGIMENT

247. VIRGINIA 64TH CAVALRY REGIMENT

See: VIRGINIA 64TH INFANTRY REGIMENT

248. VIRGINIA BALDWIN'S CAVALRY SQUADRON, PARTISAN RANGERS

Organization: Organized with two companies by the division of Baldwin's Cavalry Company Partisan Rangers prior to February 1, 1863. Companies A and B became Companies E and A, 22nd Cavalry Regiment, respectively, on October 27, 1863.

First Commander: William M. Baldwin (Major)

Assignment: Unattached, Department of Western Virginia and East Tennessee (October 1863)

249. VIRGINIA BALFOUR'S MOUNTED RIFLES CAVALRY COMPANY, STATE LINE

Organization: Probably organized in 1862. Became Company A, Jackson's Artillery Battalion, State Line, in early 1863.

250. VIRGINIA CALDWELL'S CAVALRY BATTALION

Organization: Organized, without authority, as a temporary field organization with two companies by Captain Caldwell on August 7, 1862. Increased to four companies in October 1862. Consolidated with Ferguson's Cavalry Battalion and designated as the 16th Cavalry Regiment on January 15, 1863.

First Commander: Otis Caldwell (Major)

Assignment: District of Abingdon, Department of Southwestern Virginia (August-September 1862)

251. VIRGINIA CARPENTER'S CAVALRY BATTALION

See: VIRGINIA SWANN'S CAVALRY BATTALION

252. VIRGINIA DAVIS' CAVALRY BATTALION

Organization: Organized, apparently with about nine companies, in 1864. Disbanded shortly thereafter.
First Commander: Thomas S. Davis (Major)
Assignment: Northwestern Virginia brigade, Valley District, Department of Northern Virginia (May 1864)
Battle: New Market (May 15, 1864)

253. VIRGINIA FERGUSON'S CAVALRY BATTALION

Nickname: Virginia Guyandotte Cavalry Battalion
Organization: Organized with seven companies from August 4, 1862, to January 12, 1863. One company became 2nd Company D, 8th Cavalry Regiment. Remaining six companies were consolidated with Caldwell's Cavalry Battalion and designated as the 16th Cavalry Regiment on January 15, 1863.
First Commander: Milton J. Ferguson (Captain)

254. VIRGINIA GUYANDOTTE CAVALRY REGIMENT

See: VIRGINIA FERGUSON'S CAVALRY BATTALION

255. VIRGINIA HERNDON'S CAVALRY BATTALION

Organization: Failed to complete organization and broken up in February 1863.
First Commander: William E. Herndon (Major)

256. VIRGINIA HOUNSHELL'S CAVALRY BATTALION

Also Known As: Virginia Morris' Cavalry Battalion
Virginia Thurmond's Cavalry Battalion
Organization: Organized apparently in late 1863. Does not appear in the *Official Records.*
First Commander: David S. Hounshell (Lieutenant Colonel)

257. VIRGINIA LEE'S CAVALRY SQUADRON

Organization: Organized as an unofficial field organization with two companies in late 1861. Consolidated (as Companies G and H) with the 1st (Johnson's) Cavalry Battalion and designated as the 9th Cavalry Regiment on January 18, 1862, per S.O. #6, Headquarters, Aquia District, Department of Northern Virginia.

First Commander: William H. F. Lee (Captain, Major)
Assignment: Unattached, Aquia District, Department of Northern Virginia (December 1861-January 1862)

258. VIRGINIA LEE'S LEGION CAVALRY BATTALION

See: VIRGINIA 1ST (JOHNSON'S) CAVALRY BATTALION

259. VIRGINIA MCFARLANE'S CAVALRY SQUADRON

Organization: Organized with two companies by the division of McFarlane's Cavalry Company on May 28, 1863. Temporarily attached to the 27th Cavalry Battalion as Companies L and K, respectively. Assigned as Companies F and E, 3rd (Jesse's) Cavalry Battalion, respectively, ca. July 1863.
First Commander: John A. McFarlane (Captain)

260. VIRGINIA MCNEILL'S CAVALRY COMPANY, PARTISAN RANGERS

Organization: Organized from 2nd Company E, 18th Virginia Cavalry Regiment, ca. February 1863. Surrendered near Romney, West Virginia, on May 8, 1865.
First Commander: John Hanson McNeill (Captain)
Captain: Jesse Cunningham McNeill
Assignments: Northwestern Virginia Brigade, Department of Northern Virginia (March-July 1863)
Valley District, Department of Northern Virginia (July-December 1863)
Imboden's Command, Valley District, Department of Northern Virginia (December 1863-January 1864)
Northwestern Virginia Brigade, Department of Northern Virginia (February-June 1864)
Imboden's Brigade, Ransom's-Lomax's Cavalry Division, Valley District, Department of Northern Virginia (June 1864-April 1865)
Battles: Patterson's Creek (February 16, 1863)
Burlington, West Virginia (April 26, 1863)
Raid on the Baltimore and Ohio Railroad (May 5, 1864)
New Market (May 15, 1864)
Mt. Jackson (October 3, 1864)
New Creek (November 28, 1864)
Cumberland, Maryland (February 21, 1865)
near Patterson's Creek (March 30, 1865)

261. VIRGINIA MORRIS' CAVALRY BATTALION

See: VIRGINIA HOUNSHELL'S CAVALRY BATTALION

262. VIRGINIA MOSBY'S CAVALRY REGIMENT, PARTISAN RANGERS

Organization: Organized by the increase of the 43rd Partisan Rangers Battalion to a regiment on December 7, 1864. Disbanded at Salem, Fauquier County, on April 21, 1865. Portion of the regiment formally surrendered by Lieutenant Colonel William H. Chapman at Winchester on April 22, 1865.

First Commander: John S. Mosby (Colonel)

Field Officers: William Henry Chapman (Lieutenant Colonel)
Adolphus E. Richards (Major)

Assignment: Unattached, Department of Northern Virginia (December 1864-April 1865)

Battles: near Millwood (December 17, 1864)
near Vienna (December 19, 1864)
Mt. Carmel and Shepherd's Mill (February 19, 1865)
near Lewinsville (March 12, 1865)
near Hamilton and Harmony (March 21, 1865)
near Middleburg (March 23, 1865)
near Charlestown (April 6, 1865)
near Berryville (April 8, 1865)
Arundel's Farm (April 9, 1865)

Further Reading: Mosby, John Singleton, *Memoirs*. Williamson, James J., *Mosby's Rangers: A Record of the Operations of the Forty-third Battalion Virginia Cavalry*.

263. VIRGINIA O'FERRALL'S CAVALRY BATTALION

Organization: Battalion organization authorized on October 26, 1863. Failed to complete its organization and companies transferred to the 23rd Cavalry Regiment on April 28, 1864, per S.O. #99, Adjutant and Inspector General's Office.

First Commander: Charles T. O'Ferrall (Lieutenant Colonel)

Assignment: Northwestern Virginia Brigade, Department of Northern Virginia (February-April 1864)

264. VIRGINIA PATTERSON'S CAVALRY BATTALION

Organization: Organized with four companies at Harrisonburg on April 19, 1861. Broken up during the late spring or early summer of 1861 with two companies assigned to the 1st Cavalry Regiment and one each to the 5th and 25th Infantry Regiments. Does not appear in the *Official Records*.

First Commander: Benjamin C. Patterson (Major)

265. VIRGINIA SWANN'S CAVALRY BATTALION

Also Known As: Virginia Carpenter's Cavalry Battalion

Organization: Organized with six companies on December 28, 1864, per S.O. #130, Headquarters, Department of Western Virginia and East Tennessee. Increased to seven companies on January 19, 1865. Disbanded by Brigadier General John Echols, commanding Department of Southwestern Virginia and East Tennessee, at Christianburg, Virginia, on April 12, 1865.

First Commander: Thomas B. Swann (Lieutenant Colonel)

Assignment: Witcher's Cavalry Brigade, Department of Western Virginia and East Tennessee (February-March 1865)

266. VIRGINIA THURMOND'S CAVALRY BATTALION

See: VIRGINIA HOUNSHELL'S CAVALRY BATTALION

267. VIRGINIA TRIGG'S CAVALRY BATTALION, PARTISAN RANGERS

See: VIRGINIA 27TH CAVALRY BATTALION, PARTISAN RANGERS

268. VIRGINIA WALKER'S CAVALRY BATTALION

Organization: Failed to complete its organization.

First Commander: Elias M. Walker (Captain)

269. VIRGINIA WISE LEGION CAVALRY REGIMENT

See: VIRGINIA 10TH CAVALRY REGIMENT

INFANTRY

270. VIRGINIA 1ST INFANTRY BATTALION, LOCAL DEFENSE TROOPS

Nickname: Armory Battalion
Ordnance Battalion
Organization: Organized with six companies at Richmond from the employees of the armory for local defense as needed on May 28, 1863. Mustered into Confederate service on June 15, 1863. Apparently discontinued upon the fall of Richmond on April 2, 1865.
First Commander: William S. Downer (Major)
Field Officers: Thomas H. Ayres (Major)
Charles H. Ford (Major)
Assignments: Local Defense Brigade, Department of Richmond (May 1863-March 1865)
————Brigade, G. W. C. Lee's Division, Department of Richmond (March-April 1865)
Battles: Petersburg Siege (June 1864-April 1865)
Roper's Farm (September 30, 1864)

271. VIRGINIA 1ST INFANTRY BATTALION, PROVISIONAL ARMY

Nicknames: Irish Battalion
1st Battalion Virginia Regulars
Organization: Organized with five companies in state service in May 1861. Mustered into Confederate service for three years on June 30, 1861. Reorganized during the spring of 1862. Surrendered at Appomattox Court House, Virginia, on April 9, 1865.
First Commander: John D. Munford (Major)
Field Officers: David B. Bridgford (Major)
John Seddon (Major)

Assignments: Gilham's Brigade, Army of the Northwest (September 1861-January 1862)

Gilham's-Burks'-Campbell's Brigade, Valley District, Department of Northern Virginia (March-May 1862)

Campbell's Brigade, Jackson's Division, Valley District, Department of Northern Virginia (May-June 1862)

Campbell's-Cunningham's-J. R. Jones' Brigade, Jackson's Division, 2nd Corps, Army of Northern Virginia (June-December 1862)

Provost Guard, Army of Northern Virginia (December 1863-April 1865)

Battles: Kernstown (March 23, 1862)
McDowell (May 8, 1862)
Shenandoah Valley Campaign of 1862 (May-June 1862)
Seven Days Battles (June 25-July 1, 1862)
Gaines' Mill (June 27, 1862)
Cedar Mountain (August 9, 1862)
2nd Bull Run (August 28-30, 1862)
Harpers Ferry (September 12-15, 1862)
Antietam (September 17, 1862)
Fredericksburg (December 13, 1862)
Petersburg Siege (June 1864-April 1865)
Appomattox Court House (April 9, 1865)

272. VIRGINIA 1ST INFANTRY BATTALION RESERVES

Organization: Organized with eight companies on May 31, 1864. Company I added to the battalion on September 6, 1864. Surrendered at Appomattox Court House, Virginia, on April 9, 1865.

First Commander: Richard T. W. Duke (Lieutenant Colonel)

Field Officer: James M. Strange (Major)

Assignments: Unattached, Department of Richmond (June-October 1864)
Barton's Brigade, Department of Richmond (October 1864-January 1865)
Moore's Brigade, Department of Richmond (February-March 1865)
Barton's Brigade, G. W. C. Lee's Division, Department of Richmond (March-April 1865)
Barton's Brigade, G. W. C. Lee's Division, Army of Northern Virginia (April 1865)

Battles: Petersburg Siege (June 1864-April 1865)
Fort Harrison (September 29-30, 1864)
Sayler's Creek (April 6, 1865)
Appomattox Court House (April 9, 1865)

273. VIRGINIA 1ST INFANTRY BATTALION, STATE LINE

Organization: Organized with a mixture of infantry and cavalry companies in the summer or fall of 1862. No rolls for this battalion on file at the National Archives. It also does not appear in the *Official Records*. Probably became one of the regiments of the State Line.

274. VIRGINIA 1ST INFANTRY BATTALION, VALLEY RESERVES

See: VIRGINIA 8TH INFANTRY BATTALION RESERVES

275. VIRGINIA 1ST INFANTRY REGIMENT

Nickname: Williams Rifles

Organization: Organized as a volunteer militia regiment from militia companies from Chesterfield and Henrico Counties and the City of Richmond on May 1, 1851, per G.O. #1, Virginia Adjutant General's Office. Called into state service in April 1861. Mustered into state service on April 21, 1861. Transferred to Confederate service on July 1, 1861. Reorganized with only six companies on April 27, 1862. Surrendered at Appomattox Court House, Virginia, on April 9, 1865.

First Commander: Patrick T. Moore (Colonel)

Field Officers: John Dooley (Major)

William H. Fry (Lieutenant Colonel)

Francis H. Langley (Major, Lieutenant Colonel)

William P. Munford (Major)

George F. Norton (Major)

William H. Palmer (Major)

Frederick G. Skinner (Major, Lieutenant Colonel)

Lewis B. Williams, Jr. (Colonel)

Assignments: Terrett's-Longstreet's Brigade, Army of the Potomac (June-July 1861)

Longstreet's Brigade, 1st Corps, Army of the Potomac (July-October 1861)

Clark's-Griffith's-Ewell's Brigade, Longstreet's Division, 1st Corps, Potomac District, Department of Northern Virginia (October 1861-January 1862)

Ewell's-A. P. Hill's Brigade, Longstreet's Division, Potomac District, Department of Northern Virginia (January-March 1862)

A. P. Hill's-Kemper's Brigade, Longstreet's Division, Army of Northern Virginia (March-June 1862)

Kemper's Brigade, Longstreet's Division, 1st Corps, Army of Northern Virginia (June-August 1862)

Kemper's Brigade, Kemper's Division, 1st Corps, Army of Northern Virginia (August-September 1862)

Kemper's Brigade, D. R. Jones Brigade, 1st Corps, Army of Northern Virginia (September 1862)

Kemper's Brigade, Pickett's Division, 1st Corps, Army of Northern Virginia (September 1862-February 1863)

Kemper's Brigade, Pickett's Division, Department of Virginia and North Carolina (February-April 1863)

Kemper's Brigade, Pickett's Division, Department of Southern Virginia (April-May 1863)

Kemper's Brigade, Pickett's Division, 1st Corps, Army of Northern Virginia (May-September 1863)

Kemper's Brigade, Department of Richmond (September 1863-May 1864)

Kemper's-Terry's Brigade, Pickett's Division, 1st Corps, Army of Northern Virginia (May 1864-April 1865)

Battles: Blackburn's Ford (July 18, 1861)
1st Bull Run (July 21, 1861)
Yorktown Siege (April-May 1862)
Williamsburg (May 5, 1862)
Seven Pines (May 31-June 1, 1862)
Seven Days Battles (June 25-July 1, 1862)
Frayser's Farm (June 30, 1862)
2nd Bull Run (August 28-30, 1862)
South Mountain (September 14, 1862)
Antietam (September 17, 1862)
Fredericksburg (December 13, 1862)
Suffolk Campaign (April-May 1863)
Gettysburg (July 1-3, 1863)
Plymouth (April 17-20, 1864)
Drewry's Bluff (May 16, 1864)
Howlett House (May 18, 1864)
North Anna (May 22-26, 1864)
Cold Harbor (June 1-3, 1864)
Clay Farm (June 16, 1864)
Petersburg Siege (June 1864-April 1865)
Dinwiddie Court House (March 31, 1865)
Five Forks (April 1, 1865)
Sayler's Creek (April 6, 1865)
Appomattox Court House (April 9, 1865)

Further Reading: Loehr, Charles T., *War History of the Old First Virginia Infantry Regiment, Army of Northern Virginia.* Wallace, Lee A., Jr., *1st Virginia Infantry.*

276. VIRGINIA 1ST INFANTRY REGIMENT, LOCAL DEFENSE TROOPS

Organization: Organized from the staff of the Nitre and Mining Bureau in Richmond ca. October 2, 1863.

First Commander: James F. Jones (Colonel)

277. VIRGINIA 1ST INFANTRY REGIMENT RESERVES

Organization: Organized by the consolidation of Averett's and Farinholt's Infantry Battalion of Reserves on August 12, 1864. Officially recognized as the 1st Virginia Infantry Regiment, Reserves, on February 27, 1865, per S.O. #48, Adjutant and Inspector General's Office.

First Commander: Benjamin L. Farinholt (Colonel)

Field Officers: C. E. Averett (Major)
Thomas T. Boswell (Lieutenant Colonel)

Assignments: Unattached, Department of Richmond (August-September 1864)
Walker's Brigade (Defenses of the Danville and Southside Railroad), 1st Military District, Department of Northern Virginia (September-December 1864)
Moore's Brigade (Virginia Reserves), Department of Richmond (December-post-March 1865)

Battle: Staunton River Bridge (June 25, 1864)

278. VIRGINIA 1ST INFANTRY REGIMENT, STATE LINE

Organization: Organized with a mixture of infantry and cavalry companies for one year in state service in late 1862. Disbanded ca. March 31, 1863.

First Commander: Richard C. W. Carlton (Colonel)

Field Officers: Henry M. Beckley (Lieutenant Colonel)
James A. Nighbert (Major)

Assignment: 1st Brigade, Virginia State Line (December 1862-March 1863)

Battle: Prestonburg, Kentucky (detachment) (December 4-5, 1862)

279. VIRGINIA 1ST INFANTRY REGIMENT, WISE LEGION

See: VIRGINIA 46TH INFANTRY REGIMENT

280. VIRGINIA 1ST KANAWHA INFANTRY REGIMENT

See: VIRGINIA 22ND INFANTRY REGIMENT

281. VIRGINIA 2ND INFANTRY BATTALION

Organization: Organized with two companies at Fredericksburg in April 1860. Became part of the 30th Infantry Regiment on June 13, 1861.

First Commander: William Burton (Major)

282. VIRGINIA 2ND INFANTRY BATTALION, LOCAL DEFENSE TROOPS

Nickname: Quartermaster Battalion

Organization: Organized with three companies from employees of the Quartermaster Department in Richmond on June 18, 1863. Company D organized on June 19, 1863. Company E organized on July 28, 1863. Company F organized March 26, 1864. Company G mustered in on May 8, 1864. Battalion consolidated with 6th Infantry Battalion, Local Defense Troops, and designated the 22nd Infantry Regiment, Local Defense Troops, on September 2, 1864, per S.O. #208, Adjutant and Inspector General's Office.

First Commander: Richard P. Waller (Major)

Field Officer: Daniel E. Scruggs (Major)

Assignment: Local Defense Troops Brigade, Department of Richmond (May-July 1863)

283. VIRGINIA 2ND INFANTRY BATTALION RESERVES

Organization: Organized with six companies (previously organized and mustered in for the war) on July 6, 1864. Company G organized and mustered in on July 30, 1864. Company G organized and mustered in on August 6, 1864. Presumably surrendered at Appomattox Court House, Virginia, on April 9, 1865.

First Commander: John H. Guy (Lieutenant Colonel)

Field Officer: Edward B. Cook (Major)

Assignments: Unattached, Department of Richmond (September-October 1864)

G. W. C. Lee's Brigade, Department of Richmond (October 1864-January 1865)

Moore's Brigade, Department of Richmond (February-March 1865)

Barton's Brigade, G. W. C. Lee's Division, Department of Richmond (April 1865)

Battles: Petersburg Siege (June 1864-April 1865)

Fort Harrison (September 29-30, 1864)

Sayler's Creek (presumably) (April 6, 1865)

Appomattox Court House (presumably) (April 9, 1865)

284. VIRGINIA 2ND INFANTRY BATTALION, VALLEY RESERVES

See: VIRGINIA 9TH INFANTRY BATTALION RESERVES

285. VIRGINIA 2ND INFANTRY REGIMENT

Organization: Organized on April 18, 1861, at Charlestown from the 2nd Regiment Virginia Volunteers (Militia), which had been organized on June 8, 1860, from the companies of the 55th Militia Regiment. Mustered into state service by companies on May 11-13, 1861. Designated 2nd Infantry Regiment on June 1, 1861. Regiment mustered in June 8, 1861. Transferred to Confederate service on July 1, 1861. Reorganized ca. April 20, 1862. Field consolidation with the 4th, 5th, 27th and 33rd Infantry Regiments from May 1864 to April 1865. Surrendered at Appomattox Court House, Virginia, on April 9, 1865.

First Commander: James W. Allen (Colonel)

Field Officers: Lawson Botts (Major, Lieutenant Colonel, Colonel)
Raleigh T. Colston (Major, Lieutenant Colonel)
Francis B. Jones (Major)
Francis Lackland (Lieutenant Colonel)
Edwin L. Moore (Major)
John Q. A. Nadenbousch (Lieutenant Colonel, Major)
William W. Randolph (Lieutenant Colonel)
Charles R. Stewart (Major)

Assignments: 1st Brigade, Army of the Shenandoah (June-July 1861)
1st Brigade, 2nd Corps, Army of the Potomac (July-October 1861)
Stonewall Brigade, 2nd Corps, Potomac District, Department of Northern Virginia (October-November 1861)
Stonewall Brigade, Valley District, Department of Northern Virginia (November 1861-May 1862)
Stonewall Brigade, Jackson's Division, Valley District, Department of Northern Virginia (May-June 1862)
Stonewall Brigade, Jackson's-Johnson's Division, 2nd Corps, Army of Northern Virginia (June 1862-May 1864)
Terry's Consolidated Brigade, Gordon's Division, 2nd Corps, Army of Northern Virginia (May-June 1864)
Terry's Consolidated Brigade, Gordon's Division, Valley District, Department of Northern Virginia (June-December 1864)
Terry's Consolidated Brigade, Gordon's Division, 2nd Corps, Army of Northern Virginia (December 1864-April 1865)

Battles: Seizure of Harpers Ferry (April 19, 1861)
Falling Waters (July 2, 1861)
1st Bull Run (July 21, 1861)

Romney Campaign (January 1862)
Kernstown (March 23, 1862)
McDowell (not engaged) (May 8, 1862)
1st Winchester (May 25, 1862)
Front Royal (not engaged) (May 23, 1862)
Port Republic (June 9, 1862)
Seven Days Battles (June 25-July 1, 1862)
Gaines' Mill (June 27, 1862)
White Oak Swamp (June 30, 1862)
Malvern Hill (July 1, 1862)
Cedar Mountain (August 9, 1862)
Groveton (August 28, 1862)
2nd Bull Run (August 28-30, 1862)
Chantilly (in reserve) (September 1, 1862)
Harpers Ferry (September 12-15, 1862)
Antietam (September 17, 1862)
Kearneyville (October 17, 1862)
Fredericksburg (December 13, 1862)
Chancellorsville (May 1-4, 1863)
2nd Winchester (June 14-15, 1863)
Gettysburg (July 1-3, 1863)
Bealton (November 5, 1863)
Mine Run Campaign (November-December 1863)
Morton's Ford (February 10, 1864)
The Wilderness (May 5-6, 1864)
Spotsylvania Court House (May 8-21, 1864)
North Anna (May 22-26, 1864)
Bethesda Church (May 30, 1864)
Cold Harbor (June 1-3, 1864)
Lynchburg Campaign (June 1864)
Monocacy (July 9, 1864)
Snicker's Ferry (July 18, 1864)
2nd Kernstown (July 24, 1864)
Winchester (July 24, 1864)
Newton (August 11, 1864)
Winchester (August 17, 1864)
Shepherdstown (August 25, 1864)
3rd Winchester (September 19, 1864)
Fisher's Hill (September 22, 1864)
Cedar Creek (October 19, 1864)
Petersburg Siege (from December 1864) (June 1864-April 1865)

Hatcher's Run (February 5-7, 1865)
Fort Stedman (March 25, 1865)
Sayler's Creek (April 6, 1865)
Appomattox Court House (April 9, 1865)
Further Reading: Robertson, James I., *The Stonewall Brigade.* Frye, Dennis E. *2nd Virginia Infantry.*

286. VIRGINIA 2ND INFANTRY REGIMENT, LOCAL DEFENSE TROOPS

Nickname: Quartermaster Regiment
Organization: Organized by the consolidation of the 2nd and 6th Infantry Battalions, Local Defense Troops, per S.O. #208, Adjutant and Inspector General's Office, on September 2, 1864. Apparently discontinued upon the fall of Richmond on April 2, 1865.
First Commander: Daniel E. Scruggs (Colonel)
Field Officers: John W. Carter (Major, Lieutenant Colonel)
William E. Tanner (Lieutenant Colonel)
Assignments: Local Defense Troops Brigade, Department of Richmond (September 1864-March 1865)
Brigade, G. W. C. Lee's Division, Department of Richmond (March-April 1865)
Battles: Petersburg Siege (June 1864-April 1865)
Roper's Farm (September 30, 1864)

287. VIRGINIA 2ND INFANTRY REGIMENT RESERVES

Organization: Organized in the Northern Neck of Virginia, per S.O. #150, Headquarters, Reserve Forces of Virginia, dated November 25, 1864. Officially designated as the 2nd Infantry Regiment Reserves on February 27, 1865, per S.O. #48, Adjutant and Inspector General's Office. No rolls on file at the National Archives.
First Commander: John M. Brockenbrough (Colonel)

288. VIRGINIA 2ND INFANTRY REGIMENT, STATE LINE

Organization: Organized with a mixture of infantry and cavalry companies in late 1862. Disbanded ca. March 31, 1863.
First Commander: William E. Peters (Colonel)
Field Officers: Martin V. Ball (Major)
James Harrison (Lieutenant Colonel)
Assignment: 1st Brigade, Virginia State Line
Battle: Prestonburg, Kentucky (detachment) (December 4-5, 1862)

289. VIRGINIA 2ND INFANTRY REGIMENT, WISE LEGION
See: VIRGINIA 59TH INFANTRY REGIMENT

290. VIRGINIA 2ND KANAWHA INFANTRY REGIMENT
See: VIRGINIA 36TH INFANTRY REGIMENT

291. VIRGINIA 3RD INFANTRY BATTALION, LOCAL DEFENSE TROOPS
Nicknames: Departmental Battalion
Clerk's Battalion
Organization: Organized with seven companies at Richmond for local defense as needed on June 29, 1863. 1st Company G mustered out on December 28, 1863. 2nd Company G organized on July 27, 1864. Company H organized on February 19, 1864. Company I organized on October 3, 1863, and later assigned to this battalion. Company K organized on October 23, 1863, and later assigned to this battalion. Having been increased to a regiment, the battalion was redesignated as the 3rd Infantry Regiment, Local Defense Troops, on September 23, 1863, per S.O. #226, Adjutant and Inspector General's Office.
First Commander: John A. Henley (Major)
Field Officers: Sanders G. Jamison (Major)
John McAnerney, Jr. (Lieutenant Colonel)
St. Clair F. Sutherland (Major)

292. VIRGINIA 3RD INFANTRY BATTALION RESERVES
Organization: Organized as Archer's Infantry Battalion Reserves early in 1864 and finally comprised six companies. Officially organized as the 3rd Infantry Battalion Reserves at Petersburg on June 15, 1864. Presumably surrendered at Appomattox Court House, Virginia, on April 9, 1865.
First Commander: Fletcher H. Archer (Major, Lieutenant Colonel)
Field Officer: William H. Jarvis (Major)
Assignments: 1st Military District, Department of North Carolina and Southern Virginia (June-October 1864)
Barton's Brigade, Department of Richmond (October 1864-April 1865)
Barton's Brigade, G. W. C. Lee's Division, Army of Northern Virginia (April 1865)
Battles: Petersburg (June 9, 1864)
Petersburg Siege (June 1864-April 1865)
Sayler's Creek (presumably) (April 6, 1865)
Appomattox Court House (presumably) (April 9, 1865)

293. VIRGINIA 3RD (CHRISMAN'S) INFANTRY BATTALION RESERVES

Organization: Organized as a temporary command of six companies composed of members of the various battalions of Valley Reserves in the fall of 1864.
First Commander: George Chrisman (Major)

294. VIRGINIA 3RD INFANTRY BATTALION VALLEY RESERVES

Nickname: Augusta County Reserves
Organization: Organized with four companies in August County on August 9, 1864. Broken up and merged into the 3rd (Chrisman's) Infantry Battalion Reserves in the fall of 1864.
First Commander: Samuel McCune (Major)

295. VIRGINIA 3RD INFANTRY BATTALION VOLUNTEERS (MILITIA)

Organization: Organized with two companies in 1860 as part of the volunteer forces drawn from the state militia. Merged into the 6th Infantry Regiment on May 13, 1861.
First Commander: William E. Taylor (Major)

296. VIRGINIA 3RD INFANTRY REGIMENT

Organization: Organized at Portsmouth on April 20, 1861. Reorganized on April 27, 1862. Surrendered at Appomattox Court House, Virginia, on April 9, 1865.
First Commander: Roger A. Pryor (Colonel)
Field Officers: Alexander D. Callcote (Major, Lieutenant Colonel)
Joseph Mayo, Jr. (Major, Lieutenant Colonel, Colonel)
William H. Pryor (Major, Lieutenant Colonel)
Joseph V. Scott (Major, Lieutenant Colonel)
Charles F. Urquhart (Major)
Assignments: Department of the Peninsula (detachment) (June 1861)
Department of Norfolk (July-October 1861)
Colston's Brigade, Department of Norfolk (January-April 1862)
Colston's Brigade, Longstreet's Division, Army of Northern Virginia (April-June 1862)
Pryor's Brigade, Longstreet's Division, Army of Northern Virginia (June 1862)
Pryor's Brigade, Longstreet's Division, 1st Corps, Army of Northern Virginia (June-August 1862)
Pryor's Brigade, Wilcox's Division, 1st Corps, Army of Northern Virginia (August-September 1862)

Pryor's Brigade, Anderson's Division, 1st Corps, Army of Northern Virginia (September 1862)

Pryor's Brigade, Pickett's Division, 1st Corps, Army of Northern Virginia (September-November 1862)

Kemper's Brigade, Pickett's Division, 1st Corps, Army of Northern Virginia (November 1862-February 1863)

Kemper's Brigade, Pickett's Division, Department of Virginia and North Carolina (February-April 1863)

Kemper's Brigade, Pickett's Division, Department of Southern Virginia (April-May 1863)

Kemper's Brigade, Pickett's Division, 1st Corps, Army of Northern Virginia (May-September 1863)

Kemper's Brigade, Department of Richmond (September 1863-May 1864)

Kemper's-Terry's Brigade, Pickett's Division, 1st Corps, Army of Northern Virginia (May 1864-April 1865)

Battles: Big Bethel (detachment) (June 10, 1861)

Yorktown Siege (April-May 1862)

Williamsburg (May 5, 1862)

Seven Pines (May 31-June 1, 1862)

Seven Days Battles (June 25-July 1, 1862)

Gaines' Mill (June 27, 1862)

Frayser's Farm (June 30, 1862)

2nd Bull Run (August 28-30, 1862)

Antietam (September 17, 1862)

Fredericksburg (December 13, 1862)

Suffolk Campaign (April-May 1863)

Gettysburg (July 1-3, 1863)

Drewry's Bluff (May 16, 1864)

North Anna (May 22-26, 1864)

Cold Harbor (June 1-3, 1864)

Petersburg Siege (June 1864-April 1865)

Five Forks (April 1, 1865)

Sayler's Creek (April 6, 1865)

Appomattox Court House (April 9, 1865)

Further Reading: Wallace, Lee, *3rd Virginia Infantry.*

297.   VIRGINIA 3RD INFANTRY REGIMENT, LOCAL DEFENSE TROOPS

Nickname: Departmental Regiment

Organization: Organized at Richmond by the increase of the 3rd Infantry Battalion, Local Defense Troops, to a regiment on September 23, 1864 per S.O.

#226, Adjutant and Inspector General's Office. Apparently discontinued upon the fall of Richmond on April 2, 1865.

First Commander: John McAnerney, Jr. (Colonel)
Field Officers: Bolling Baker (Major)
St. Clair F. Sutherland (Lieutenant Colonel)
Assignments: Local Defense Troops Brigade, Department of Richmond (September 1864-February 1865)
————Brigade, G. W. C. Lee's Division, Department of Richmond (March-April 1865)
Battles: Petersburg Siege (June 1864-April 1865)
Roper's Farm (September 30, 1864)

298. VIRGINIA 3RD INFANTRY REGIMENT RESERVES

Organization: Organized from 10 independent companies of reserves, which had been organized in April and May 1864, on September 30, 1864. Officially designated as the 3rd Infantry Regiment Reserves on February 27, 1865, per S.O. #48, Adjutant and Inspector General's Office.
First Commander: Richard A. Booker (Colonel)
Field Officers: William M. Ewers (Major)
Joel B. Leftwich (Lieutenant Colonel)
Assignments: Walker's Brigade, 1st Military District, Department of North Carolina and Southern Virginia (September-December 1864)
Richmond and Danville Railroad Defenses (Walker's), Army of Northern Virginia (January-March 1865)

299. VIRGINIA 3RD INFANTRY REGIMENT, STATE LINE

Organization: Three companies organized and mustered in for this regiment on November 1, 1862. Eventually comprised nine infantry and cavalry companies. Unit failed to complete its organization and was disbanded in January 1862. The three original companies were assigned to the 23rd Infantry Battalion and the rest to the other regiments of the State Line.
First Commander: John N. Clarkson (Colonel)
Field Officers: Peachy G. Breckinridge (Major)
James W. Massie (Lieutenant Colonel)
Assignment: 1st Brigade, Virginia State Line (November 1862-January 1863)
Battle: Prestonburg, Kentucky (detachment) (December 4-5, 1862)

300. VIRGINIA 3RD INFANTRY REGIMENT, WISE LEGION

See: VIRGINIA 60TH INFANTRY REGIMENT

301. VIRGINIA 3RD KANAWHA INFANTRY REGIMENT

Organization: Failed to complete its organization, having comprised only eight companies. Some companies transferred to the 22nd and 36th Infantry Regiments.

First Commander: Christopher Q. Tompkins (Colonel)

302. VIRGINIA 4TH INFANTRY BATTALION

Organization: Ordered to be organized with seven companies at Lewisburg on November 23, 1861, per S.O. #236, Adjutant and Inspector General's Office. Failed to complete organization.

First Commander: Nathaniel Tyler (Lieutenant Colonel)

303. VIRGINIA 4TH INFANTRY BATTALION, LOCAL DEFENSE TROOPS

Nickname: Naval Battalion

Organization: Organized with five companies at Richmond from the employees of the Navy Department for local defense as needed on June 22, 1863. Mustered into Confederate service at Richmond on June 23, 1863. Company F temporarily assigned on June 27, 1863. Apparently discontinued upon the fall of Richmond on April 2, 1865.

First Commander: Robert D. Minor (Major [1st Lieutenant, CSN])

Field Officer: Martin W. Curlin (Major)

Assignments: G. W. C. Lee's Brigade, Department of Richmond (May-July 1863)

Local Defense Troops Brigade, Department of Richmond (September 1864-February 1865)

———Brigade, G. W. C. Lee's Division, Department of Richmond (March-April 1865)

Battles: Petersburg Siege (June 1864-April 1865)

Roper's Farm (September 30, 1864)

304. VIRGINIA 4TH INFANTRY BATTALION MILITIA

Organization: Organized at Petersburg with five companies in December 1860. Increased to a regiment and designated as the 12th Infantry Regiment on July 12, 1861, per S.O. #39, Norfolk Harbor.

305. VIRGINIA 4TH INFANTRY BATTALION RESERVES

Organization: Organized with four companies in Greensville County on August 27, 1864. Officially designated as the 4th Infantry Battalion Reserves on February 27, 1865, per S.O. #48, Adjutant and Inspector General's Office.

Presumably surrendered at Appomattox Court House, Virginia, on April 9, 1865.

First Commander: David E. Godwin (Major)

Assignments: 1st Military District, Department of North Carolina and Southern Virginia (August-October 1864)

Barton's Brigade, Department of Richmond (October 1864-February 1865)

Barton's Brigade, G. W. C. Lee's Division, Department of Richmond (February-April 1865)

Barton's Brigade, G. W. C. Lee's Division, Army of Northern Virginia (April 1865)

Battles: Petersburg Siege (June 1864-April 1865)

Sayler's Creek (presumably) (April 6, 1865)

Appomattox Court House (presumably) (April 9, 1865)

306. VIRGINIA 4TH INFANTRY BATTALION, VALLEY RESERVES

See: VIRGINIA 10TH INFANTRY BATTALION RESERVES

307. VIRGINIA 4TH INFANTRY BATTALION VOLUNTEERS (MILITIA)

Organization: Organized at Petersburg with four companies from the militia in December 1860. Became part of the 12th Infantry Regiment on July 12, 1861.

First Commander: David A. Weisiger (Major)

308. VIRGINIA 4TH INFANTRY REGIMENT

Organization: Organized April 26, 1861. Designated the 4th Infantry Regiment on June 1, 1861. Mustered into Confederate service at Harpers Ferry on June 8, 1861. Reorganized April 22, 1862. Field consolidation with the 2nd, 5th, 27th and 33rd Infantry Regiments from May 1864 to April 1865. Surrendered at Appomattox Court House, Virginia, on April 9, 1865.

First Commander: James F. Preston (Colonel)

Field Officers: Matthew D. Bennett (Major)

Robert D. Gardner (Lieutenant Colonel)

Joseph F. Kent (Major)

Lewis T. Moore (Lieutenant Colonel)

Albert G. Pendleton (Major)

Charles A. Ronald (Colonel)

William Terry (Major, Colonel)

Assignments: 1st Brigade, Army of the Shenandoah (June-July 1861)

1st Brigade, 2nd Corps, Army of the Potomac (July-October 1861)

Stonewall Brigade, 2nd Corps, Potomac District, Department of Northern Virginia (October-November 1861)

Stonewall Brigade, Valley District, Department of Northern Virginia (November 1861-May 1862)

Stonewall Brigade, Jackson's Division, Valley District, Department of Northern Virginia (May-June 1862)

Stonewall Brigade, Jackson's-Johnson's Division, 2nd Corps, Army of Northern Virginia (June 1862-May 1864)

Terry's Consolidated Brigade, Gordon's Division, 2nd Corps, Army of Northern Virginia (May-June 1864)

Terry's Consolidated Brigade, Gordon's Division, Valley District, Department of Northern Virginia (June-December 1864)

Terry's Consolidated Brigade, Gordon's Division, 2nd Corps, Army of Northern Virginia (December 1864-April 1865)

Battles: Falling Waters (July 2, 1861)

1st Bull Run (July 21, 1861)

Romney Campaign (January 1862)

Kernstown (March 23, 1862)

McDowell (not engaged) (May 8, 1862)

Front Royal (not engaged) (May 23, 1862)

1st Winchester (May 25, 1862)

Port Republic (June 9, 1862)

Seven Days Battles (June 25-July 1, 1862)

Gaines' Mill (June 27, 1862)

White Oak Swamp (June 30, 1862)

Malvern Hill (July 1, 1862)

Cedar Mountain (August 9, 1862)

Groveton (August 28, 1862)

2nd Bull Run (August 28-30, 1862)

Chantilly (in reserve) (September 1, 1862)

Harpers Ferry (September 12-15, 1862)

Antietam (September 17, 1862)

Kearneyville (October 17, 1862)

Fredericksburg (December 13, 1862)

Chancellorsville (May 1-4, 1863)

2nd Winchester (June 14-15, 1863)

Gettysburg (July 1-3, 1863)

Bealton Station (October 26, 1863)

Bealton (November 5, 1863)

Mine Run Campaign (November-December 1863)

Morton's Ford (February 10, 1864)

The Wilderness (May 5-6, 1864)

Spotsylvania Court House (May 8-21, 1864)

North Anna (May 22-26, 1864)
Bethesda Church (May 30, 1864)
Cold Harbor (June 1-3, 1864)
Lynchburg Campaign (June 1864)
Monocacy (July 9, 1864)
Snicker's Ford (July 18, 1864)
2nd Kernstown (July 24, 1864)
Winchester (July 24, 1864)
Newton (August 11, 1864)
Winchester (August 17, 1864)
Shepherdstown (August 25, 1864)
3rd Winchester (September 19, 1864)
Fisher's Hill (September 22, 1864)
Cedar Creek (October 19, 1864)
Petersburg Siege (from December 1864) (June 1864-April 1865)
Hatcher's Run (February 5-7, 1865)
Fort Stedman (March 25, 1865)
Sayler's Creek (April 6, 1865)
Appomattox Court House (April 9, 1865)

Further Reading: Robertson, James I., *The Stonewall Brigade.* Robertson, James I., *4th Virginia Infantry.*

309. VIRGINIA 4TH INFANTRY REGIMENT RESERVES

Also Known As: 5th Infantry Regiment Reserves

Organization: Organized by increasing of Preston's Infantry Battalion Reserves to a regiment on November 24, 1864, per orders from the Department of Western Virginia and East Tennessee, dated September 20, 1864. Officially recognized by the War Department and designated as the 4th Infantry Regiment Reserves on February 27, 1865, per S.O. #48, Adjutant and Inspector General's Office. Disbanded by Brigadier General John Echols, commanding Department of Southwestern Virginia and East Tennessee, at Christianburg, Virginia, on April 12, 1865.

First Commander: Robert T. Preston (Colonel)

Field Officer: Alpheus W. Poague (Lieutenant Colonel)

Assignment: Preston's Brigade, Department of Western Virginia and East Tennessee (February-April 1865)

310. VIRGINIA 4TH INFANTRY REGIMENT, STATE LINE

Organization: Organized with a mixture of infantry and cavalry companies in late 1862 or early 1863. Disbanded ca. March 31, 1863.

First Commander: N. McC. Menifee (Colonel)

Field Officer: David S. Hounshell (Colonel)

311.   VIRGINIA 4TH INFANTRY REGIMENT VOLUNTEERS (MILITIA)

Organization: Organized with seven companies in Rockingham County in 1860. Four companies consolidated with other companies in May 1861 at Harpers Ferry and designated as the 10th Infantry Regiment.
First Commander: Simeon B. Gibbons (Colonel)

312.   VIRGINIA 5TH INFANTRY BATTALION

Organization: Organized with six companies April 29, 1861. Reorganized May 22, 1862. Disbanded September 6, 1862, per S.O. #209, Adjutant and Inspector General's Office. Those men liable to the draft assigned to the 53rd Infantry Regiment.
First Commander: Fletcher H. Archer (Lieutenant Colonel)
Field Officers: William R. Foster (Major)
John P. Wilson, Jr. (Major)
Assignments: Armistead's Brigade, Department of Norfolk (April 1862)
Armistead's Brigade, Huger's-Anderson's Division, Army of Northern Virginia (April-July 1862)
Armistead's Brigade, Anderson's Division, 1st Corps, Army of Northern Virginia (July-September 1862)
Battles: Seven Pines (May 31-June 1, 1862)
Seven Days Battles (June 25-July 1, 1862)
Malvern Hill (July 1, 1862)

313.   VIRGINIA 5TH INFANTRY BATTALION, LOCAL DEFENSE TROOPS

Nickname: Arsenal Battalion
Organization: Organized with six companies at Richmond from employees of the arsenal for local defense as needed on June 24, 1863. Mustered into Confederate service at Richmond on June 24, 1863. Company G organized on July 4, 1863. Company H organized on July 1, 1863. Company D consolidated with 1st Company A to form 2nd Company A on February 17, 1864, per S.O. #40, Adjutant and Inspector General's Office. Apparently discontinued upon the fall of Richmond on April 2, 1865.
First Commander: William L. Broun (Lieutenant Colonel)
Field Officers: Philip J. Ennis (Lieutenant Colonel)
John B. Vaughan (Major)
Assignments: G. W. C. Lee's Brigade, Department of Richmond (May 1863-July 1863)

Local Defense Troops Brigade, Department of Richmond (September 1864-February 1865)

———Brigade, Department of Richmond (March-April 1865)

Battles: Petersburg Siege (June 1864-April 1865)

Roper's Farm (September 30, 1864)

314. VIRGINIA 5TH INFANTRY BATTALION RESERVES

Nickname: Henry's Infantry Regiment Reserves

Organization: Organized as a battalion of nine companies on September 12, 1864. Redesignated as the 5th Infantry Battalion Reserves on February 27, 1865 per S.O. #48, Adjutant and Inspector General's Office.

First Commander: Patrick M. Henry (Lieutenant Colonel)

Field Officer: A. D. Reynolds (Major)

Assignments: Walker's Brigade, 1st Military District, Department of North Carolina and Southern Virginia (September-December 1864)

Richmond and Danville Railroad (Walker), Army of Northern Virginia (January 1865-? 1865)

Battle: Petersburg Siege (June 1864-April 1865)

315. VIRGINIA 5TH INFANTRY BATTALION, VALLEY RESERVES

See: VIRGINIA 7TH INFANTRY BATTALION RESERVES

316. VIRGINIA 5TH INFANTRY REGIMENT

Organization: Organized in Augusta County from a regiment of volunteer militia on May 7, 1861, with 12 companies. Designated as the 5th Infantry Regiment on June 1, 1861. Mustered into state service at Harpers Ferry on June 8, 1861. Transferred to Confederate service with 11 companies on July 1, 1861. Reorganized on April 21, 1862. Field consolidation with the 2nd, 4th, 27th and 33rd Infantry Regiments from May 1864 to April 1865. Surrendered at Appomattox Court House, Virginia, on April 9, 1865.

First Commander: Kenton Harper (Colonel)

Field Officers: William S. H. Baylor (Major, Lieutenant Colonel, Colonel)

John H. S. Funk (Lieutenant Colonel, Colonel)

William H. Harman (Lieutenant Colonel, Colonel)

Absalom Koiner (Major)

James W. Newton (Major)

Hazael J. Williams (Major, Lieutenant Colonel)

Assignments: 1st Brigade, Army of the Shenandoah (June-July 1861)

1st Brigade, 2nd Corps, Army of the Potomac (July-October 1861)

Stonewall Brigade, 2nd Corps, Potomac District, Department of Northern Virginia (October-November 1861)

Stonewall Brigade, Valley District, Department of Northern Virginia (November 1861-May 1862)

Stonewall Brigade, Jackson's Division, Valley District, Department of Northern Virginia (May-June 1862)

Stonewall Brigade, Jackson's-Johnson's Division, 2nd Corps, Army of Northern Virginia (June 1862-May 1864)

Terry's Consolidated Brigade, Gordon's Division, 2nd Corps, Army of Northern Virginia (May-June 1864)

Terry's Consolidated Brigade, Gordon's Division, Valley District, Department of Northern Virginia (June-December 1864)

Terry's Consolidated Brigade, Gordon's Division, 2nd Corps, Army of Northern Virginia (December 1864-April 1865)

Battles: Falling Waters (July 2, 1861)

1st Bull Run (July 21, 1861)

Romney Campaign (January 1862)

Kernstown (March 23, 1862)

McDowell (not engaged) (May 8, 1862)

Front Royal (not engaged) (May 23, 1862)

1st Winchester (May 25, 1862)

Port Republic (June 9, 1862)

Seven Days Battles (June 25-July 1, 1862)

Gaines' Mill (June 27, 1862)

White Oak Swamp (June 30, 1862)

Malvern Hill (July 1, 1862)

Cedar Mountain (August 9, 1862)

Groveton (August 28, 1862)

2nd Bull Run (August 28-30, 1862)

Chantilly (in reserve) (September 1, 1862)

Harpers Ferry (September 12-15, 1862)

Antietam (September 17, 1862)

Kearneyville (October 17, 1862)

Fredericksburg (December 13, 1862)

Chancellorsville (May 1-4, 1863)

2nd Winchester (June 14-15, 1863)

Gettysburg (July 1-3, 1863)

Bealton Station (October 26, 1863)

Bealton (November 5, 1863)

Mine Run Campaign (November-December 1863)

Morton's Ford (February 10, 1864)

The Wilderness (May 5-6, 1864)

Spotsylvania Court House (May 8-21, 1864)

North Anna (May 22-26, 1864)
Bethesda Church (May 30, 1864)
Cold Harbor (June 1-3, 1864)
Lynchburg Campaign (June 1864)
Monocacy (July 9, 1864)
Snicker's Ferry (July 18, 1864)
2nd Kernstown (July 24, 1864)
Winchester (July 24, 1864)
Newton (August 11, 1864)
Winchester (August 17, 1864)
Shepherdstown (August 25, 1864)
3rd Winchester (September 19, 1864)
Fisher's Hill (September 22, 1864)
Cedar Creek (October 19, 1864)
Petersburg Siege (from December 1864) (June 1864-April 1865)
Hatcher's Run (February 5-7, 1865)
Fort Stedman (March 25, 1865)
Sayler's Creek (April 6, 1865)
Appomattox Court House (April 9, 1865)
Further Reading: Robertson, James I., *The Stonewall Brigade*. Wallace, Lee
A., Jr., *5th Virginia Infantry*.

317.   VIRGINIA 5TH INFANTRY REGIMENT, STATE LINE

Organization: Organized with a mixture of nine infantry, cavalry and artillery
companies on February 9, 1863. Disbanded ca. March 31, 1863.
First Commander: David S. Hounshell (Lieutenant Colonel)
Field Officers: David Edmondson (Lieutenant Colonel)
C. H. Preston (Major)

318.   VIRGINIA 6TH INFANTRY BATTALION, LOCAL DEFENSE TROOPS

Nickname: Tredegar Battalion
Organization: Organized with four companies at Richmond from the employees of the Tredegar iron works for local defense as needed in May 1861.
Designated as the 8th Infantry Battalion by Governor Letcher on June 3, 1861.
Reorganized with three companies in 1863. Mustered into Confederate service
on October 16, 1863, for the term of "Residence in Richmond." Consolidated
with the 2nd Infantry Battalion, Local Defense Troops, and redesignated as the
2nd Infantry Regiment, Local Defense Troops, on September 2, 1864, per S.O.
#208, Adjutant and Inspector General's Office.
First Commander: Joseph R. Anderson (Major)

Field Officers: Robert S. Archer (Major)
William E. Tanner (Major)

319.   VIRGINIA 6TH INFANTRY BATTALION RESERVES

Also Known As: Virginia 13th Infantry Battalion Reserves
Organization: Organized by the redesignation of the nine companies of the 13th Infantry Battalion Reserves on February 27, 1865, per S.O. #48, Adjutant and Inspector General's Office. Disbanded by Brigadier General John Echols, commanding the Department of Southwestern Virginia and East Tennessee, at Christianburg, Virginia, on April 12, 1865.
First Commander: Robert Smith (Lieutenant Colonel)
Field Officer: John H. A. Smith (Major)
Assignment: Preston's Brigade, Department of Western Virginia and East Tennessee (February-April 1865)

320.   VIRGINIA 6TH INFANTRY BATTALION VOLUNTEERS (MILITIA)

Organization: Organized with six companies at Alexandria on April 10, 1861. Increased to a regiment and designated as the 17th Infantry Regiment at Manassas Junction on June 10, 1861.
First Commander: Montgomery D. Corse (Major)
Assignment: Department of Alexandria (April-June 1861)
Further Reading: Wise, George, *History of the Seventeenth Virginia Infantry, C.S.A.*

321.   VIRGINIA 6TH INFANTRY REGIMENT

Organization: Organized at Norfolk on May 13, 1861. Two companies had been in service previously as the 3rd Battalion Virginia Volunteers (Militia). Transferred to Confederate service on July 1, 1861. Reorganized on May 3, 1862. Surrendered at Appomattox Court House, Virginia, on April 9, 1865.
First Commander: William Mahone (Colonel)
Field Officers: Thomas J. Corprew (Lieutenant Colonel, Major)
William T. Lundy (Major, Lieutenant Colonel)
George T. Rogers (Major, Colonel)
Robert B. Taylor (Major)
Henry W. Williamson (Lieutenant Colonel)
Assignments: Department of Norfolk (July ? 1861)
Mahone's Brigade, Department of Norfolk (? 1861-April 1862)
Mahone's Brigade, Huger's-Anderson's Division, Army of Northern Virginia (April-July 1862)

Mahone's Brigade, Anderson's Division, 1st Corps, Army of Northern Virginia (July 1862-May 1863)

Mahone's-Weisiger's Brigade, Anderson's-Mahone's Division, 3rd Corps, Army of Northern Virginia (May 1863-April 1865)

Battles: Sewell's Point (Company C) (May 1861)

Seven Days Battles (June 25-July 1, 1862)

King's School House (June 25, 1862)

Brackett's (June 30, 1862)

Malvern Hill (July 1, 1862)

2nd Bull Run (August 28-30, 1862)

South Mountain (September 14, 1862)

Antietam (September 17, 1862)

Fredericksburg (December 13, 1862)

Chancellorsville (May 1-4, 1863)

Gettysburg (July 1-3, 1863)

Bristoe Campaign (October 1863)

Mine Run Campaign (November-December 1863)

The Wilderness (May 5-6, 1864)

Spotsylvania Court House (May 8-21, 1864)

North Anna (May 22-26, 1864)

Cold Harbor (June 1-3, 1864)

Petersburg Siege (June 1864-April 1865)

The Crater (July 30, 1864)

Appomattox Court House (April 9, 1865)

Further Reading: Cavanaugh, Michael A., *6th Virginia Infantry*.

322.   VIRGINIA 7TH INFANTRY BATTALION

Organization: Organized with eight companies as heavy artillery in 1861. Attempted to organize as a regiment at Jarrett's Hotel, Petersburg, on May 22, 1862. Increased to 10 companies in August 1862 and reorganized as the 61st Infantry Regiment on October 1, 1862.

First Commander: Samuel M. Wilson (Lieutenant Colonel)

323.   VIRGINIA 7TH INFANTRY BATTALION RESERVES

Also Known As: Virginia 5th Infantry Battalion Valley Reserves

Organization: Organized with four companies on August 9, 1864. Officially designated as the 7th Infantry Battalion Reserves on February 27, 1865, per S.O. #48, Adjutant and Inspector General's Office.

First Commander: George Chrisman (Major)

324. VIRGINIA 7TH INFANTRY REGIMENT

Organization: Organized in May 1861. Transferred to Confederate service on July 1, 1861. Reorganized April 26, 1862. Surrendered at Appomattox Court House, Virginia, on April 9, 1865.

First Commander: James J. Kemper (Colonel)

Field Officers: Charles C. Flowerree (Major, Lieutenant Colonel, Colonel)
Waller T. Patton (Major, Lieutenant Colonel, Colonel)
Aylett A. Swindler (Major)
Lewis B. Williams, Jr. (Lieutenant Colonel)

Assignments: Early's Brigade, Army of the Potomac (June-July 1861)
Early's Brigade, 1st Corps, Army of the Potomac (July 1861)
Longstreet's Brigade, 1st Corps, Army of the Potomac (July-October 1861)
Clark's-Griffith's-Ewell's Brigade, Longstreet's Division, 1st Corps, Potomac District, Department of Northern Virginia (October 1861-January 1862)
Ewell's-A. P. Hill's Brigade, Longstreet's Division, Potomac District, Department of Northern Virginia (January-March 1862)
A. P. Hill's-Kemper's Brigade, Longstreet's Division, Army of Northern Virginia (March-June 1862)
Kemper's Brigade, Longstreet's Division, 1st Corps, Army of Northern Virginia (June-August 1862)
Kemper's Brigade, Kemper's Division, 1st Corps, Army of Northern Virginia (August-September 1862)
Kemper's Brigade, D. R. Jones' Brigade, 1st Corps, Army of Northern Virginia (September 1862)
Kemper's Brigade, Pickett's Division, 1st Corps, Army of Northern Virginia (September 1862-February 1863)
Kemper's Brigade, Pickett's Division, Department of Virginia and North Carolina (February-April 1863)
Kemper's Brigade, Pickett's Division, Department of Southern Virginia (April-May 1863)
Kemper's Brigade, Pickett's Division, 1st Corps, Army of Northern Virginia (May-September 1863)
Kemper's Brigade, Department of Richmond (September 1863-May 1864)
Kemper's-Terry's Brigade, Pickett's Division, 1st Corps, Army of Northern Virginia (May 1864-April 1865)

Battles: Blackburn's Ford (July 18, 1861)
1st Bull Run (July 21, 1861)
Yorktown Siege (April-May 1862)
Williamsburg (May 5, 1862)
Seven Pines (May 31-June 1, 1862)
Seven Days Battles (June 25-July 1, 1862)

Frayser's Farm (June 30, 1862)
2nd Bull Run (August 28-30, 1862)
South Mountain (September 14, 1862)
Antietam (September 17, 1862)
Fredericksburg (December 13, 1862)
Suffolk Campaign (April-May 1863)
Gettysburg (July 1-3, 1863)
Milford Station (April 15, 1864)
Drewry's Bluff (May 16, 1864)
Howlett House (May 18, 1864)
North Anna (May 22-26, 1864)
Cold Harbor (June 1-3, 1864)
Clay Farm (June 16, 1864)
Petersburg Siege (June 1864-April 1865)
Dinwiddie Court House (March 31, 1865)
Five Forks (April 1, 1865)
Sayler's Creek (April 6, 1865)
Appomattox Court House (April 9, 1865)
Further Reading: Riggs, David F., *7th Virginia Infantry*.

325.   Virginia 8th Infantry Battalion
See: VIRGINIA 6TH INFANTRY BATTALION, LOCAL DEFENSE TROOPS

326.   Virginia 8th Infantry Battalion Reserves
Also Known As: Virginia 1st Infantry Battalion Valley Reserves
Organization: Organized with four companies on August 9, 1864. Officially designated as the 8th Infantry Battalion Reserves on February 27, 1865, per S.O. #48, Adjutant and Inspector General's Office.
First Commander: William A. J. Miller (Major)

327.   Virginia 8th Infantry Regiment
Nickname: Old Bloody Eighth
Organization: Organized in state service on May 8, 1861. Transferred to Confederate service in July 1861. Reorganized April 27, 1862. Surrendered at Appomattox Court House, Virginia, on April 9, 1865.
First Commander: Eppa Hunton (Colonel)
Field Officers: Edmund Berkeley (Major, Lieutenant Colonel)
Norborne Berkeley (Major, Lieutenant Colonel, Colonel)
William N. Berkeley (Major)
Charles B. Tebbs (Lieutenant Colonel)
James Thrift (Major)

Assignments: 5th (Cocke's) Brigade, Army of the Potomac (June-July 1861)
5th (Cocke's) Brigade, 1st Corps, Army of the Potomac (July 1861)
Unattached, 1st Corps, Army of the Potomac (July 1861)
7th (Evans') Brigade, 1st Corps, Army of the Potomac (October 1861)
5th (Cocke's) Brigade, Longstreet's Division, 1st Corps, Potomac District, Department of Northern Virginia (January 1862)
5th (Cocke's-Pickett's) Brigade, Longstreet's Division, Potomac District, Department of Northern Virginia (January-March 1862)
Pickett's Brigade, Longstreet's Division, Army of Northern Virginia (March-June 1862)
Pickett's Brigade, Longstreet's Division, 1st Corps, Army of Northern Virginia (June-August 1862)
Pickett's Brigade, Kemper's Division, 1st Corps, Army of Northern Virginia (August-September 1862)
Pickett's Brigade, D. R. Jones' Division, 1st Corps, Army of Northern Virginia (September 1862)
Pickett's-Garnett's Brigade, Pickett's Division, 1st Corps, Army of Northern Virginia (September 1862-February 1863)
Garnett's Brigade, Pickett's Division, Department of Virginia and North Carolina (February-April 1863)
Garnett's Brigade, Pickett's Division, Department of Southern Virginia (April-May 1863)
Garnett's-Hunton's Brigade, Pickett's Division, 1st Corps, Army of Northern Virginia (May-September 1863)
Hunton's Brigade, Department of Richmond (September 1863-May 1864)
Hunton's Brigade, Pickett's Division, 1st Corps, Army of Northern Virginia (May 1864-April 1865)

Battles: 1st Bull Run (July 21, 1861)
Ball's Bluff (October 21, 1861)
Yorktown Siege (April-May 1862)
Williamsburg (May 5, 1862)
Seven Pines (May 5, 1862)
Seven Days Battles (June 25-July 1, 1862)
Gaines' Mill (June 27, 1862)
Frayser's Farm (June 30, 1862)
2nd Bull Run (August 28-30, 1862)
South Mountain (September 14, 1862)
Antietam (September 17, 1862)
Fredericksburg (December 13, 1862)
Gettysburg (July 1-3, 1863)
North Anna (May 22-26, 1864)

Cold Harbor (June 1-3, 1864)
Petersburg Siege (June 1864-April 1865)
Five Forks (April 1, 1865)
Sayler's Creek (April 6, 1865)
Appomattox Court House (April 9, 1865)
Further Reading: Divine, John E., *8th Virginia Infantry.*

328. VIRGINIA 9TH INFANTRY BATTALION

Organization: Organized with four companies in June 1861. Merged into the 25th Infantry Regiment on May 1, 1862, by order of Brigadier General Edward Johnson. Consolidation declared illegal by the War Department, and Lieutenant Colonel Hansborough ordered to reorganize the battalion on November 4, 1862, per S.O. #258, Adjutant and Inspector General's Office. He failed to comply with the order. It was revoked, and the merger with the 25th Infantry Regiment was confirmed on February 28, 1863, per S.O. #50, Adjutant and Inspector General's Office.
First Commander: George W. Hansborough (Lieutenant Colonel)
Field Officer: Gideon D. Camden, Jr. (Major)
Assignments: Jackson's Brigade, Army of the Northwest (September-November 1861)
Johnson's Brigade, Jackson's Division, Army of the Northwest (November 1861-January 1862)
Army of the Northwest (March-May 1862)
Battles: Greenbrier River (October 3, 1861)
Camp Alleghany, West Virginia (December 13, 1861)

329. VIRGINIA 9TH INFANTRY BATTALION RESERVES

Also Known As: Virginia 2nd Infantry Battalion Valley Reserves
Organization: Organized with four companies on August 9, 1864. Officially designated as the 9th Infantry Battalion Reserves on February 27, 1865, per S.O. #48, Adjutant and Inspector General's Office.
First Commander: Archibald Taylor (Major)

330. VIRGINIA 9TH INFANTRY REGIMENT

Organization: Organized on July 7, 1861. Reorganized on May 20, 1862. Surrendered at Appomattox Court House, Virginia, on April 9, 1865.
First Commander: Francis H. Smith (Colonel)
Field Officers: Stapleton Crutchfield (Major)
James S. Gilliam (Major, Lieutenant Colonel)
David J. Godwin (Lieutenant Colonel, Colonel)
Mark B. Hardin (Major)

John C. Owens (Major)

James J. Phillips (Colonel)

John T. L. Preston (Lieutenant Colonel)

William J. Richardson (Lieutenant Colonel)

Assignments: Department of Norfolk (July 1861-January 1862)

Armistead's Brigade, Department of Norfolk (January-April 1862)

Armistead's Brigade, Huger's-Anderson's Division, Army of Northern Virginia (April-July 1862)

Armistead's Brigade, Anderson's Division, 1st Corps, Army of Northern Virginia (July-September 1862)

Armistead's Brigade, Pickett's Division, 1st Corps, Army of Northern Virginia (September-February 1863)

Armistead's Brigade, Pickett's Division, Department of Virginia and North Carolina (February-April 1863)

Armistead's Brigade, Pickett's Division, Department of Southern Virginia (April-May 1863)

Armistead's Brigade, Pickett's Division, 1st Corps, Army of Northern Virginia (May-September 1863)

Armistead's-Barton's Brigade, Pickett's Division, Department of North Carolina (September-October 1863)

Barton's Brigade, Department of North Carolina (December 1863-February 1864)

Barton's Brigade, Department of Richmond (February-May 1864)

Barton's-Steuart's Brigade, Pickett's Division, 1st Corps, Army of Northern Virginia (May 1864-April 1865)

Battles: Seven Pines (May 31-June 1, 1862)

Seven Days Battles (June 25-July 1, 1862)

Malvern Hill (July 1, 1862)

2nd Bull Run (August 28-30, 1862)

South Mountain (September 14, 1862)

Antietam (September 17, 1862)

Shepherdstown Ford (September 20, 1862)

Fredericksburg (December 13, 1862)

Suffolk Campaign (April-May 1863)

Gettysburg (July 1-3, 1863)

Chester Station (May 10, 1864)

Drewry's Bluff (May 16, 1864)

North Anna (May 22-26, 1864)

Cold Harbor (June 1-3, 1864)

Petersburg Siege (June 1864-April 1865)

Five Forks (April 1, 1865)

Sayler's Creek (April 6, 1865)
Appomattox Court House (April 9, 1865)
Further Reading: Trask, Benjamin H., *9th Virginia Infantry*.

331. Virginia 10th Infantry Battalion Reserves

Also Known As: Virginia 4th Infantry Battalion Valley Reserves
Organization: Organized with five companies on August 23, 1864. Officially designated as the 10th Infantry Battalion Reserves on February 27, 1865, per S.O #48, Adjutant and Inspector General's Office.
First Commander: William W. Byrd (Major)

332. Virginia 10th Infantry Regiment

Organization: Organized at Harpers Ferry in May 1861 from four companies of the 4th Infantry Regiment Volunteers (Militia) and other companies organized for one year. Transferred to Confederate service on July 1, 1861. 1st Company C disbanded on April 18, 1862. Company L assigned to this regiment on April 19, 1862. 2nd Company C assigned to this regiment on April 23, 1862. Reorganized ca. April 23, 1862. Served in a field consolidation with the 23rd and 37th Infantry Regiments from May 1864 to April 1865. Surrendered at Appomattox Court House, Virginia, on April 9, 1865.
First Commander: Simeon B. Gibbons (Colonel)
Field Officers: Isaac G. Coffman (Major)
Dorilas H. L. Martz (Lieutenant Colonel)
Joshua Stover (Major)
Samuel T. Walker (Major, Lieutenant Colonel)
Edward T. H. Warren (Lieutenant Colonel, Colonel)
Assignments: 4th (E. K. Smith's) Brigade, Army of the Shenandoah (July 1861)
4th (E. K. Smith's-Elzey's) Brigade, 2nd Corps, Army of the Potomac (July-October 1861)
4th (Elzey's) Brigade, 2nd Corps, Potomac District, Department of Northern Virginia (October-November 1861)
Elzey's Brigade, E. K. Smith's-Ewell's Division, Potomac District, Department of Northern Virginia (November 1861-April 1862)
Taliaferro's Brigade, Valley District, Department of Northern Virginia (April-May 1862)
Taliaferro's-Fulkerson's Brigade, Jackson's Division, Valley District, Department of Northern Virginia (May-June 1862)
Fulkerson's-Warren's-Hampton's-Taliaferro's-Colston's-Steuart's Brigade, Jackson's-Trimble's-Johnson's Division, 2nd Corps, Army of Northern Virginia (June 1862-May 1864)

Terry's Consolidated Brigade, Gordon's Division, 2nd Corps, Army of Northern Virginia (May-June 1864)

Terry's Consolidated Brigade, Gordon's Division, Valley District, Department of Northern Virginia (June-December 1864)

Terry's Consolidated Brigade, Gordon's Division, 2nd Corps, Army of Northern Virginia (December 1864-April 1865)

Battles: 1st Bull Run (July 21, 1861)

McDowell (May 8, 1862)

Shenandoah Valley Campaign of 1862 (May-June 1862)

Seven Days Battles (June 25-July 1, 1862)

Gaines' Mill (June 27, 1862)

Malvern Hill (July 1, 1862)

Cedar Mountain (August 9, 1862)

2nd Bull Run (August 28-30, 1862)

Harpers Ferry (September 12-15, 1862)

Antietam (September 17, 1862)

Fredericksburg (December 13, 1862)

Chancellorsville (May 1-4, 1863)

2nd Winchester (June 14-15, 1863)

Gettysburg (July 1-3, 1863)

Bristoe Campaign (October 1863)

Mine Run Campaign (November-December 1863)

The Wilderness (May 5-6, 1864)

Spotsylvania Court House (May 8-21, 1864)

North Anna (May 22-26, 1864)

Cold Harbor (June 1-3, 1864)

Monocacy (July 9, 1864)

3rd Winchester (September 19, 1864)

Fisher's Hill (September 22, 1864)

Cedar Creek (October 19, 1864)

Petersburg Siege (from December 1864) (June 1864-April 1865)

Fort Stedman (March 25, 1865)

Appomattox Court House (April 9, 1865)

333. VIRGINIA 11TH INFANTRY BATTALION RESERVES

Also Known As: Virginia 4th Infantry Battalion Reserves

Organization: Organized as the 4th Infantry Battalion Reserves with six companies on August 13, 1864. Officially designated as the 11th Infantry Battalion Reserves on February 27, 1865 per S.O. #48, Adjutant and Inspector General's Office. Disbanded by Brigadier General John Echols, commanding

the Department of Southwestern Virginia and East Tennessee, at Christian-
burg, Virginia, on April 12, 1865.
First Commander: Samuel M. Wallace (Lieutenant Colonel)
Field Officer: William H. Bosang (Major)
Assignment: Preston's Brigade, Department of Western Virginia and East
Tennessee (February-April 1865)

334. VIRGINIA 11TH INFANTRY REGIMENT

Organization: Organized in state service in May 1861. Transferred to Con-
federate service on July 1, 1861. Reorganized on April 26, 1865. Surrendered
at Appomattox Court House, Virginia, on April 9, 1865.
First Commander: Samuel Garland, Jr. (Colonel)
Field Officers: Adam Clement (Major)
David Funsten (Lieutenant Colonel, Major)
Carter H. Harrison (Major)
James R. Hutter (Major)
Maurice S. Langhorne (Major, Lieutenant Colonel, Colonel)
Kirkwood Otey (Major, Lieutenant Colonel, Colonel)
Assignments: Terrett's-Longstreet's Brigade, Army of the Potomac (June-July
    1861)
Longstreet's Brigade, 1st Corps, Army of the Potomac (July-October 1861)
Clark's-Griffith's-Ewell's Brigade, Longstreet's Division, 1st Corps, Potomac
    District, Department of Northern Virginia (October 1861-January 1862)
Ewell's-A. P. Hill's Brigade, Longstreet's Division, Potomac District, Depart-
    ment of Northern Virginia (January-March 1862)
A. P. Hill's-Kemper's Brigade, Longstreet's Division, Army of Northern Vir-
    ginia (March-June 1862)
Kemper's Brigade, Longstreet's Division, 1st Corps, Army of Northern Virginia
    (June-August 1862)
Kemper's Brigade, Kemper's Division, 1st Corps, Army of Northern Virginia
    (August-September 1862)
Kemper's Brigade, D. R. Jones Brigade, 1st Corps, Army of Northern Virginia
    (September 1862)
Kemper's Brigade, Pickett's Division, 1st Corps, Army of Northern Virginia
    (September-February 1863)
Kemper's Brigade, Pickett's Division, Department of Virginia and North Car-
    olina (February-April 1863)
Kemper's Brigade, Pickett's Division, Department of Southern Virginia (April-
    May 1863)
Kemper's Brigade, Pickett's Division, 1st Corps, Army of Northern Virginia
    (May-September 1863)

Kemper's Brigade, Department of Richmond (September 1863-May 1864)

Kemper's-Terry's Brigade, Pickett's Division, 1st Corps, Army of Northern Virginia (May 1864-April 1865)

Battles: Blackburn's Ford (July 18, 1861)

1st Bull Run (July 21, 1861)

Dranesville (December 20, 1861)

Yorktown Siege (April-May 1862)

Williamsburg (May 5, 1862)

Seven Pines (May 31-June 1, 1862)

Seven Days Battles (June 25-July 1, 1862)

Frayser's Farm (June 30, 1862)

2nd Bull Run (August 28-30, 1862)

South Mountain (September 14, 1862)

Antietam (September 17, 1862)

Fredericksburg (December 13, 1862)

Suffolk Campaign (April-May 1863)

Gettysburg (July 1-3, 1863)

Drewry's Bluff (May 16, 1864)

North Anna (May 22-26, 1864)

Cold Harbor (June 1-3, 1864)

Petersburg Siege (June 1864-April 1865)

Dinwiddie Court House (March 31, 1865)

Five Forks (April 1, 1865)

Sayler's Creek (April 6, 1865)

Appomattox Court House (April 9, 1865)

Further Reading: Bell, Robert T., *11th Virginia Infantry.*

335.   VIRGINIA 12TH INFANTRY REGIMENT

Organization: Organized beginning in May 1861 from the 4th Infantry Battalion Volunteers (Militia). Organization completed on July 12, 1861, per S.O. #39, Headquarters Forces Norfolk Harbor. Transferred to Confederate service on July 1, 1861. Reorganized on May 3, 1862.

First Commander: David A. Weisiger (Colonel)

Field Officers: Edgar L. Brockett (Major)

Everard M. Field (Major, Lieutenant Colonel, Colonel)

John R. Lewellen (Major, Lieutenant Colonel)

John P. May (Major)

Fielding L. Taylor (Lieutenant Colonel)

Assignments: Department of Norfolk (July ? 1861)

Mahone's Brigade, Department of Norfolk (? 1861-April 1862)

Mahone's Brigade, Huger's-Anderson's Division, Army of Northern Virginia (April-July 1862)

Mahone's Brigade, Anderson's Division, 1st Corps, Army of Northern Virginia (July 1862-May 1863)

Mahone's-Weisiger's Brigade, Anderson's-Mahone's Division, 3rd Corps, Army of Northern Virginia (May 1863-April 1865)

Battles: Sewell's Point (detachment of Company H) (May 18-19, 1861)
Seven Days Battles (June 25-July 1, 1862)
King's School House (June 25, 1862)
Malvern Hill (July 1, 1862)
2nd Bull Run (August 28-30, 1862)
South Mountain (September 14, 1862)
Antietam (September 17, 1862)
Fredericksburg (December 13, 1862)
Chancellorsville (May 1-4, 1863)
Gettysburg (July 1-3, 1863)
Bristoe Campaign (October 1863)
Mine Run Campaign (November-December 1863)
The Wilderness (May 5-6, 1864)
Spotsylvania Court House (May 8-21, 1864)
North Anna (May 22-26, 1864)
Cold Harbor (June 1-3, 1864)
Petersburg Siege (June 1864-April 1865)
The Crater (July 30, 1864)
Appomattox Court House (April 9, 1865)
Further Reading: Henderson, William D., *12th Virginia Infantry*.

336. VIRGINIA 13TH INFANTRY BATTALION RESERVES

Organization: Organized and mustered in for the war with nine companies on June 3, 1864. Redesignated as the 6th Infantry Battalion Reserves on February 27, 1865, per S.O. #48, Adjutant and Inspector General's Office.
First Commander: Robert Smith (Lieutenant Colonel)
Field Officer: John H. A. Smith (Major)
Assignment: Unattached, Department of Western Virginia and East Tennessee (June 1864-February 1865)

337. VIRGINIA 13TH INFANTRY REGIMENT

Organization: Organized in state service on May 9, 1861. Transferred to Confederate service on July 1, 1861. Reorganized on April 23, 1862.
First Commander: Ambrose P. Hill (Colonel)
Field Officers: Charles T. Crittenden (Major)

George A. Goodman (Major, Lieutenant Colonel)

John B. Sherrard (Major)

James B. Terrill (Major, Lieutenant Colonel, Colonel)

James A. Walker (Lieutenant Colonel, Colonel)

Assignments: 4th (Elzey's-E. K. Smith's) Brigade, Army of the Potomac (July 1861)

4th (E. K. Smith's-Elzey's) Brigade, 2nd Corps, Army of the Potomac (July-November 1861)

4th (Elzey's) Brigade, E. K. Smith's Division, 1st Corps, Army of the Potomac (November 1861-January 1862)

4th (Elzey's) Brigade, E. K. Smith's-Ewell's Division, Potomac District, Department of Northern Virginia (January-March 1862)

4th (Elzey's) Brigade, Ewell's Division, Department of Northern Virginia (March-May 1862)

4th (Elzey's) Brigade, Ewell's Division, Valley District, Department of Northern Virginia (May-June 1862)

Elzey's-Early's-Smith's-Pegram's Brigade, Ewell's-Early's-Ramseur's Division, 2nd Corps, Army of Northern Virginia (June 1862-June 1864)

Pegram's Brigade, Ramseur's-Pegram's Division, Valley District, Department of Northern Virginia (June-December 1864)

Pegram's-Walker's Brigade, Pegram's Division, 2nd Corps, Army of Northern Virginia (December 1864-April 1865)

Battles: New Creek, West Virginia (two companies) (June 19, 1861)

Lewinsville, Virginia (battalion) (September 11, 1861)

Shenandoah Valley Campaign of 1862 (May-June 1862)

Cross Keys (June 8, 1862)

Port Republic (June 9, 1862)

Sangster's Station (March 9, 1862)

Seven Days Battles (June 25-July 1, 1862)

Gaines' Mill (June 27, 1862)

Cedar Mountain (August 9, 1862)

Bristoe and Manassas Junction (August 26-27, 1862)

2nd Bull Run (August 28-30, 1862)

Chantilly (September 1, 1862)

Harpers Ferry (September 12-15, 1862)

Antietam (September 17, 1862)

Fredericksburg (December 13, 1862)

Chancellorsville (May 1-4, 1863)

2nd Winchester (June 14-15, 1863)

Bristoe Campaign (October 1863)

Mine Run Campaign (November-December 1863)

The Wilderness (May 5-6, 1864)
Spotsylvania Court House (May 8-21, 1864)
North Anna (May 22-26, 1864)
Bethesda Church (May 31, 1864)
Cold Harbor (June 1-3, 1864)
Monocacy (July 9, 1864)
Fort Stevens (July 11, 1864)
3rd Winchester (September 19, 1864)
Fisher's Hill (September 22, 1864)
Cedar Creek (October 19, 1864)
Petersburg Siege (from December 1864) (June 1864-April 1865)
Fort Stedman (March 25, 1865)
Appomattox Court House (April 9, 1865)
Further Reading: Riggs, David F., *13th Virginia Infantry*.

338.   VIRGINIA 14TH INFANTRY REGIMENT

Organization: Organized in state service on May 23, 1861. Transferred to Confederate service on July 1, 1861. Reorganized on May 6, 1862. Surrendered at Appomattox Court House, Virginia, on April 9, 1865.
First Commander: James G. Hodges (Colonel)
Field Officers: Moses F. T. Evans (Lieutenant Colonel)
David J. Godwin (Lieutenant Colonel)
Parke Poindexter (Lieutenant Colonel)
Robert H. Poore (Major)
William D. Shelton (Major)
William White (Major, Lieutenant Colonel, Colonel)
William W. Wood (Major, Lieutenant Colonel)
Assignments: Department of the Peninsula (July-October 1861)
August's Brigade, Department of the Peninsula (October 1861-January 1862)
McLaws' Division, Department of the Peninsula (January-April 1862)
Armistead's Brigade, Huger's-Anderson's Division, Army of Northern Virginia (April-July 1862)
Armistead's Brigade, Anderson's Division, 1st Corps, Army of Northern Virginia (July-September 1862)
Armistead's Brigade, Pickett's Division, 1st Corps, Army of Northern Virginia (September 1862-February 1863)
Armistead's Brigade, Pickett's Division, Department of Virginia and North Carolina (February-April 1863)
Armistead's Brigade, Pickett's Division, Department of Southern Virginia (April-May 1863)

Armistead's Brigade, Pickett's Division, 1st Corps, Army of Northern Virginia (May-September 1863)

Armistead's-Barton's Brigade, Pickett's Division, Department of North Carolina (September-October 1863)

Barton's Brigade, Department of North Carolina (December 1863-February 1864)

Barton's Brigade, Department of Richmond (February-May 1864)

Barton's-Steuart's Brigade, Pickett's Division, 1st Corps, Army of Northern Virginia (May-April 1865)

Battles: Seven Pines (May 31-June 1, 1862)

Seven Days Battles (June 25-July 1, 1862)

Malvern Hill (July 1, 1862)

2nd Bull Run (August 28-30, 1862)

South Mountain (September 14, 1862)

Antietam (September 17, 1862)

Shepherdstown Ford (September 20, 1862)

Fredericksburg (December 13, 1862)

Suffolk Campaign (April-May 1863)

Edenton Road (April 24, 1863)

Gettysburg (July 1-3, 1863)

Chester Station (May 10, 1864)

Drewry's Bluff (May 16, 1864)

North Anna (May 22-26, 1864)

Cold Harbor (June 1-3, 1864)

Petersburg Siege (June 1864-April 1865)

Five Forks (April 1, 1865)

Sayler's Creek (April 6, 1865)

Appomattox Court House (April 9, 1865)

339. VIRGINIA 15TH INFANTRY REGIMENT

Organization: Organized at Richmond May 17, 1861. Sometimes referred to as the 3rd Infantry Regiment. Given its official designation as the 15th Infantry Regiment on June 1, 1861, per G.O. #24, Headquarters Virginia Forces. Transferred to Confederate service on July 1, 1861. Companies F and K refused to reorganize and were disbanded on June 20, 1862, per S.O. #142, Adjutant and Inspector General's Office. Regiment reorganized with eight companies on April 25, 1862.

First Commander: Thomas P. August (Colonel)

Field Officers: Charles H. Clarke (Major)

James R. Crenshaw (Lieutenant Colonel)

Emmett M. Morrison (Major, Lieutenant Colonel)

Thomas G. Peyton (Major, Lieutenant Colonel)
Henry St. G. Tucker, Jr. (Major, Lieutenant Colonel)
John S. Walker (Major)
Assignments: Department of the Peninsula (May-October 1861)
August's Brigade, Department of the Peninsula (October 1861-January 1862)
McLaws' Division, Department of the Peninsula (January-February 1862)
McLaws' Brigade, McLaws' Division, Magruder's Command, Department of Northern Virginia (April-May 1862)
McLaws' Brigade, Magruder's Division, Army of Northern Virginia (May-June 1862)
Semmes' Brigade, McLaws' Division, Magruder's Command, Army of Northern Virginia (June-July 1862)
Semmes' Brigade, McLaws' Division, Army of Northern Virginia (July 1862)
Semmes' Brigade, McLaws' Division, 1st Corps, Army of Northern Virginia (July-November 1862)
Corse's Brigade, Pickett's Division, 1st Corps, Army of Northern Virginia (November 1862-February 1863)
Corse's Brigade, Pickett's Division, Department of Virginia and North Carolina (February-April 1863)
Corse's Brigade, Pickett's Division, Department of Southern Virginia (April-May 1863)
Corse's Brigade, Pickett's Division, 1st Corps, Army of Northern Virginia (May-September 1863)
Corse's Brigade, Pickett's Division, Department of North Carolina (September-October 1863)
Corse's Brigade, Army of Western Virginia and East Tennessee (October-November 1863)
Corse's Brigade, Ransom's Division, Department of Western Virginia and East Tennessee (November 1863-January 1864)
Corse's Brigade, Department of Southwestern Virginia and East Tennessee (January 1864)
Corse's Brigade, Department of North Carolina (February-May 1864)
Corse's Brigade, Hoke's Division, Department of North Carolina and Southern Virginia (May 1864)
Corse's Brigade, Pickett's Division, 1st Corps, Army of Northern Virginia (May 1864-April 1865)
Battles: Yorktown Siege (April-May 1862)
Williamsburg [skirmish] (May 4, 1862)
Seven Days Battles (June 25-July 1, 1862)
Savage Stations (June 29, 1862)
Malvern Hill (July 1, 1862)

South Mountain (September 14, 1862)
Harpers Ferry (September 12-15, 1862)
Antietam (September 17, 1862)
Fredericksburg (December 13, 1862)
Knoxville Siege (November-December 1863)
Plymouth Siege (April 1864)
Drewry's Bluff (May 16, 1864)
North Anna (May 22-26, 1864)
Cold Harbor (June 1-3, 1864)
Petersburg Siege (June 1864-April 1865)
Five Forks (April 1, 1865)
Sayler's Creek (April 6, 1865)
Appomattox Court House (April 9, 1865)

340. VIRGINIA 16TH INFANTRY REGIMENT

Organization: Organized in state service as the 26th Infantry Regiment on May 17, 1861. Redesignated as 16th Infantry Regiment. Transferred to Confederate service on July 1, 1861. Reorganized May 1, 1862. Surrendered at Appomattox Court House, Virginia, on April 9, 1865.
First Commander: Raleigh E. Colston (Colonel)
Field Officers: Charles A. Crump (Lieutenant Colonel, Colonel)
Stapleton Crutchfield (Colonel)
Joseph H. Ham (Lieutenant Colonel, Colonel)
Francis D. Holladay (Major)
John C. Page, Jr. (Major, Lieutenant Colonel)
Henry T. Parrish (Lieutenant Colonel, Colonel)
Richard O. Whitehead (Major, Lieutenant Colonel)
John T. Woodhouse (Major)
Assignments: Department of Norfolk (July 1861-January 1862)
Mahone's Brigade, Department of Norfolk (January-April 1862)
Mahone's Brigade, Huger's-Anderson's Division, Army of Northern Virginia (April-July 1862)
Mahone's Brigade, Anderson's Division, 1st Corps, Army of Northern Virginia (July 1862-May 1863)
Mahone's-Weisiger's Brigade, Anderson's-Mahone's Division, 3rd Corps, Army of Northern Virginia (May 1863-April 1865)
Battles: Seven Days Battles (June 25-July 1, 1862)
Malvern Hill (July 1, 1862)
2nd Bull Run (August 28-30, 1862)
South Mountain (September 14, 1862)
Antietam (September 17, 1862)

Fredericksburg (December 13, 1862)
Chancellorsville (May 1-4, 1863)
Gettysburg (July 1-4, 1863)
Bristoe Campaign (October 1863)
Mine Run Campaign (November-December 1863)
The Wilderness (May 5-6, 1864)
Spotsylvania Court House (May 8-21, 1864)
North Anna (May 22-26, 1864)
Cold Harbor (June 1-3, 1864)
Petersburg Siege (June 1864-April 1865)
The Crater (July 30, 1864)
Appomattox Court House (April 9, 1865)
Further Reading: Trask, Benjamin H., *16th Virginia Infantry.*

341. VIRGINIA 17TH INFANTRY REGIMENT

Organization: Organized at Manassas Junction on June 10, 1861, from four companies of the 6th Infantry Battalion Volunteers (Militia) and other companies. Transferred to Confederate service on July 1, 1861. Reorganized on April 27, 1862. Surrendered at Appomattox Court House, Virginia, on April 9, 1865.

First Commander: Montgomery D. Corse (Colonel)

Field Officers: George W. Brent (Major)

Arthur Herbert (Major, Lieutenant Colonel, Colonel)

Morton Marye (Lieutenant Colonel, Colonel)

William Munford (Lieutenant Colonel)

Robert H. Simpson (Major)

Grayson Tyler (Major, Lieutenant Colonel)

Assignments: Department of Alexandria (June 1861)

Terrett's-Longstreet's Brigade, Army of the Potomac (June-July 1861)

Longstreet's Brigade, 1st Corps, Army of the Potomac (July-October 1861)

Clark's-Griffith's-Ewell's Brigade, Longstreet's Division, 1st Corps, Potomac District, Department of Northern Virginia (October 1861-January 1862)

Ewell's-A. P. Hill's Brigade, Longstreet's Division, Potomac District, Department of Northern Virginia (January-March 1862)

A. P. Hill's-Kemper's Brigade, Longstreet's Division, Army of Northern Virginia (March-June 1862)

Kemper's Brigade, Longstreet's Division, 1st Corps, Army of Northern Virginia (June-August 1862)

Kemper's Brigade, Kemper's Division, 1st Corps, Army of Northern Virginia (August-September 1862)

Kemper's Brigade, D. R. Jones Brigade, 1st Corps, Army of Northern Virginia
(September 1862)

Kemper's Brigade, Pickett's Division, 1st Corps, Army of Northern Virginia
(September-November 1862)

Corse's Brigade, Pickett's Division, 1st Corps, Army of Northern Virginia
(November 1862-February 1863)

Corse's Brigade, Pickett's Division, Department of Virginia and North Carolina
(February-April 1863)

Corse's Brigade, Pickett's Division, Department of Southern Virginia (April-
May 1863)

Corse's Brigade, Pickett's Division, 1st Corps, Army of Northern Virginia
(May-September 1863)

Corse's Brigade, Pickett's Division, Department of North Carolina (September-October 1863)

Unattached, Department of North Carolina (October 1863-January 1864)

Corse's Brigade, Department of North Carolina (February-May 1864)

Corse's Brigade, Hoke's Division, Department of North Carolina and Southern
Virginia (May 1864)

Corse's Brigade, Pickett's Division, 1st Corps, Army of Northern Virginia (May
1864-April 1865)

Battles: Fairfax Court House (Company F; prior to organization of the regiment) (June 1, 1861)

Blackburn's Ford (July 18, 1861)

1st Bull Run (July 21, 1861)

Yorktown Siege (April-May 1862)

Williamsburg (May 5, 1862)

Seven Pines (May 31-June 1, 1862)

Seven Days Battles (June 25-July 1, 1862)

Frayser's Farm (June 30, 1862)

2nd Bull Run (August 28-30, 1862)

Harpers Ferry (September 12-15, 1862)

South Mountain (September 14, 1862)

Antietam (September 17, 1862)

Fredericksburg (December 13, 1862)

Suffolk (November 11, 1863)

Plymouth Siege (April 1864)

Flat Creek Bridge (May 16, 1864)

Drewry's Bluff (May 16, 1864)

North Anna (May 22-26, 1864)

Cold Harbor (June 1-3, 1864)

Petersburg Siege (June 1864-April 1865)

Five Forks (April 1, 1865)
Sayler's Creek (April 6, 1865)
Appomattox Court House (April 9, 1865)
Further Reading: Wise, George, *History of the Seventeenth Virginia Infantry,*
C.S.A.

342. VIRGINIA 18TH INFANTRY REGIMENT

Organization: Organized in late May 1861. Transferred to Confederate ser-
vice on July 1, 1861. Reorganized in April 1862. Surrendered at Appomattox
Court House, Virginia, on April 9, 1865.
First Commander: Robert E. Withers (Colonel)
Field Officers: George C. Cabell (Major, Lieutenant Colonel)
Henry A. Carrington (Lieutenant Colonel, Colonel)
Assignments: 5th (Cocke's) Brigade, Army of the Potomac (June-July 1861)
5th (Cocke's) Brigade, 1st Corps, Army of the Potomac (July-October 1861)
5th (Cocke's) Brigade, Longstreet's Division, 1st Corps, Potomac District,
    Department of Northern Virginia (October 1861-January 1862)
5th (Cocke's-Pickett's) Brigade, Longstreet's Division, Potomac District, De-
    partment of Northern Virginia (January-March 1862)
Pickett's Brigade, Longstreet's Division, Army of Northern Virginia (March-
    June 1862)
Pickett's Brigade, Longstreet's Division, 1st Corps, Army of Northern Virginia
    (June-August 1862)
Pickett's Brigade, Kemper's Division, 1st Corps, Army of Northern Virginia
    (August-September 1862)
Pickett's Brigade, D. R. Jones' Division, 1st Corps, Army of Northern Virginia
    (September 1862)
Pickett's-Garnett's Brigade, Pickett's Division, 1st Corps, Army of Northern
    Virginia (September 1862-February 1863)
Garnett's Brigade, Pickett's Division, Department of Virginia and North Car-
    olina (February-April 1863)
Garnett's Brigade, Pickett's Division, Department of Southern Virginia (April-
    May 1863)
Garnett's-Hunton's Brigade, Pickett's Division, 1st Corps, Army of Northern
    Virginia (May-September 1863)
Hunton's Brigade, Department of Richmond (September 1863-May 1864)
Department of Henrico (Company G) (March-April 1864)
Hunton's Brigade, Pickett's Division, 1st Corps, Army of Northern Virginia
    (May 1864-April 1865)
Battles: Blackburn's Ford (July 18, 1861)
1st Bull Run (July 21, 1861)

Yorktown Siege (April-May 1862)
Williamsburg (May 5, 1862)
Seven Pines (May 31-June 1, 1862)
Seven Days Battles (June 25-July 1, 1862)
Gaines' Mill (June 27, 1862)
Frayser's Farm (June 30, 1862)
2nd Bull Run (August 28-30, 1862)
South Mountain (September 14, 1862)
Antietam (September 17, 1862)
Fredericksburg (December 13, 1862)
Gettysburg (July 1-3, 1863)
Plymouth Siege (April 1864)
Drewry's Bluff (May 16, 1864)
North Anna (May 22-26, 1864)
Cold Harbor (June 1-3, 1864)
Petersburg Siege (June 1864-April 1865)
Five Forks (April 1, 1865)
Sayler's Creek (April 6, 1865)
Appomattox Court House (April 9, 1865)
Further Reading: Robertson, James I., *18th Virginia Infantry*.

343. VIRGINIA 19TH INFANTRY REGIMENT

Organization: Organized for one year at Manassas Junction in May 1861. Transferred to Confederate service on July 1, 1861. Reorganized on April 29, 1862. Surrendered at Appomattox Court House, Virginia, on April 9, 1865.
First Commander: P. St. George Cocke (Colonel)
Field Officers: Waller M. Boyd (Major)
John T. Ellis (Major, Lieutenant Colonel)
Henry Gantt (Major, Lieutenant Colonel, Colonel)
Charles S. Peyton (Major, Lieutenant Colonel)
Armistead T. M. Rust (Colonel)
John B. Strange (Lieutenant Colonel, Colonel)
Bennett Taylor (Major, Lieutenant Colonel)
William Watts (Major)
Assignments: 5th (Cocke's) Brigade, Army of the Potomac (June-July 1861)
5th (Cocke's) Brigade, 1st Corps, Army of the Potomac (July-October 1861)
5th (Cocke's) Brigade, Longstreet's Division, 1st Corps, Potomac District, Department of Northern Virginia (October 1861-January 1862)
5th (Cocke's-Pickett's) Brigade, Longstreet's Division, Potomac District, Department of Northern Virginia (January-March 1862)

Pickett's Brigade, Longstreet's Division, Army of Northern Virginia (March-June 1862)

Pickett's Brigade, Longstreet's Division, 1st Corps, Army of Northern Virginia (June-August 1862)

Pickett's Brigade, Kemper's Division, 1st Corps, Army of Northern Virginia (August-September 1862)

Pickett's Brigade, D. R. Jones' Division, 1st Corps, Army of Northern Virginia (September 1862)

Pickett's-Garnett's Brigade, Pickett's Division, 1st Corps, Army of Northern Virginia (September 1862-February 1863)

Garnett's Brigade, Pickett's Division, Department of Virginia and North Carolina (February-April 1863)

Garnett's Brigade, Pickett's Division, Department of Southern Virginia (April-May 1863)

Garnett's-Hunton's Brigade, Pickett's Division, 1st Corps, Army of Northern Virginia (May-September 1863)

Hunton's Brigade, Department of Richmond (September 1863-May 1864)

Chaffin's Bluff, Department of Richmond (Companies B and G) (October 1863)

Hunton's Brigade, Pickett's Division, 1st Corps, Army of Northern Virginia (May 1864-April 1865)

Battles: 1st Bull Run (July 21, 1861)

Yorktown Siege (April-May 1862)

Williamsburg (May 5, 1862)

Seven Pines (May 31-June 1, 1862)

Gaines' Mill (June 27, 1862)

Seven Days Battles (June 25-July 1, 1862)

Frayser's Farm (June 30, 1862)

2nd Bull Run (August 28-30, 1862)

South Mountain (September 14, 1862)

Antietam (September 17, 1862)

Fredericksburg (December 13, 1862)

Gettysburg (July 1-3, 1863)

North Anna (May 22-26, 1864)

Cold Harbor (June 1-3, 1864)

Petersburg Siege (June 1864-April 1865)

Five Forks (April 1, 1865)

Sayler's Creek (April 6, 1865)

Appomattox Court House (April 9, 1865)

Further Reading: Jordan, Ervin L., Jr., and Thomas, Herbert A., Jr., *19th Virginia Infantry*.

344. VIRGINIA 20TH INFANTRY REGIMENT

Organization: Organized for one year in early June 1861. Transferred to Confederate service on July 1, 1861. Companies G and H captured at Rich Mountain on July 11, 1861. Both companies later mistakenly disbanded while on parole. Companies A, B, C, D and E disbanded on September 10, 1861, per S.O. #270, Adjutant and Inspector General's Office, dated September 5, 1861. Company F became Company A, 57th Infantry Regiment, on September 23, 1861, per S.O. #285, Adjutant and Inspector General's Office. Remaining two companies of the regiment, I and K, slated to become part of the 4th Infantry Battalion, along with several Georgia companies, per S.O. #236, Adjutant and Inspector General's Office, dated November 23, 1861. However, battalion failed to complete its organization and order was revoked on December 10, 1861, per S.O. #262, Adjutant and Inspector General's Office. Companies I and K assigned to the 46th Infantry Regiment as Companies D and F, respectively, from May 9, 1862, to September 24, 1862. Companies I and K again served as part of the 20th Infantry regiment until October 27, 1862, when they became Companies B and C, respectively, 59th Infantry Regiment, per S.O. #244, Adjutant and Inspector General's Office, dated October 18, 1862.

First Commander: John Pegram (Lieutenant Colonel)

Field Officers: James R. Crenshaw (Lieutenant Colonel)

Nathaniel Tyler (Major, Lieutenant Colonel)

Assignments: Army of the Northwest (June-July 1861)

Wise's Brigade, Unattached, Department of North Carolina and Southern Virginia (August-October 1862)

Battles: Middle Fork Bridge (one company) (July 7, 1861)

Rich Mountain (July 11, 1861)

Seven Days Battles (Companies I and K) (June 25-July 1, 1862)

345. VIRGINIA 21ST INFANTRY BATTALION

Nicknames: Pound Gap Battalion

Special Service Battalion

Organization: Organized for one year with six companies in the fall of 1861. Reorganized on April 16, 1862. Consolidated with the 29th Infantry Battalion and designated as the 64th Infantry Regiment (AKA: 64th Cavalry Regiment and 64th Mounted Infantry Regiment) on November 24, 1862, per S.O. #275, Adjutant and Inspector General's Office.

First Commander: John B. Thompson (Major)

Field Officers: Auburn L. Pridemore (Major)

Campbell Slemp (Lieutenant Colonel)

Assignments: Marshall's Brigade, Army of Eastern Kentucky, Department #2 (March 1862)

District of Abingdon (May 1862)

District of Abingdon, Department of Southwestern Virginia (May-November 1862)

Battle: Pound Gap, Kentucky (March 16, 1862)

346. VIRGINIA 21ST INFANTRY REGIMENT

Organization: Organized in state service on April 21, 1861. Mustered into state service on June 28, 1861, to date from April 21, 1861. Transferred to Confederate service on July 1, 1861. Reorganized on April 21, 1862. Field consolidation with 25th, 42nd,44th, 48th and 50th Infantry Regiments from May 14, 1864, to April 9, 1865. 50th Infantry Regiment detached from this field consolidation of some time prior to July 9, 1864. Surrendered at Appomattox Court House, Virginia, on April 9, 1865.

First Commander: William Gilham (Colonel)

Field Officers: William R. Berkeley (Major)

Richard H. Cunningham, Jr. (Lieutenant Colonel)

Alfred Kelley (Major)

John B. Moseley (Major)

William P. Moseley (Lieutenant Colonel)

John M. Patton, Jr. (Lieutenant Colonel, Colonel)

Scott Shipp (Major)

William A. Witcher (Lieutenant Colonel, Colonel)

Assignments: Gilham's Brigade, Army of the Northwest (August-November 1861)

Gilham's Brigade, Loring's Division, Army of the Northwest (November-December 1861)

2nd (Burks'-Campbell's) Brigade, Valley District, Department of Northern Virginia (December 1861-May 1862)

2nd (Campbell's) Brigade, Jackson's Division, Valley District, Department of Northern Virginia (May-June 1862)

J. R. Jones'-J. M. Jones' Brigade, Jackson's-Trimble's-Johnson's Division, 2nd Corps, Army of Northern Virginia (June 1862-May 1864)

Terry's Consolidated Brigade, Gordon's Division, 2nd Corps, Army of Northern Virginia (May-June 1864)

Terry's Consolidated Brigade, Gordon's Division, Valley District, Department of Northern Virginia (June-December 1864)

Terry's Consolidated Brigade, Gordon's Division, 2nd Corps, Army of Northern Virginia (December 1864-April 1865)

Battles: Aquia Creek (May 29, 1861)

Aquia Creek (June 7-8, 1861)

Crouch's (August 15, 1861)

Bath (January 4, 1862)
Sir John's Run (January 6, 1862)
Hancock, Maryland (January 17, 1862)
Kernstown (March 23, 1862)
McDowell (May 8, 1862)
Franklin (May 11, 1862)
Front Royal (May 23, 1862)
Middletown (May 24, 1862)
1st Winchester (May 25, 1862)
Cross Keys (June 8, 1862)
Port Republic (June 9, 1862)
Seven Days Battles (June 25-July 1, 1862)
Gaines' Mill (June 27, 1862)
White Oak Swamp (June 30, 1862)
Malvern Hill (July 1, 1862)
Cedar Mountain (August 9, 1862)
2nd Bull Run (August 28-30, 1862)
Chantilly (September 1, 1862)
Harpers Ferry (September 12-15, 1862)
Antietam (September 17, 1862)
Fredericksburg (December 13, 1862)
Chancellorsville (May 1-4, 1863)
2nd Winchester (June 14-15, 1863)
Gettysburg (July 1-3, 1863)
Williamsport (Company F) (July 6, 1863)
Hagerstown, Maryland (July 8, 1863)
Mine Run Campaign (November-December 1863)
Payne's Farm (November 27, 1863)
The Wilderness (May 5-6, 1864)
Spotsylvania Court House (May 8-21, 1864)
North Anna (May 22-26, 1864)
Bethesda Church (May 30, 1864)
Cold Harbor (June 1, 1864-June 3, 1864)
Lynchburg (June 18, 1864)
Monocacy (July 9, 1864)
Fort Stevens (July 11, 1864)
Kernstown (July 24, 1864)
Newtown (August 11, 1864)
Winchester (August 17, 1864)
3rd Winchester (September 19, 1864)
Fisher's Hill (September 22, 1864)

Cedar Creek (October 19, 1864)

Petersburg Siege (from December 1864) (June 1864-April 1865)

Hatcher's Run (February 5-7, 1865)

Fort Stedman (March 25, 1865)

Petersburg Final Assault (April 2, 1865)

Appomattox Court House (April 9, 1865)

Further Reading: Worsham, John H., *One of Jackson's Foot Cavalry.*

347. VIRGINIA 22ND INFANTRY BATTALION

Organization: Organized with six companies from the 2nd Artillery Regiment ca. May 1862. Also known as the 2nd Infantry Battalion. Battalion disbanded per S.O. #303, Adjutant and Inspector General's Office, dated December 22, 1864. Order apparently not carried out. Surrendered at Appomattox Court House, Virginia, on April 9, 1865.

First Commander: James C. Johnson (Lieutenant Colonel)

Field Officers: John S. Bowles (Major)

Edward P. Tayloe (Lieutenant Colonel)

Assignments: Pender's Brigade, A. P. Hill's Division, Army of Northern Virginia (June 1862)

Pender's Brigade, A. P. Hill's Division, 1st Corps, Army of Northern Virginia (June-July 1862)

Field's Brigade, A. P. Hill's Division, 2nd Corps, Army of Northern Virginia (August 1862-May 1863)

Field's-Walker's Brigade, Heth's Division, 3rd Corps, Army of Northern Virginia (May 1863-January 1865)

Mayo's-Barton's Brigade, Department of Richmond (January-March 1865)

Barton's Brigade, G. W. C. Lee's Division, Department of Richmond (March-April 1865)

Barton's Brigade, G. W. C. Lee's Division, Army of Northern Virginia (April 1865)

Battles: Seven Days Battles (June 25-July 1, 1862)

Mechanicsville (June 26, 1862)

Cedar Mountain (August 9, 1862)

2nd Bull Run (August 28-30, 1862)

Harpers Ferry (September 12-15, 1862)

Antietam (September 17, 1862)

Shepherdstown Ford (September 20, 1862)

Fredericksburg (December 13, 1862)

Chancellorsville (May 1-4, 1863)

Gettysburg (July 1-3, 1863)

Bristoe Campaign (October 1863)

Mine Run Campaign (November-December 1863)
The Wilderness (May 5-6, 1864)
Spotsylvania Court House (May 8-21, 1864)
North Anna (May 22-26, 1864)
Cold Harbor (June 1-3, 1864)
Petersburg Siege (June 1864-April 1865)
Squirrel Level Road (September 30, 1864)
Jones' Farm (September 30, 1864)
Pegram's Farm (October 1, 1864)
Harman Road (October 2, 1864)
Sayler's Creek (April 6, 1865)
Appomattox Court House (April 9, 1865)

348. VIRGINIA 22ND INFANTRY REGIMENT

Nickname: Virginia 1st Kanawha Infantry Regiment
Organization: Organized in state service ca. April 25, 1861. Transferred to Confederate service on July 1, 1861. Reorganized May 1, 1862. Disbanded at Christianburg, Virginia, on April 12, 1865, by Brigadier General John Echols, commanding the Department of Southwestern Virginia and East Tennessee.
First Commander: Christopher Q. Tompkins (Colonel)
Field Officers: Robert A. Bailey (Major)
Andrew R. Barbee (Lieutenant Colonel)
William A. Jackson (Lieutenant Colonel)
John C. McDonald (Major, Lieutenant Colonel)
Patrick H. Moore (Major)
George S. Patton (Lieutenant Colonel, Colonel)
Isaac N. Smith (Major)
Assignments: Army of the Kanawha (September-December 1861)
District of Lewisburg (January-May 1862)
Army of the Kanawha, Department of Western Virginia (May-November 1862)
Patton's Brigade, Department of Western Virginia (November 1862-March 1863)
Echols' Brigade, Department of Western Virginia (April 1863-May 1864)
Echols' Brigade, Breckinridge's Division, Army of Northern Virginia (May-June 1864)
Echols' Brigade, Breckinridge's-Wharton's Division, Valley District, Department of Northern Virginia (June 1864-January 1865)
Echols' Brigade, Department of Southwestern Virginia and East Tennessee (January-April 1865)
Battles: Scarey Creek, West Virginia (July 17, 1861)

Giles Court House, West Virginia (May 10, 1862)
Lewisburg, West Virginia (May 23, 1862)
Kanawha Campaign (September 1862)
Jones' and Imboden's West Virginia Raid (April 1863)
White Sulphur Springs (August 26-27, 1863)
Droop Mountain (December 6, 1863)
New Market (May 15, 1864)
North Anna (May 22-26, 1864)
Cold Harbor (June 1-3, 1864)
Lynchburg Campaign (June 1864)
Monocacy (July 9, 1864)
3rd Winchester (September 19, 1864)
Fisher's Hill (September 22, 1864)
Cedar Creek (October 19, 1864)
Further Reading: Lowry, Terry, *22nd Virginia Infantry.*

349. VIRGINIA 23RD INFANTRY BATTALION

Organization: Organized with five companies on January 15, 1862. Three of the original companies had served in the 3rd Regiment, Floyd's Brigade, which had failed to complete its organization. Was also known as the 1st Infantry Battalion. Reorganized May 21, 1862. Increased to eight companies by April 1863. Disbanded at Christianburg, Virginia, on April 12, 1865, by Brigadier General John Echols, commanding the Department of Southwestern Virginia and East Tennessee.

First Commander: David S. Hounsell (Major)
Field Officers: William Blessing (Major)
William P. Cecil (Major)
Clarence Derrick (Lieutenant Colonel)
Assignments: Echols' Brigade, Department of Western Virginia (August 1862-May 1864)
Echols' Brigade, Breckinridge's Division, Army of Northern Virginia (May-June 1864)
Echol's Brigade, Breckinridge's-Wharton's Division, Valley District, Department of Northern Virginia (June 1864-January 1865)
Echols' Brigade, Department of Southwestern Virginia and East Tennessee (January-April 1865)
Battles: Kanawha Campaign (September 1862)
White Sulphur Springs (August 26-27, 1863)
Droop Mountain (December 6, 1863)
New Market (May 15, 1864)
North Anna (May 22-26, 1864)

Cold Harbor (June 1-3, 1864)
Lynchburg Campaign (June 1864)
Monocacay (July 9, 1864)
3rd Winchester (September 19, 1864)
Fisher's Hill (September 22, 1864)
Cedar Creek (October 19, 1864)

350. VIRGINIA 23RD INFANTRY REGIMENT

Organization: Organized at Richmond for one year in May 1861. Transferred to Confederate service on July 1, 1861. Reorganized April 21, 1862. Field consolidation with 10th and 37th Infantry Regiments from May 14, 1865, to April 9, 1865. Surrendered at Appomattox Court House, Virginia, on April 9, 1865.

First Commander: William B. Taliaferro (Colonel)

Field Officers: J. D. Camden (Major)
Clayton G. Coleman (Major, Lieutenant Colonel)
James H. Crenshaw (Lieutenant Colonel)
George W. Curtis (Lieutenant Colonel)
John P. Fitzgerald (Major, Lieutenant Colonel)
Joseph H. Pendleton (Major)
Andrew J. Richardson (Major)
Andrew V. Scott (Major)
Alexander G. Taliaferro (Lieutenant Colonel, Colonel)
Simeon T. Walton (Major, Lieutenant Colonel)

Assignments: Taliaferro's Brigade, Army of the Northwest (July-November 1861)

Taliaferro's Brigade, Jackson's Division, Army of the Northwest (November-December 1861)

3rd (Taliaferro's) Brigade, Valley District, Department of Northern Virginia (December 1861-May 1862)

3rd (Taliaferro's) Brigade, Jackson's Division, Valley District, Department of Northern Virginia (May-June 1862)

3rd (Taliaferro's-Warren's-Hampton's-Taliaferro's-Colston's-Steuart's) Brigade, Jackson's-Trimble's-Johnson's Division, 2nd Corps, Army of Northern Virginia (June 1862-May 1864)

Terry's Consolidated Brigade, Gordon's Division, 2nd Corps, Army of Northern Virginia (May-June 1864)

Terry's Consolidated Brigade, Gordon's Division, Valley District, Department of Northern Virginia (June-December 1864)

Terry's Consolidated Brigade, Gordon's Division, 2nd Corps, Army of Northern Virginia (December 1864-April 1865)

Battles: Laurel Hill (July 7, 1861)
Corrick's Ford, West Virginia (July 13, 1861)
Cheat Mountain (September 12, 1861)
Greenbrier River (October 3, 1861)
Camp Alleghany, West Virginia (December 13, 1861)
Kernstown (March 23, 1862)
McDowell (May 8, 1862)
Shenandoah Valley Campaign of 1862 (May-June 1862)
1st Winchester (May 25, 1862)
Seven Days Battles (June 25-July 1, 1862)
Gaines' Mill (June 27, 1862)
Malvern Hill (July 1, 1862)
Cedar Mountain (August 9, 1862)
2nd Bull Run (August 28-30, 1862)
Harpers Ferry (September 12-15, 1862)
Antietam (September 17, 1862)
Fredericksburg (December 13, 1862)
Chancellorsville (May 1-4, 1863)
2nd Winchester (June 14-15, 1863)
Gettysburg (July 1-3, 1863)
Bristoe Campaign (October 1863)
Bealeton (October 26, 1863)
Mine Run Campaign (November-December 1863)
Payne's Farm (November 27, 1863)
The Wilderness (May 5-6, 1864)
Spotsylvania Court House (May 8-21, 1864)
North Anna (May 22-26, 1864)
Cold Harbor (June 1-3, 1864)
Lynchburg Campaign (June 1864)
Monocacy (July 9, 1864)
3rd Winchester (September 19, 1864)
Fisher's Hill (September 22, 1864)
Harrisonburg (September 28, 1864)
Cedar Creek (October 19, 1864)
Petersburg Siege (from December 1864) (June 1864-April 1865)
Hatcher's Run (February 5-7, 1865)
Fort Stedman (March 25, 1865)
Petersburg Final Assault (April 2, 1865)
Appomattox Court House (April 9, 1865)

Further Reading: Rankin, Thomas M., *23rd Virginia Infantry*.

351. VIRGINIA 24TH INFANTRY REGIMENT

Organization: Organized at Lynchburg for one year on May 17, 1861. Transferred to Confederate service on July 1, 1861. Reorganized on May 10, 1862. Surrendered at Appomattox Court House, Virginia, on April 9, 1865.

First Commander: Jubal A. Early (Colonel)

Field Officers: William W. Bentley (Major)

Peter Hairston, Jr. (Lieutenant Colonel)

Joseph A. Hambrick (Major)

James P. Hammet (Major)

Richard L. Maury (Major, Lieutenant Colonel)

William R. Terry (Colonel)

Assignments: Early's Brigade, Army of the Potomac (June-July 1861)

Early's Brigade, 1st Corps, Army of the Potomac (July-October 1861)

Early's Brigade, Van Dorn's Division, 1st Corps, Army of the Potomac (October 1861-January 1862)

Early's Brigade, Van Dorn's-D. H. Hill's Division, Potomac District, Department of Northern Virginia (January-March 1862)

Early's-Garland's Brigade, D. H. Hill's Division, Army of Northern Virginia (March-June 1862)

Kemper's Brigade, Longstreet's Division, Army of Northern Virginia (June 1862)

Kemper's Brigade, Longstreet's Division, 1st Corps, Army of Northern Virginia (June-August 1862)

Kemper's Brigade, Kemper's Division, 1st Corps, Army of Northern Virginia (August-September 1862)

Kemper's Brigade, D. R. Jones' Division, 1st Corps, Army of Northern Virginia (September 1862)

Kemper's Brigade, Pickett's Division, 1st Corps, Army of Northern Virginia (September 1862-February 1863)

Kemper's Brigade, Pickett's Division, Department of Virginia and North Carolina (February-April 1863)

Kemper's Brigade, Pickett's Division, Department of Southern Virginia (April-May 1863)

Kemper's Brigade, Pickett's Division, 1st Corps, Army of Northern Virginia (May-September 1863)

Kemper's Brigade, Department of Richmond (September 1863-May 1864)

Kemper's-Terry's Brigade, Pickett's Division, 1st Corps, Army of Northern Virginia (May 1864-April 1865)

Battles: Blackburn's Ford (July 18, 1861)

1st Bull Run (July 21, 1861)

Yorktown Siege (April-May 1862)

Williamsburg (May 5, 1862)
Seven Pines (May 31-June 1, 1862)
Seven Days Battles (June 25-July 1, 1862)
Frayser's Farm (June 30, 1862)
2nd Bull Run (August 28-30, 1862)
Antietam (September 17, 1862)
Fredericksburg (December 13, 1862)
Suffolk Campaign (April-May 1863)
Gettysburg (July 1-3, 1863)
Drewry's Bluff (May 16, 1864)
North Anna (May 22-26, 1864)
Cold Harbor (June 1-3, 1864)
Petersburg Siege (June 1864-April 1865)
Chaffin's Farm (September 27, 1864)
Five Forks (April 1, 1865)
Sayler's Creek (April 6, 1865)
Appomattox Court House (April 9, 1865)
Further Reading: Gunn, Ralph White, *24th Virginia Infantry*.

352. VIRGINIA 25TH INFANTRY BATTALION

Nickname: Richmond City Battalion
Organization: Organized with five companies at Richmond as a local defense unit for six months on August 15, 1862. Mustered in for the war during January and February 1862. Surrendered at Appomattox Court House, Virginia, on April 9, 1865.
First Commander: Wyatt M. Elliott (Major, Lieutenant Colonel)
Field Officer: Louis J. Bossieux (Major)
Assignments: Department of Henrico (August 1862-May 1864)
Unattached, Department of Richmond (May-October 1864)
Barton's Brigade, Department of Richmond (October 1864-March 1865)
Barton's Brigade, G. W. C. Lee's Division, Department of Richmond (March-April 1865)
Barton's Brigade, G. W. C. Lee's Division, Army of Northern Virginia (April 1865)
Battles: Petersburg Siege (June 1864-April 1865)
Fort Gilmer (September 29-30, 1864)
Sayler's Creek (April 6, 1865)
Appomattox Court House (April 9, 1865)

353. VIRGINIA 25TH INFANTRY REGIMENT

Organization: Organized in state service for one year probably during June 1861. Transferred to Confederate service on July 1, 1861. Much of the regiment captured at Rich Mountain on July 11, 1861. 1st Company G disbanded following its capture and parole. Many of the other companies did not reorganize until October 1862. Regiment reorganized on May 1, 1862, with the addition of the four companies of the 9th Infantry Battalion. 1st Company K transferred to the 62nd (Mounted) Infantry Regiment on September 24, 1862. 1st Companies E, F, H and I assigned to the 62nd (Mounted) Infantry Regiment, following their exchange and reorganization, per S.O. #23, Adjutant and Inspector General's Office, dated January 28, 1863. Field Consolidation with the 21st, 42nd, 44th, 48th and 50th Infantry Regiments from May 14, 1864, to April 9, 1865. 50th Infantry Regiment detached from this field consolidation prior to July 9, 1864. Surrendered at Appomattox Court House, Virginia, on April 9, 1865.

First Commander: George A. Porterfield (Colonel)

Field Officers: Patrick B. Duffy (Lieutenant Colonel)

Wilson Harper (Major)

Jonathan M. Heck (Lieutenant Colonel)

John C. Higginbotham (Major, Lieutenant Colonel)

Robert D. Lilley (Major, Lieutenant Colonel)

Albert G. Reger (Major)

John A. Robinson (Major, Lieutenant Colonel)

George H. Smith (Colonel)

William P. Thompson (Major)

Assignments: Taliaferro's Brigade, Army of the Northwest (July-November 1861)

Johnson's Brigade, Jackson's Division, Army of the Northwest (November-December 1861)

Army of the Northwest (March 1862)

Conner's Brigade, Army of the Northwest (May 1862)

Elzey's-Early's Brigade, Ewell's Division, Valley District, Department of Northern Virginia (May-June 1862)

Early's Brigade, Ewell's-Early's Division, 2nd Corps, Army of Northern Virginia (June 1862-April 1863)

Northwest Virginia Brigade, Department of Northern Virginia (April-June 1863)

J. M. Jones' Brigade, Johnson's Division, 2nd Corps, Army of Northern Virginia (June 1863-May 1864)

Terry's Consolidated Brigade, Gordon's Division, 2nd Corps, Army of Northern Virginia (May-June 1864)

Terry's Consolidated Brigade, Gordon's Division, Valley District, Department of Northern Virginia (June-December 1864)

Terry's Consolidated Brigade, Gordon's Division, 2nd Corps, Army of Northern Virginia (December 1864-April 1865)

Battles: Middle Fork Bridge (One Company) (July 7, 1861)
Rich Mountain (July 11, 1861)
Greenbrier River (October 3, 1861)
Camp Alleghany, West Virginia (December 13, 1861)
Kernstown (March 23, 1862)
McDowell (May 8, 1862)
Shenandoah Valley Campaign of 1862 (May-June 1862)
Port Republic (June 9, 1862)
Seven Days Battles (June 25-July 1, 1862)
Gaines' Mill (June 27, 1862)
White Oak Swamp (June 30, 1862)
Malvern Hill (July 1, 1862)
Cedar Mountain (August 9, 1862)
2nd Bull Run (August 28-30, 1862)
Chantilly (September 1, 1862)
Harpers Ferry (September 12-15, 1862)
Antietam (September 17, 1862)
Fredericksburg (December 13, 1862)
Jones' and Imboden's West Virginia Raid (April 1863)
Gettysburg (July 1-3, 1863)
Bristoe Campaign (October 1863)
Mine Run Campaign (November-December 1863)
The Wilderness (May 5-6, 1864)
Spotsylvania Court House (May 8-21, 1864)
North Anna (May 22-26, 1864)
Cold Harbor (June 1-3, 1864)
Monocacy (July 9, 1864)
3rd Winchester (September 19, 1864)
Fisher's Hill (September 22, 1864)
Cedar Creek (October 19, 1864)
Petersburg Siege (from December 1864) (June 1864-April 1865)
Fort Stedman (March 25, 1865)
Appomattox Court House (April 9, 1865)

354. VIRGINIA 26TH INFANTRY BATTALION

Organization: Organized with seven companies on May 20, 1862, from those members of the 59th Infantry Regiment not captured at Roanoke Island on February 8, 1862. Companies H and I organized on June 12 and 6, 1863, respectively. Disbanded at Christianburg, Virginia, on April 12, 1865, by Brigadier General John Echols, commanding the Department of Southwestern Virginia and East Tennessee.

First Commander: George M. Edgar (Major, Lieutenant Colonel)
Field Officer: Richard Woodrum (Major)
Assignments: Echols' Brigade, Department of Western Virginia (August 1862-May 1864)
Echols' Brigade, Breckinridge's Division, Army of Northern Virginia (May-June 1864)
Echols' Brigade, Breckinridge's-Wharton's Division, Valley District, Department of Northern Virginia (June 1864-January 1865)
Echols' Brigade, Department of Southwestern Virginia and East Tennessee (January-April 1865)
Battles: Lewisburg, West Virginia (May 23, 1862)
Kanawha Campaign (September 1862)
Lewisburg (May 2, 1863)
White Sulphur Springs (August 26-27, 1863)
Droop Mountain (December 6, 1863)
New Market (May 15, 1864)
North Anna (May 22-26, 1864)
Totopotomoy Creek (May 30, 1864)
Cold Harbor (June 1-3, 1864)
Lynchburg Campaign (June 1864)
Monocacy (July 9, 1864)
3rd Winchester (September 19, 1864)
Fisher's Hill (September 22, 1864)
Cedar Creek (October 19, 1864)

355.   VIRGINIA 26TH INFANTRY REGIMENT

Organization: Organized in state service for one year ca. June 1862. Transferred to Confederate service on July 1, 1861. 1st Company B, a Mississippi unit, transferred to the 2nd Mississippi Infantry Battalion on October 16, 1861, per S.O. #181, Adjutant and Inspector General's Office. Companies relettered at this time and the same order assigned a new company, K, to the regiment. Reorganized on May 13, 1862. Surrendered at Appomattox Court House, Virginia, on April 9, 1865.
First Commander: Charles A. Crump (Colonel)
Field Officers: James C. Councill (Lieutenant Colonel)
Patrick H. Fitzhugh (Major)
Joshua L. Garrett (Major)
Powhatan R. Page (Lieutenant Colonel, Colonel)
William K. Perrin (Major)
William H. Wheelwright (Major)
Assignments: Department of the Peninsula (July-October 1861)

Gloucester Point (Crump's Command), Department of the Peninsula (October 1861-April 1862)

Gloucester Point (Crump's Command), Rains' Division, D. H. Hill's Command, Department of Northern Virginia (April-May 1862)

Gloucester Point (Crump's Command), D. H. Hill's Division, Department of Northern Virginia (May 1862)

Rodes' Brigade, D. H. Hill's Division, Department of Northern Virginia (May 1862)

Wise's Brigade, D. H. Hill's Division, Army of Northern Virginia (May-June 1862)

Wise's Brigade, Army of Northern Virginia (June-July 1862)

Wise's Brigade, D. H. Hill's Division, Army of Northern Virginia (July 1862)

Wise's Brigade, Unattached, Department of North Carolina and Southern Virginia (August-December 1862)

Wise's Brigade, Elzey's Command, Department of North Carolina and Southern Virginia (December 1862-April 1863)

Wise's Brigade, Department of Richmond (April-September 1863)

Wise's Brigade, 1st Military District of South Carolina, Department of South Carolina, Georgia and Florida (September-October 1863)

6th Military District of South Carolina, Department of South Carolina, Georgia and Florida (October-November 1863)

Wise's Brigade, 6th Military District of South Carolina, Department of South Carolina, Georgia and Florida (December 1863-April 1864)

District of Florida, Department of South Carolina, Georgia and Florida (April 1864)

Wise's Brigade, Johnson's Division, Department of North Carolina and Southern Virginia (May-October 1864)

Wise's Brigade, Johnson's Division, 4th Corps, Army of Northern Virginia (October 1864-April 1865)

Battles: Yorktown Siege (April-May 1862)

Williamsburg (May 5, 1862)

Seven Days Battles (June 25-July 1, 1862)

Blake's Farm, near Deep Bottom, James River (August 6, 1863)

Charleston Harbor (August-September 1863)

Legaresville, South Carolina, vs. USS *Marblehead* (December 25, 1863)

Nottoway Bridge (two companies) (May 8, 1864)

Drewry's Bluff (May 16, 1864)

Bermuda Hundred (May 17-June 14, 1864)

Petersburg Siege (June 1864-April 1865)

Jordan's Farm (June 15, 1864)

Taylor's Farm (June 17, 1864)

Sayler's Creek (April 6, 1865)

Appomattox Court House (April 9, 1865)
Further Reading: Wiatt, Alex L., *26th Virginia Infantry.*

356. VIRGINIA 27TH INFANTRY REGIMENT

Organization: Organized May 30, 1861, as the 6th Infantry Regiment in state service. Designated the 27th Infantry Regiment on June 1, 1861. Mustered into state service at Harpers Ferry on June 8, 1861. Transferred to Confederate service with seven companies on July 1, 1861. Reorganized on March 23, 1862. Field consolidation with the 2nd, 4th, 5th and 33rd Infantry Regiments from May 1864 to April 1865. Surrendered at Appomattox Court House, Virginia, on April 9, 1865.

First Commander: William W. Gordon (Colonel)
Field Officers: Joseph H. Carpenter (Lieutenant Colonel)
John Echols (Lieutenant Colonel, Colonel)
James K. Edmondson (Lieutenant Colonel, Colonel)
Philip F. Frazer (Major)
Andrew J. Grigsby (Major, Lieutenant Colonel, Colonel)
Charles L. Haynes (Lieutenant Colonel)
Elisha F. Paxton (Major)
Daniel M. Shriver (Major, Lieutenant Colonel)
Assignments: 1st Brigade, Army of the Shenandoah (June-July 1861)
1st Brigade, 2nd Corps, Army of the Potomac (July-October 1861)
Stonewall Brigade, 2nd Corps, Potomac District, Department of Northern Virginia (October-November 1861)
Stonewall Brigade, Valley District, Department of Northern Virginia (November 1861-May 1862)
Stonewall Brigade, Jackson's Division, Valley District, Department of Northern Virginia (May-June 1862)
Stonewall Brigade, Jackson's-Johnson's Division, 2nd Corps, Army of Northern Virginia (June 1862-May 1864)
Terry's Consolidated Brigade, Gordon's Division, 2nd Corps, Army of Northern Virginia (May-June 1864)
Terry's Consolidated Brigade, Gordon's Division, Valley District, Department of Northern Virginia (June-December 1864)
Terry's Consolidated Brigade, Gordon's Division, 2nd Corps, Army of Northern Virginia (December 1864-April 1865)
Battles: Falling Waters (July 2, 1861)
1st Bull Run (July 21, 1861)
Romney Campaign (January 1862)
Kernstown (March 23, 1862)
Cedar Creek (March 24, 1862)

Shenandoah Valley Campaign of 1862 (May-June 1862)
McDowell (not engaged) (May 23, 1862)
Front Royal (not engaged) (May 23, 1862)
1st Winchester (May 25, 1862)
Port Republic (June 9, 1862)
Seven Days Battles (June 25-July 1, 1862)
Gaines' Mill (June 27, 1862)
White Oak Swamp (June 30, 1862)
Malvern Hill (July 1, 1862)
Cedar Mountain (August 9, 1862)
Groveton (August 28, 1862)
2nd Bull Run (August 28-30, 1862)
Chantilly (in reserve) (September 1, 1862)
Harpers Ferry (September 12-15, 1862)
Antietam (September 17, 1862)
Kearneyville (October 17, 1862)
Fredericksburg (December 13, 1862)
Chancellorsville (May 1-4, 1863)
2nd Winchester (June 14-15, 1863)
Gettysburg (July 1-3, 1863)
Bealton (November 5, 1863)
Mine Run Campaign (November-December 1863)
Morton's Ford (February 10, 1864)
The Wilderness (May 5-6, 1864)
Spotsylvania Court House (May 8-21, 1864)
North Anna (May 22-26, 1864)
Bethesda Church (May 30, 1864)
Cold Harbor (June 1-3, 1864)
Lynchburg Campaign (June 1864)
Monocacy (July 9, 1864)
Snicker's Ferry (July 18, 1864)
2nd Kernstown (July 24, 1864)
Winchester (July 24, 1864)
Newton (August 11, 1864)
Winchester (August 17, 1864)
Shepherdstown (August 25, 1864)
3rd Winchester (September 19, 1864)
Fisher's Hill (September 22, 1864)
Cedar Creek (October 19, 1864)
Petersburg Siege (from December 1864) (June 1864-April 1865)
Hatcher's Run (February 5-7, 1865)

Fort Stedman (March 25, 1865)
Sayler's Creek (April 6, 1865)
Appomattox Court House (April 9, 1865)
Further Reading: Robertson, James I., *The Stonewall Brigade.*

357.   VIRGINIA 28TH INFANTRY BATTALION

Nickname: Virginia 28th Heavy Artillery Battalion
Organization: Organized with four companies previously guarding prisoners
of war in Richmond on September 9, 1862, per S.O. #211, Adjutant and
Inspector General's Office. Companies A and B detached from the battalion
on October 29, 1862, per S.O. #253, Adjutant and Inspector General's Office.
Battalion merged into 59th Infantry Regiment on November 1, 1862, per S.O.
#244, Adjutant and Inspector General's Office.

358.   VIRGINIA 28TH INFANTRY REGIMENT

Organization: Organized in state service for one year at Lynchburg on May
17, 1861. Transferred to Confederate service on July 1, 1861. Reorganized in
late April 1862. Surrendered at Appomattox Court House, Virginia, on April
9, 1865.
First Commander: Robert T. Preston (Colonel)
Field Officers: Robert C. Allen (Major, Colonel)
Samuel B. Paul (Lieutenant Colonel)
Michael P. Spessard (Major)
William Watts (Major, Lieutenant Colonel)
Nathaniel C. Wilson (Major)
William L. Wingfield (Lieutenant Colonel)
Assignments: 5th (Cocke's) Brigade, Army of the Potomac (June-July 1861)
5th (Cocke's) Brigade, 1st Corps, Army of the Potomac (July-October 1861)
5th (Cocke's) Brigade, Longstreet's Division, 1st Corps, Potomac District,
    Department of Northern Virginia (October 1861-January 1862)
5th (Cocke's-Pickett's) Brigade, Longstreet's Division, Potomac District, De-
    partment of Northern Virginia (January-March 1862)
Pickett's Brigade, Longstreet's Division, Army of Northern Virginia (March-
    June 1862)
Pickett's Brigade, Longstreet's Division, 1st Corps, Army of Northern Virginia
    (June-August 1862)
Pickett's Brigade, Kemper's Division, 1st Corps, Army of Northern Virginia
    (August-September 1862)
Pickett's Brigade, D. R. Jones' Division, 1st Corps, Army of Northern Virginia
    (September 1862)

Pickett's-Garnett's Brigade, Pickett's Division, 1st Corps, Army of Northern Virginia (September 1862-February 1863)

Garnett's Brigade, Pickett's Division, Department of Virginia and North Carolina (February-April 1863)

Garnett's Brigade, Pickett's Division, Department of Southern Virginia (April-May 1863)

Garnett's-Hunton's Brigade, Pickett's Division, 1st Corps, Army of Northern Virginia (May-September 1863)

Hunton's Brigade, Department of Richmond (September 1863-May 1864)

Department of Henrico (Company I) (March-April 1864)

Hunton's Brigade, Pickett's Division, 1st Corps, Army of Northern Virginia (May 1864-April 1865)

Battles: 1st Bull Run (July 21, 1861)

Yorktown Siege (April-May 1862)

Williamsburg (May 5, 1862)

Seven Pines (May 31-June 1, 1862)

Seven Days Battles (June 25-July 1, 1862)

Gaines' Mill (June 27, 1862)

Frayser's Farm (June 30, 1862)

2nd Bull Run (August 28-30, 1862)

South Mountain (September 14, 1862)

Antietam (September 17, 1862)

Fredericksburg (December 13, 1862)

Gettysburg (July 1-3, 1863)

North Anna (May 22-26, 1864)

Cold Harbor (June 1-3, 1864)

Howlett House (May 18, 1864)

Petersburg Siege (June 1864-April 1865)

White Oak Road (March 31, 1865)

Five Forks (April 1, 1865)

Sayler's Creek (April 6, 1865)

Appomattox Court House (April 9, 1865)

Further Reading: Fields, Frank E., Jr., *28th Virginia Infantry.*

359. VIRGINIA 29TH INFANTRY BATTALION

Organization: Organized with five companies in August and September 1862. Apparently mustered as a cavalry unit. Reduced to four companies and consolidated with the 21st Infantry Battalion and designated as the 64th Infantry Regiment on November 24, 1862, per S.O. #275, Adjutant and Inspector General's Office. Does not appear in the *Official Records.*

360.   VIRGINIA 29TH INFANTRY REGIMENT

Organization: Organized by S.O. #206, Adjutant and Inspector General's Office, dated November 5, 1861. Five companies illegally assigned to this battalion since they had been raised for Local and Special Service and were then serving as part of the 21st Infantry Battalion ("Pound Gap Battalion"). Company G organized on March 27, 1862. Companies H, I and K organized on April 2 and 3, 1862. Reorganized with only nine companies during May 1862. 1st Company F disbanded in about May 1862. Company K became 2nd Company I in about May 1862. 1st Company I became 2nd Company F in about May 1862. Surrendered at Appomattox Court House, Virginia, on April 9, 1865.

First Commander: Alfred C. Moore (Colonel)

Field Officers: Ebenezer Bruster (Major)

James Giles (Major, Lieutenant Colonel, Colonel)

Alexander Haynes (Major, Lieutenant Colonel)

William R. B. Horne (Major)

William Leigh (Lieutenant Colonel)

Edwin R. Smith (Major, Lieutenant Colonel)

Isaac White (Major)

Assignments: Marshall's Brigade, Department #2 (November-December 1861)

Marshall's Brigade, Army of Eastern Kentucky, Department #2 (January-May 1862)

District of Abingdon (May 1862)

District of Abingdon, Department of Southwestern Virginia (May-? 1862)

Unattached, Elzey's Command, Department of North Carolina and Southern Virginia (December 1862)

Colston's Brigade, Elzey's Command, Department of North Carolina and Southern Virginia (December 1862)

Colston's Brigade, French's Command, Department of North Carolina and Southern Virginia (December 1862-February 1863)

Unattached, French's Command, Department of North Carolina and Southern Virginia (February-April 1863)

Unattached, Department of Southern Virginia (April-May 1863)

Corse's Brigade, Pickett's Division, 1st Corps, Army of Northern Virginia (May-September 1863)

Corse's Brigade, Pickett's Division, Department of North Carolina (September-October 1863)

Corse's Brigade, Army of Western Virginia and East Tennessee (October-November 1863)

Corse's Brigade, Ransom's Division, Department of Western Virginia and East Tennessee (November 1863-January 1864)

Corse's Brigade, Department of Southwestern Virginia and East Tennessee (January 1864)

Corse's Brigade, Department of North Carolina (February-May 1864)

Corse's Brigade, Hoke's Division, Department of North Carolina and Southern Virginia (May 1864)

Corse's Brigade, Pickett's Division, 1st Corps, Army of Northern Virginia (May 1864-April 1865)

Battles: Wolf Creek, West Virginia (May 15, 1862)

Princeton, West Virginia (May 15-17, 1862)

Suffolk Campaign (April-May 1863)

Edenton Road (April 24, 1863)

Knoxville Siege (November-December 1863)

Plymouth Siege (April 1864)

Drewry's Bluff (May 16, 1864)

North Anna (May 22-26, 1864)

Cold Harbor (June 1-3, 1864)

Petersburg Siege (June 1864-April 1865)

Five Forks (April 1, 1865)

Sayler's Creek (April 6, 1865)

Appomattox Court House (April 9, 1865)

Further Reading: Alderman, John Perry, *29th Virginia Infantry.*

361.   VIRGINIA 30TH INFANTRY BATTALION, SHARPSHOOTERS

Organization: Organized with six companies on September 1, 1862. Company A formerly Adams' Artillery Battery. Company B formerly French's Artillery Battery. Company C formerly Vawter's Western Artillery Battery. Battalion officers commissioned on October 5, 1862. Dispersed at Waynesborough on March 2, 1865.

First Commander: J. Lyle Clarke (Lieutenant Colonel)

Field Officer: Peter J. Ofey (Major)

Assignments: Wharton's Brigade, Department of Southwestern Virginia (September 1862)

Unattached, Elzey's Command, Department of North Carolina (December 1862)

Colston's Brigade, Elzey's Command, Department of North Carolina and Southern Virginia (December 1862)

Colston's-Pryor's Brigade, French's Command, Department of North Carolina and Southern Virginia (December 1862-February 1863)

Wharton's Brigade, Department of Western Virginia (April-October 1863)

Wharton's Brigade, Ransom's Division, Department of Western Virginia and East Tennessee (October-November 1863)

Wharton's Brigade, Ransom's Division, Department of East Tennessee (November 1863-March 1864)

Wharton's Brigade, Department of Western Virginia (March-May 1864)

Wharton's Brigade, Breckinridge's Division, Army of Northern Virginia (May-June 1864)

Wharton's Brigade, Breckinridge's-Wharton's Division, Valley District, Department of Northern Virginia (June 1864-March 1865)

Battles: Middle Creek, Kentucky (January 10, 1862)

Kanawha Campaign (September 1862)

Knoxville Siege (November-December 1863)

New Market (May 15, 1864)

Cold Harbor (June 1-3, 1864)

Lynchburg Campaign (June 1864)

Monocacy (July 9, 1864)

3rd Winchester (September 19, 1864)

Fisher's Hill (September 22, 1864)

Cedar Creek (October 19, 1864)

Waynesborough (March 2, 1865)

362.   VIRGINIA 30TH INFANTRY REGIMENT

Organization: Organized from 2nd Infantry Battalion Volunteers (Militia) and eight other companies in state service on June 13, 1861. Transferred to Confederate service on July 1, 1861. Reorganized on April 19, 1862. Surrendered at Appomattox Court House, Virginia, on April 9, 1865.

First Commander: R. Milton Cary (Colonel)

Field Officers: William S. Barton (Major)

Robert S. Chew (Lieutenant Colonel, Colonel)

John M. Gouldin (Major, Lieutenant Colonel)

Archibald T. Harrison (Lieutenant Colonel, Colonel)

Robert O. Peatross (Major)

Assignments: Department of Fredericksburg (July 1861)

District of Aquia, Department of Fredericksburg (July-September 1861)

Walker's Brigade, District of Aquia, Department of Fredericksburg (September-October 1861)

Walker's Brigade, Aquia District, Department of Northern Virginia (October 1861-March 1862)

Walker's Brigade, Department of North Carolina (March-August 1862)

Walker's-Cooke's Brigade, Walker's Ransom's Division, 1st Corps, Army of Northern Virginia (September-November 1862)

Corse's Brigade, Pickett's Division, 1st Corps, Army of Northern Virginia (November 1862-February 1863)

Corse's Brigade, Pickett's Division, Department of Virginia and North Carolina (February-April 1863)

Corse's Brigade, Pickett's Division, Department of Southern Virginia (April-May 1863)

Corse's Brigade, Pickett's Division, 1st Corps, Army of Northern Virginia (May-September 1863)

Corse's Brigade, Pickett's Division, Department of North Carolina (September-October 1863)

Corse's Brigade, Army of Western Virginia and East Tennessee (October-November 1863)

Corse's Brigade, Ransom's Division, Department of Western Virginia and East Tennessee (November 1863-January 1864)

Corse's Brigade, Department of Southwestern Virginia and East Tennessee (January 1864)

Corse's Brigade, Department of North Carolina (February-May 1864)

Corse's Brigade, Hoke's Division, Department of North Carolina and Southern Virginia (May 1864)

Corse's Brigade, Pickett's Division, 1st Corps, Army of Northern Virginia (May 1864-April 1865)

Battles: Seven Days Battles (June 25-July 1, 1862)
Malvern Cliff (June 30, 1862)
Antietam (September 17, 1862)
Harpers Ferry (September 12-15, 1862)
Fredericksburg (December 13, 1862)
Knoxville Siege (November-December 1863)
Plymouth Siege (April 1864)
Drewry's Bluff (May 16, 1864)
North Anna (May 22-26, 1864)
Cold Harbor (June 1-3, 1864)
Petersburg Siege (June 1864-April 1865)
Five Forks (April 1, 1865)
Sayler's Creek (April 6, 1865)
Appomattox Court House (April 9, 1865)
Further Reading: Krick, Robert K., *30th Virginia Infantry*.

363.   VIRGINIA 31ST INFANTRY REGIMENT

Organization: Organized in state service for one year in June 1861. Transferred to Confederate service on July 1, 1861. Reorganized on May 1, 1862. Surrendered at Appomattox Court House, Virginia, on April 9, 1865.

First Commander: William L. Jackson (Lieutenant Colonel)

Field Officers: James C. Arbogast (Major)

Francis M. Boykin (Major, Lieutenant Colonel)

Joseph H. Chenoweth (Major)

William P. Cooper (Major)

Joseph S. Hoffman (Major, Colonel)

Alfred H. Jackson (Lieutenant Colonel)

James S. K. McCutchen (Major, Lieutenant Colonel)

Samuel H. Reynolds (Colonel)

Assignments: 1st (H. R. Jackson's) Brigade, Army of the Northwest (September-November 1861)

Johnson's Brigade, Jackson's Division, Army of the Northwest (November 1861-January 1862)

Army of the Northwest (March 1862)

Conner's Brigade, Army of the Northwest (May 1862)

Elzey's Brigade, Ewell's Division, Valley District, Department of Northern Virginia (May-June 1862)

Elzey's-Early's-Smith's Brigade, Ewell's-Early's Division, 2nd Corps, Army of Northern Virginia (June 1862-April 1863)

Northwestern Virginia Brigade, Department of Northern Virginia (April-June 1863)

Smith's-Pegram's Brigade, Early's-Ramseur's Division, 2nd Corps, Army of Northern Virginia (June 1863-June 1864)

Pegram's Brigade, Ramseur's-Pegram's Division, Valley District, Department of Northern Virginia (June-December 1864)

Pegram's-Walker's Brigade, Pegram's Division, 2nd Corps, Army of Northern Virginia (December 1864-April 1865)

Battles: Greenbrier River (October 3, 1861)

Camp Alleghany, West Virginia (December 13, 1861)

McDowell (May 8, 1862)

Shenandoah Valley Campaign of 1862 (May-June 1862)

Port Republic (June 9, 1862)

Seven Days Battles (June 25-July 1, 1862)

Gaines' Mill (June 27, 1862)

Malvern Hill (July 1, 1862)

Rappahannock Station (August 23, 1862)

Cedar Mountain (August 9, 1862)

Bristoe and Manassas Junction (August 26-27, 1862)

2nd Bull Run (August 28-30, 1862)

Chantilly (September 1, 1862)

Harpers Ferry (September 12-15, 1862)

Antietam (September 17, 1862)

Fredericksburg (December 13, 1862)

Jones' and Imboden's West Virginia Raid (April 1863)
2nd Winchester (June 14-15, 1863)
Gettysburg (July 1-3, 1863)
Bristoe Campaign (October 1863)
Mine Run Campaign (November-December 1863)
The Wilderness (May 5-6, 1864)
Spotsylvania Court House (May 8-21, 1864)
North Anna (May 22-26, 1864)
Cold Harbor (June 1-3, 1864)
Lynchburg Campaign (June 1864)
Monocacy (July 9, 1864)
Fort Stevens (July 11, 1864)
3rd Winchester (September 19, 1864)
Fisher's Hill (September 22, 1864)
Cedar Creek (October 19, 1864)
Petersburg Siege (from December 1864) (June 1864-April 1865)
Appomattox Court House (April 9, 1865)
Further Reading: Ashcraft, John M., Jr., *31st Virginia Infantry.*

364. VIRGINIA 32ND INFANTRY REGIMENT

Organization: Organized in state service for one year in May 1861. Trans-
ferred to Confederate service on July 1, 1861. Montague's Infantry Battalion
temporarily attached to this regiment from August 1861 to September 1861.
Companies G, 1st H and 1st I transferred to the 1st Artillery Regiment ca.
September 1861. Reorganized with seven companies on May 21, 1862. Surren-
dered at Appomattox Court House, Virginia, on April 9, 1865.
First Commander: Benjamin S. Ewell (Colonel)
Field Officers: John B. Cary (Lieutenant Colonel)
James M. Goggin (Major)
Baker P. Lee, Jr. (Major)
Edgar P. Montague (Colonel)
Jefferson Sinclair (Major)
William R. Willis (Lieutenant Colonel)
Assignments: Department of the Peninsula (July-October 1861)
B. S. Ewell's Brigade, Department of the Peninsula (October 1861)
Rains' Division, Department of the Peninsula (two companies) (January-April
   1862)
McLaws' Division, Department of the Peninsula (two companies) (January-
   April 1862)
Williamsburg and Spratley's (B. S. Ewell's Command), Department of the
   Peninsula (two companies) (January-April 1862)

Williamsburg (B. S. Ewell's Command), Magruder's Command, Department of
Northern Virginia (one company) (April-May 1862)

Pryor's Brigade, Longstreet's Division, Department of Northern Virginia (May
1862)

Semmes' Brigade, McLaws' Division, Magruder's Command, Army of Northern
Virginia (June-July 1862)

Semmes' Brigade, McLaws' Division, Army of Northern Virginia (July 1862)

Semmes' Brigade, McLaws' Division, 1st Corps, Army of Northern Virginia
(July-November 1862)

Corse's Brigade, Pickett's Division, 1st Corps, Army of Northern Virginia
(November 1862-February 1863)

Corse's Brigade, Pickett's Division, Department of Virginia and North Carolina
(February-April 1863)

Corse's Brigade, Pickett's Division, Department of Southern Virginia (April-
May 1863)

Corse's Brigade, Pickett's Division, 1st Corps, Army of Northern Virginia
(May-September 1863)

Corse's Brigade, Pickett's Division, Department of North Carolina (September-October 1863)

Hunton's Brigade, Department of Richmond (February-May 1864)

Corse's Brigade, Pickett's Division, 1st Corps, Army of Northern Virginia (May
1864-April 1865)

Battles: Yorktown Siege (April-May 1862)

Williamsburg (detachment) (May 5, 1862)

Seven Days Battles (June 25-July 1, 1862)

Savage Station (June 29, 1862)

Malvern Hill (July 1, 1862)

Harpers Ferry (September 12-15, 1862)

South Mountain (September 14, 1862)

Antietam (September 17, 1862)

Fredericksburg (December 13, 1862)

North Anna (May 22-26, 1864)

Cold Harbor (June 1-3, 1864)

Petersburg Siege (June 1864-April 1865)

Chaffin's Farm (September 29, 1864)

Five Forks (April 1, 1865)

Appomattox Court House (April 9, 1865)

365. VIRGINIA 33RD INFANTRY REGIMENT

Organization: Organized in June 1861 for one year. Regiment transferred to
Confederate service on July 1, 1861. Reorganized on April 22, 1862. Field

consolidation with the 2nd, 4th, 5th and 27th Infantry Regiments from May 1864 to April 1865. Surrendered at Appomattox Court House, Virginia, on April 9, 1865.

First Commander: Arthur C. Cummings (Colonel)

Field Officers: Jacob B. Golladay (Major)

Philip T. Grace (Major)

Frederick W. M. Holliday (Colonel)

George Huston (Major, Lieutenant Colonel)

John R. Jones (Lieutenant Colonel)

Edwin G. Lee (Major, Lieutenant Colonel, Colonel)

John F. Neff (Colonel)

Abraham Spengler (Lieutenant Colonel, Colonel)

Assignments: 1st Brigade, Army of the Shenandoah (June-July 1861)

1st Brigade, 2nd Corps, Army of the Potomac (July-October 1861)

Stonewall Brigade, 2nd Corps, Potomac District, Department of Northern Virginia (October-November 1861)

Stonewall Brigade, Valley District, Department of Northern Virginia (November 1861-May 1862)

Stonewall Brigade, Jackson's Division, Valley District, Department of Northern Virginia (May-June 1862)

Stonewall Brigade, Jackson's-Johnson's Division, 2nd Corps, Army of Northern Virginia (June 1862-May 1864)

Terry's Consolidated Brigade, Gordon's Division, 2nd Corps, Army of Northern Virginia (May-June 1864)

Terry's Consolidated Brigade, Gordon's Division, Valley District, Department of Northern Virginia (June-December 1864)

Terry's Consolidated Brigade, Gordon's Division, 2nd Corps, Army of Northern Virginia (December 1864-April 1865)

Battles: Falling Waters (July 2, 1861)

1st Bull Run (July 21, 1861)

Romney Campaign (January 1862)

Kernstown (March 23, 1862)

McDowell (not engaged) (May 8, 1862)

Front Royal (not engaged) (May 23, 1862)

1st Winchester (May 25, 1862)

Port Republic (June 9, 1862)

Seven Days Battles (June 25-July 1, 1862)

Gaines' Mill (June 27, 1862)

White Oak Swamp (June 30, 1862)

Malvern Hill (July 1, 1862)

Cedar Mountain (August 9, 1862)

Groveton (August 28, 1862)

2nd Bull Run (August 28-30, 1862)

Chantilly (in reserve) (September 1, 1862)

Harpers Ferry (September 12-15, 1862)

Antietam (September 17, 1862)

Kearneyville (October 17, 1862)

Fredericksburg (December 13, 1862)

Chancellorsville (May 1-4, 1863)

2nd Winchester (June 14-15, 1863)

Gettysburg (July 1-3, 1863)

Bealton (November 5, 1863)

Mine Run Campaign (November-December 1863)

Morton's Ford (February 10, 1864)

The Wilderness (May 5-6, 1864)

Spotsylvania Court House (May 8-21, 1864)

North Anna (May 22-26, 1864)

Bethesda Church (May 30, 1864)

Cold Harbor (June 1-3, 1864)

Lynchburg Campaign (June 1864)

Monocacy (July 9, 1864)

Snicker's Ferry (July 18, 1864)

2nd Kernstown (July 24, 1864)

Winchester (July 24, 1864)

Newton (August 11, 1864)

Winchester (August 17, 1864)

Shepherdstown (August 25, 1864)

3rd Winchester (September 19, 1864)

Fisher's Hill (September 22, 1864)

Cedar Creek (October 19, 1864)

Petersburg Siege (from December 1864) (June 1864-April 1865)

Hatcher's Run (February 5-7, 1865)

Fort Stedman (March 25, 1865)

Sayler's Creek (April 6, 1865)

Appomattox Court House (April 9, 1865)

Further Reading: Robertson, James I., *The Stonewall Brigade*. Reidenbaugh, Lowell, *33rd Virginia Infantry*.

366.   VIRGINIA 34TH INFANTRY REGIMENT

Organization: Organized by the change of designation of the 4th Heavy Artillery Regiment on March 8, 1864, per S.O. #56, Adjutant and Inspector

General's Office. Surrendered at Appomattox Court House, Virginia, on April 9, 1865.

First Commander: John Thomas Goode (Colonel)

Field Officers: John R. Bagby (Major)

Randolph Harrison (Lieutenant Colonel)

Assignments: Wise's Brigade, 6th Military District of South Carolina, Department of South Carolina, Georgia and Florida (March-May 1864)

Wise's Brigade, Johnson's Division, Department of North Carolina and Southern Virginia (May-October 1864)

Wise's Brigade, Johnson's Division, 4th Corps, Army of Northern Virginia (October 1864-April 1865)

Battles: Drewry's Bluff (May 16, 1864)

Bermuda Hundred (May 17-June 14, 1864)

Petersburg Siege (June 1864-April 1865)

The Crater (July 30, 1864)

Sayler's Creek (April 6, 1865)

Appomattox Court House (April 9, 1865)

367. VIRGINIA 36TH INFANTRY REGIMENT

Nickname: 2nd Kanawha Infantry Regiment

Organization: Organized on July 15, 1861. Reduced to eight companies in August 1861. Three companies assigned from the 3rd Kanawha Infantry Regiment. Reorganized with nine companies on May 15, 1862. 2nd Company K organized on April 17, 1864. Dispersed at Waynesborough on March 2, 1865.

First Commander: John A. McCausland (Colonel)

Field Officers: William E. Fife (Major, Lieutenant Colonel)

Benjamin R. Linkous (Lieutenant Colonel)

Legh W. Reid (Lieutenant Colonel)

Thomas Smith (Major, Lieutenant Colonel, Colonel)

Assignments: Forces in Kanawha Valley (July-August 1861)

Army of the Kanawha (August-December 1861)

3rd (Floyd's) Division, Central Army of Kentucky, Department #2 (January 1862)

McCausland's Brigade, 3rd (Floyd's) Division, Central Army of Kentucky, Department #2 (February 1862)

McCausland's Brigade, Floyd's Division, Fort Donelson, Department #2 (February 1862)

McCausland's Brigade, Army of the Kanawha (February-May 1862) ·

Army of the Kanawha, Department of Southwestern Virginia (May-September 1862)

McCausland's-Smith's Brigade, Department of Western Virginia and East
    Tennessee (February 1863-September 1864)
Smith's Brigade, Wharton's Division, Valley District, Department of Northern
    Virginia (September 1864-March 1865)
Battles: Scarey Creek, West Virginia (July 17, 1861)
Fort Donelson (February 12-16, 1862)
Kanawha Campaign (September 1862)
Cloyd's Mountain (May 9, 1864)
New River Bridge (May 10, 1864)
Cedar Creek (October 19, 1864)
Waynesboro (March 2, 1865)
Further Reading: Scott, J. L., *36th Virginia Infantry.*

368. VIRGINIA 37TH INFANTRY REGIMENT

Organization: Organized in state service for one year in April or May 1861.
Transferred to Confederate service on July 1, 1861. Reorganized on April 22,
1862. Field consolidation with 10th and 23rd Infantry Regiments from May 14,
1864, to April 9, 1865. Surrendered at Appomattox Court House, Virginia, on
April 9, 1865.
First Commander: Samuel V. Fulkerson (Colonel)
Field Officers: Robert P. Carson (Lieutenant Colonel)
John F. Terry (Major, Lieutenant Colonel)
Titus V. Williams (Major, Colonel)
Henry C. Wood (Major)
Assignments: Taliaferro's Brigade, Army of the Northwest (September-No-
    vember 1861)
Taliaferro's Brigade, Jackson's Division, Army of the Northwest (November-
    December 1861)
3rd (Taliaferro's) Brigade, Valley District, Department of Northern Virginia
    (December 1861-May 1862)
3rd (Taliaferro's) Brigade, Jackson's Division, Valley District, Department of
    Northern Virginia (May-June 1862)
3rd (Taliaferro's-Warren's-Hampton's-Taliaferro's-Colston's-Steuart's) Bri-
    gade, Jackson's-Trimble's-Johnson's Division, 2nd Corps, Army of Northern
    Virginia (June 1862-May 1864)
Terry's Consolidated Brigade, Gordon's Division, 2nd Corps, Army of North-
    ern Virginia (May-June 1864)
Terry's Consolidated Brigade, Gordon's Division, Valley District, Department
    of Northern Virginia (June-December 1864)
Terry's Consolidated Brigade, Gordon's Division, 2nd Corps, Army of North-
    ern Virginia (December 1864-April 1865)

Battles: Kernstown (March 23, 1862)
McDowell (May 8, 1862)
Shenandoah Valley Campaign of 1862 (May-June 1862)
Seven Days Battles (June 25-July 1, 1862)
Gaines' Mill (June 27, 1862)
Malvern Hill (July 1, 1862)
Cedar Mountain (August 9, 1862)
2nd Bull Run (August 28-30, 1862)
Harpers Ferry (September 12-15, 1862)
Antietam (September 17, 1862)
Fredericksburg (December 13, 1862)
Chancellorsville (May 1-4, 1863)
2nd Winchester (June 14-15, 1863)
Gettysburg (July 1-3, 1863)
Bristoe Campaign (October 1863)
Mine Run Campaign (November-December 1863)
The Wilderness (May 5-6, 1864)
Spotsylvania Court House (May 8-21, 1864)
North Anna (May 22-26, 1864)
Cold Harbor (June 1-3, 1864)
Lynchburg Campaign (June 1864)
Monocacy (July 9, 1864)
3rd Winchester (September 19, 1864)
Fisher's Hill (September 22, 1864)
Cedar Creek (October 19, 1864)
Petersburg Siege (from December 1864) (June 1864-April 1865)
Fort Stedman (March 25, 1865)
Appomattox Court House (April 9, 1865)
Further Reading: Rankin, Thomas M., *37th Virginia Infantry.*

369. VIRGINIA 38TH INFANTRY REGIMENT

Nickname: Pittsylvania Regiment
Organization: Organized in state service for one year on June 12, 1861. Designated as the 38th Infantry Regiment on June 14, 1861, per S.O. #192, Headquarters Virginia Forces. Transferred to Confederate service on July 1, 1861. Reorganized on May 12, 1862. Surrendered at Appomattox Court House, Virginia, on April 9, 1865.
First Commander: Edward C. Edmonds (Colonel)
Field Officers: Joseph R. Cabell (Major, Lieutenant Colonel, Colonel)
Isaac H. Carrington (Major)
George K. Griggs (Major, Lieutenant Colonel, Colonel)

Henderson L. Lee (Major)

George A. Martin (Lieutenant Colonel)

Powhatan B. Whittle (Colonel)

Assignments: 4th (E. K. Smith's) Brigade, Army of the Shenandoah (July 1861)

5th (Forney's) Brigade, Army of the Shenandoah (July 1861)

Forney's-Wilcox's Brigade, 2nd Corps, Army of the Potomac (July 1861-January 1862)

Wilcox's Brigade, G. W. Smith's Division, Potomac District, Department of Northern Virginia (January-March 1862)

Toombs' Brigade, Toombs' Division, Magruder's Command, Department of Northern Virginia (March-May 1862)

Early's-Garland's Brigade, D. H. Hill's Division, Army of Northern Virginia (May-June 1862)

Armistead's Brigade, Huger's-Anderson's Division, Army of Northern Virginia (June-July 1862)

Armistead's Brigade, Anderson's Division, 1st Corps, Army of Northern Virginia (July-September 1862)

Armistead's Brigade, Pickett's Division, 1st Corps, Army of Northern Virginia (September 1862-February 1863)

Armistead's Brigade, Pickett's Division, Department of Virginia and North Carolina (February-April 1863)

Armistead's Brigade, Pickett's Division, Department of Southern Virginia (April-May 1863)

Armistead's Brigade, Pickett's Division, 1st Corps, Army of Northern Virginia (May-September 1863)

Armistead's-Barton's Brigade, Pickett's Division, Department of North Carolina (September-October 1863)

Barton's Brigade, Department of North Carolina (December 1863-February 1864)

Barton's Brigade, Department of Richmond (February-May 1864)

Barton's-Steuart's Brigade, Pickett's Division, 1st Corps, Army of Northern Virginia (May 1864-April 1865)

Battles: Yorktown Siege (April-May 1862)

Williamsburg (May 5, 1862)

Seven Pines (May 31-June 1, 1862)

Seven Days Battles (June 25-July 1, 1862)

Malvern Hill (July 1, 1862)

2nd Bull Run (August 28-30, 1862)

South Mountain (September 14, 1862)

Antietam (September 17, 1862)

Shepherdstown Ford (September 20, 1862)
Fredericksburg (December 13, 1862)
Suffolk Campaign (April-May 1863)
Gettysburg (July 1-3, 1863)
Chester Station (May 10, 1864)
Drewry's Bluff (May 16, 1864)
North Anna (May 22-26, 1864)
Cold Harbor (June 1-3, 1864)
Petersburg Siege (June 1864-April 1865)
Five Forks (April 1, 1865)
Sayler's Creek (April 6, 1865)
Appomattox Court House (April 9, 1865)
Further Reading: Gregory, G. Howard, *38th Virginia Infantry.*

370. VIRGINIA 39TH INFANTRY REGIMENT

Organization: Organized in state service on May 28, 1861. Composed of 11 companies (eight infantry, two cavalry and one artillery). Transferred to Confederate service on July 1, 1861. Mustered out on February 3, 1862, per S.O. #20, Adjutant and Inspector General's Office, dated January 25, 1862, since the regiment had been unable to transfer from the Eastern Shore of Virginia when ordered to do so in November 1861.
First Commander: Charles Smith (Colonel)
Field Officers: Nathaniel R. Cary (Major)
Louis C. H. Finney (Lieutenant Colonel)
Assignment: Eastern Shore of Virginia (May-November 1861)

371. VIRGINIA 40TH INFANTRY REGIMENT

Organization: Organized in state service on May 30, 1861. Transferred to Confederate service on July 1, 1861. Reorganized on April 23, 1862. Surrendered at Appomattox Court House, Virginia, on April 9, 1865.
First Commander: John M. Brockenbrough (Colonel)
Field Officers: Richard A. Claybrook (Lieutenant Colonel)
Fleet W. Cox (Major, Lieutenant Colonel)
Arthur S. Cunningham (Lieutenant Colonel)
Edward T. Stakes (Major)
Warner T. Taliaferro (Major)
Henry H. Walker (Lieutenant Colonel)
Assignments: Department of Fredericksburg (September-October 1861)
Unattached, Aquia District, Department of Northern Virginia (October 1861-March 1862)
Field's Brigade, A. P. Hill's Division, Army of Northern Virginia (May-June 1862)

Field's Brigade, A. P. Hill's Division, 1st Corps, Army of Northern Virginia
    (June-July 1862)
Field's Brigade, A. P. Hill's Division, 2nd Corps, Army of Northern Virginia
    (July 1862-May 1863)
Field's-Walker's Brigade, Heth's Division, 3rd Corps, Army of Northern Vir-
    ginia (May 1863-January 1865)
Mayo's-Barton's Brigade, Department of Richmond (January-March 1865)
Barton's Brigade, G. W. C. Lee's Division, Department of Richmond (March-
    April 1865)
Barton's Brigade, G. W. C. Lee's Division, Army of Northern Virginia (April
    1865)
Battles: Mathias Point (June 27, 1861)
US Occupation of Fredericksburg (April 19, 1862)
Seven Days Battles (June 25-July 1, 1862)
Cedar Mountain (August 9, 1862)
2nd Bull Run (August 28-30, 1862)
Harpers Ferry (September 12-15, 1862)
Antietam (September 17, 1862)
Shepherdstown Ford (September 20, 1862)
Fredericksburg (December 13, 1862)
Chancellorsville (May 1-4, 1863)
Gettysburg (July 1-3, 1863)
Bristoe Campaign (October 1863)
Mine Run Campaign (November-December 1863)
The Wilderness (May 5-6, 1864)
Spotsylvania Court House (May 8-21, 1864)
North Anna (May 22-26, 1864)
Cold Harbor (June 1-3, 1864)
Petersburg Siege (June 1864-April 1865)
Squirrel Level Road (September 29, 1864)
Jones' Farm (September 30, 1864)
Pegram's Farm (October 1, 1864)
Harman Road (October 2, 1864)
Sayler's Creek (April 6, 1865)
Appomattox Court House (April 9, 1865)
Further Reading: Krick, Robert E. L., *40th Virginia Infantry*.

372. VIRGINIA 41ST INFANTRY REGIMENT

Organization: Organized for one year in July 1861. Reorganized on May 1,
1862. Surrendered at Appomattox Court House, Virginia, on April 9, 1865.
First Commander: John R. Chambliss, Jr. (Colonel)

Field Officers: George Blow, Jr. (Lieutenant Colonel)
William H. Etheridge (Major)
Joseph P. Mineteree (Major, Lieutenant Colonel)
William A. Parham (Lieutenant Colonel, Colonel)
Francis W. Smith (Major)
Assignments: Department of Norfolk (July 1861)
Mahone's Brigade, Department of Norfolk (October 1861-April 1862)
Mahone's Brigade, Huger's-Anderson's Division, Army of Northern Virginia
   (April-July 1862)
Mahone's Brigade, Anderson's Division, 1st Corps, Army of Northern Virginia
   (July 1862-May 1863)
Mahone's-Weisiger's Brigade, Anderson's-Mahone's Division, 3rd Corps,
   Army of Northern Virginia (May 1863-April 1865)
Battles: Seven Days Battles (June 25-July 1, 1862)
King's School House (June 25, 1862)
Brackett's (June 30, 1862)
Malvern Hill (July 1, 1862)
2nd Bull Run (August 20-30, 1862)
South Mountain (September 14, 1862)
Antietam (September 17, 1862)
Fredericksburg (December 13, 1862)
Chancellorsville (May 1-4, 1863)
Gettysburg (July 1-3, 1863)
Bristoe Campaign (October 1863)
Mine Run Campaign (November-December 1863)
The Wilderness (May 5-6, 1864)
Spotsylvania Court House (May 8-21, 1864)
North Anna (May 22-26, 1864)
Cold Harbor (June 1-3, 1864)
Petersburg Siege (June 1864-April 1865)
The Crater (July 30, 1864)
Appomattox Court House (April 9, 1865)
Further Reading: Henderson, William D., *41st Virginia Infantry.*

373.   VIRGINIA 42ND INFANTRY REGIMENT

Organization: Organized for one year in July 1861. Reorganized on April 21,
1861. Field consolidation with 21st, 25th, 44th, 48th and 50th Infantry Regiments from May 14, 1864, to April 9, 1865. 50th Infantry Regiment detached
from this field consolidation prior to July 9, 1864. Surrendered at Appomattox
Court House, Virginia, on April 9, 1865.
First Commander: Jesse S. Burks (Colonel)

Field Officers: Pearson B. Adams (Major)
Andrew J. Deyerle (Colonel)
Henry Lane (Major)
Daniel A. Langhorne (Lieutenant Colonel)
William Martin (Lieutenant Colonel)
John E. Penn (Major, Lieutenant Colonel, Colonel)
Jesse M. Richardson (Major)
Samuel H. Saunders (Lieutenant Colonel)
Robert W. Withers (Lieutenant Colonel, Colonel)
Assignments: Burks' Brigade, Army of the Northwest (August-November 1861)
Gilham's Brigade, Loring's Division, Army of the Northwest (November-December 1861)
2nd (Burks'-Campbell's) Brigade, Valley District, Department of Northern Virginia (December 1861-May 1862)
2nd (Campbell's) Brigade, Jackson's Division, Valley District, Department of Northern Virginia (May-June 1862)
J. R. Jones'-J. M. Jones' Brigade, Jackson's-Trimble's-Johnson's Division, 2nd Corps, Army of Northern Virginia (June 1862-May 1864)
Terry's Consolidated Brigade, Gordon's Division, 2nd Corps, Army of Northern Virginia (May-June 1864)
Terry's Consolidated Brigade, Gordon's Division, Valley District, Department of Northern Virginia (June-December 1864)
Terry's Consolidated Brigade, Gordon's Division, 2nd Corps, Army of Northern Virginia (December 1864-April 1865)
Battles: Kernstown (March 23, 1862)
McDowell (May 8, 1862)
Shenandoah Valley Campaign of 1862 (May-June 1862)
Cross Keys (June 8, 1862)
Seven Days Battles (June 25-July 1, 1862)
Gaines' Mill (June 27, 1862)
White Oak Swamp (June 30, 1862)
Malvern Hill (July 1, 1862)
Cedar Mountain (August 9, 1862)
2nd Bull Run (August 28-30, 1862)
Harpers Ferry (September 12-15, 1862)
Antietam (September 17, 1862)
Fredericksburg (December 13, 1862)
Chancellorsville (May 1-4, 1863)
2nd Winchester (June 14-15, 1863)
Gettysburg (July 1-3, 1863)

Bristoe Campaign (October 1863)
Mine Run Campaign (November-December 1863)
The Wilderness (May 5-6, 1864)
Spotsylvania Court House (May 8-21, 1864)
North Anna (May 22-26, 1864)
Cold Harbor (June 1-3, 1864)
Lynchburg Campaign (June 1864)
Monocacy (July 9, 1864)
3rd Winchester (September 19, 1864)
Fisher's Hill (September 22, 1864)
Cedar Creek (October 19, 1864)
Petersburg Siege (from December 1864) (June 1864-April 1865)
Fort Stedman (March 25, 1865)
Appomattox Court House (April 9, 1865)
Further Reading: Chapla, John D., *42nd Virginia Infantry.*

374. VIRGINIA 43RD INFANTRY REGIMENT

Organization: Apparently attempted to organize at Winchester in the summer of 1861. Failed to complete organization.
First Commander: Raphael M. Conn (Colonel)

375. VIRGINIA 44TH INFANTRY BATTALION

Nickname: Petersburg City Battalion
Organization: Organized with three companies on November 3, 1863. Companies D and E organized on February 7 and 29, 1864, respectively. Served in the Reserve Forces of Virginia. Surrendered at Appomattox Court House, Virginia, on April 9, 1865.
First Commander: Peter V. Batte (Major)
Assignments: Unattached, Department of North Carolina (November 1863-May 1864)
1st Military District, Department of North Carolina and Southern Virginia (May 1864-March 1865)
Archer's Battalion, Grimes' Division, 2nd Corps, Army of Northern Virginia (March-April 1865)
Provost Guard, Army of Northern Virginia (Company B) (March-April 1865)
Battles: Petersburg (June 9, 1864)
Petersburg Siege (June 1864-April 1865)
Sayler's Creek (April 6, 1865)
Appomattox Court House (April 9, 1865)

376. VIRGINIA 44TH INFANTRY REGIMENT

Organization: Organized in state service for one year on June 14, 1861. Transferred to Confederate service on July 1, 1861. Company A detached from the regiment on March 13, 1862, per S.O. #55, Adjutant and Inspector General's Office, dated March 10, 1862, and reorganized as Robertson's Heavy Artillery Company. Reorganized with nine companies on May 1, 1862. Field consolidation with 21st, 25th, 42nd, 48th and 50th Infantry Regiments from May 14, 1864, to April 9, 1865. 50th Infantry Regiment detached from this field consolidation prior to July 9, 1864. Surrendered at Appomattox Court House, Virginia, on April 9, 1865.

First Commander: William C. Scott (Colonel)

Field Officers: David W. Anderson (Major)

Thomas R. Buckner (Lieutenant Colonel)

Norvell Cobb (Major, Colonel)

James L. Hubard (Lieutenant Colonel)

Alexander C. Jones (Lieutenant Colonel)

Assignments: Taliaferro's Brigade, Army of the Northwest (August-November 1861)

Johnson's Brigade, Jackson's Division, Army of the Northwest (November 1861)

Army of the Northwest (March 1862)

Conner's Brigade, Army of the Northwest (May 1862)

Elzey's-Early's Brigade, Ewell's Division, Valley District, Department of Northern Virginia (May-June 1862)

Elzey's-Early's Brigade, Ewell's-Early's Division, 2nd Corps, Army of Northern Virginia (June 1862-January 1863)

J. R. Jones'-J. M. Jones' Brigade, Jackson's-Trimble's-Johnson's Division, 2nd Corps, Army of Northern Virginia (January 1863-May 1864)

Terry's Consolidated Brigade, Gordon's Division, 2nd Corps, Army of Northern Virginia (May-June 1864)

Terry's Consolidated Brigade, Gordon's Division, Valley District, Department of Northern Virginia (June-December 1864)

Terry's Consolidated Brigade, Gordon's Division, 2nd Corps, Army of Northern Virginia (December 1864-April 1865)

Battles: Greenbrier River (October 3, 1861)

Kernstown (March 23, 1862)

McDowell (May 8, 1862)

Shenandoah Valley Campaign of 1862 (May-June 1862)

Cross Keys (June 8, 1862)

Port Republic (June 9, 1862)

Seven Days Battles (June 25-July 1, 1862)

Gaines' Mill (June 27, 1862)
White Oak Swamp (June 30, 1862)
Malvern Hill (July 1, 1862)
Cedar Mountain (August 9, 1862)
Bristoe and Manassas Junction (August 26-27, 1862)
2nd Bull Run (August 28-30, 1862)
Harpers Ferry (September 12-15, 1862)
Antietam (September 17, 1862)
Fredericksburg (December 13, 1862)
Chancellorsville (May 1-4, 1863)
2nd Winchester (June 14-15, 1863)
Gettysburg (July 1-3, 1863)
Bristoe Campaign (October 1863)
Mine Run Campaign (November-December 1863)
The Wilderness (May 5-6, 1864)
Spotsylvania Court House (May 8-21, 1864)
North Anna (May 22-26, 1864)
Cold Harbor (June 1-3, 1864)
Lynchburg Campaign (June 1864)
Monocacy (July 9, 1864)
3rd Winchester (September 19, 1864)
Fisher's Hill (September 22, 1864)
Cedar Creek (October 19, 1864)
Petersburg Siege (from December 1864) (June 1864-April 1865)
Fort Stedman (March 25, 1865)
Appomattox Court House (April 9, 1865)
Further Reading: Ruffner, Kevin C., *44th Virginia Infantry.*

377. VIRGINIA 45TH INFANTRY BATTALION

Organization: Organized from April to December 1863 in Logan, Tazewell
and adjoining counties with six companies (lettered A-E and K) from former
members of the 1st Cavalry Regiment, State Line, which had been disbanded
ca. March 31, 1863. Organization completed on December 21, 1863. Dispersed
at Waynesborough on March 2, 1865.

First Commander: Henry M. Beckley (Lieutenant Colonel)

Field Officer: Blake L. Woodson (Major)

Assignments: McCausland's-Smith's Brigade, Department of Western Virginia and East Tennessee (January-September 1864)

Smith's Brigade, Wharton's Division, Valley District, Department of Northern
Virginia (September 1864-March 1865)

Battles: Cloyd's Mountain (May 9, 1864)

New River Bridge (skirmish) (May 10, 1864)
Cedar Creek (October 19, 1864)
Waynesborough (March 2, 1865)

378. VIRGINIA 45TH INFANTRY REGIMENT

Organization: Organized in state service for one year ca. May 29, 1861.
Transferred to Confederate service on July 1, 1861. Company L organized
September 3, 1861. Company L became C, 23rd Infantry Battalion, on January
15, 1862. Reorganized on May 14, 1862. Dispersed at Waynesborough on
March 2, 1865.

First Commander: Henry Heth (Colonel)
Field Officers: William H. Browne (Colonel)
Alexander M. Davis (Major, Lieutenant Colonel)
Benjamin F. Ficklin (Lieutenant Colonel)
Edwin H. Harman (Lieutenant Colonel)
Robert H. Logan (Lieutenant Colonel)
William E. Peters (Lieutenant Colonel, Colonel)
William C. Sanders (Major)
William H. Werth (Major, Lieutenant Colonel)
Gabriel C. Wharton (Major)

Assignments: Army of the Kanawha (September 1861-January 1862)
District of Lewisburg (January-May 1862)
District of Lewisburg, Department of Southwestern Virginia (May 1862)
Army of the Kanawha, Department of Southwestern Virginia (September
    1862)
Echols' Brigade, Department of Western Virginia (February-June 1863)
Wharton's Brigade, Ransom's Division, Department of Western Virginia and
    East Tennessee (October-December 1863)
Saltville, Department of Western Virginia (December 1863-May 1864)
Wharton's Brigade, Department of Western Virginia (May 1864)
Wharton's Brigade, Breckinridge's Division, Army of Northern Virginia (May-
    June 1864)
Wharton's Brigade, Breckinridge's-Wharton's Division, Valley District, De-
    partment of Northern Virginia (June 1864-March 1865)

Battles: Camp Creek, Stone River Valley, West Virginia (May 1, 1862)
Giles Court House, West Virginia (May 10, 1862)
Lewisburg, West Virginia (May 23, 1862)
Kanawha Campaign (September 1862)
White Sulphur Springs (August 26-27, 1863)
Cloyd's Mountain (May 9, 1864)
New Market (May 15, 1864)

Piedmont (June 5, 1864)
North Anna (May 22-26, 1864)
Cold Harbor (June 1-3, 1864)
Lynchburg Campaign (June 1864)
Monocacy (July 9, 1864)
3rd Winchester (September 19, 1864)
Fisher's Hill (September 22, 1864)
Cedar Creek (October 19, 1864)
Waynesborough (March 2, 1865)

379. VIRGINIA 46TH INFANTRY REGIMENT

Nickname: Virginia 1st Infantry Regiment, Wise Legion
Virginia 2nd Infantry Regiment, Wise Legion
Organization: Organized on August 8, 1861. Part of the regiment captured
and paroled at Roanoke Island, North Carolina, on February 8, 1862. Reorganized on May 24, 1862. Captured portion of the regiment declared exchanged
in September 1862.
First Commander: James Lucius Davis (Colonel)
Field Officers: Richard T. W. Duke (Colonel)
Hugh W. Fry, Jr. (Major)
Randolph Harrison (Lieutenant Colonel, Colonel)
James C. Hill (Major)
John H. Richardson (Lieutenant Colonel, Colonel)
Peyton Wise (Major, Lieutenant Colonel)
Assignments: Troops in Kanawha Valley (June-August 1861)
Wise's Brigade (August-December 1861)
District of the Albemarle (Wise's Brigade), Department of Norfolk (December
    1861-February 1862)
Gloucester Point (Crump's Command), Rains' Division, D. H. Hill's Command, Department of Northern Virginia (April-May 1862)
Crump's Brigade, D. H. Hill's Division, Department of Northern Virginia (May
    1862)
Wise's Brigade, Army of Northern Virginia (June-July 1862)
Wise's Brigade, D. H. Hill's Division, Army of Northern Virginia (July 1862)
Wise's Brigade, Unattached, Department of North Carolina and Southern
    Virginia (August-December 1862)
Wise's Brigade, Elzey's Command, Department of North Carolina and Southern Virginia (December 1862-April 1863)
Wise's Brigade, Department of Richmond (April-September 1863)
Wise's Brigade, 1st Military District of South Carolina, Department of South
    Carolina, Georgia and Florida (September-October 1863)

6th Military District of South Carolina, Department of South Carolina, Georgia and Florida (October-November 1863)

Wise's Brigade, 6th Military District of South Carolina, Department of South Carolina, Georgia and Florida (December 1863-February 1864)

District of Florida, Department of South Carolina, Georgia and Florida (February-April 1864)

Wise's Brigade, Johnson's Division, Department of North Carolina and Southern Virginia (May-October 1864)

Wise's Brigade, Johnson's Division, 4th Corps, Army of Northern Virginia (October 1864-April 1865)

Battles: Roanoke Island (February 8, 1862)

Yorktown Siege (April-May 1862)

Williamsburg (May 5, 1862)

Seven Days Battles (June 25-July 1, 1862)

Williamsburg (skirmish) (March 29, 1863)

Pamunkey River, near West Point, Virginia (April 16, 1863)

Charleston Harbor (August-September 1863)

Drewry's Bluff, South Carolina (May 16, 1864)

Bermuda Hundred (May 17-June 14, 1864)

Petersburg (June 9, 1864)

Petersburg Siege (June 1864-April 1865)

Sayler's Creek (April 6, 1865)

Appomattox Court House (April 9, 1865)

380. VIRGINIA 47TH INFANTRY REGIMENT

Organization: Organized for one year on June 11, 1861. Transferred to Confederate service on July 1, 1861. Reorganized on May 1, 1862. Field consolidation with the 55th Infantry from February to April 9, 1865. Surrendered at Appomattox Court House, Virginia, on April 9, 1865.

First Commander: George W. Richardson (Colonel)

Field Officers: James D. Bruce (Major, Lieutenant Colonel)

Charles J. Green (Major)

William J. Green (Lieutenant Colonel)

John W. Lyell (Lieutenant Colonel)

Robert M. Mayo (Major, Colonel)

Edward P. Tayloe (Major)

Assignments: Department of Fredericksburg (September-October 1861)

French's Brigade, Aquia District, Department of Northern Virginia (November 1861-March 1862)

Field's Brigade, A. P. Hill's Division, Army of Northern Virginia (May-June 1862)

Field's Brigade, A. P. Hill's Division, 1st Corps, Army of Northern Virginia (June-July 1862)

Field's Brigade, A. P. Hill's Division, 2nd Corps, Army of Northern Virginia (July 1862-May 1863)

Field's-Walker's Brigade, Heth's Division, 3rd Corps, Army of Northern Virginia (May 1863-January 1865)

Mayo's-Barton's Brigade, Department of Richmond (January-March 1865)

Barton's Brigade, G. W. C. Lee's Division, Department of Richmond (March-April 1865)

Barton's Brigade, G. W. C. Lee's Division, Army of Northern Virginia (April 1865)

Battles: Seven Days Battles (June 25-July 1, 1862)

2nd Bull Run (August 28-30, 1862)

Harpers Ferry (September 12-15, 1862)

Antietam (September 17, 1862)

Shepherdstown Ford (September 20, 1862)

Fredericksburg (December 13, 1862)

Chancellorsville (May 1-4, 1863)

Gettysburg (July 1-3, 1863)

Bristoe Campaign (October 1863)

Mine Run Campaign (November-December 1863)

The Wilderness (May 5-6, 1864)

Spotsylvania Court House (May 8-21, 1864)

North Anna (May 22-26, 1864)

Cold Harbor (June 1-3, 1864)

Petersburg Siege (June 1864-April 1865)

Squirrel Level Road (September 29, 1864)

Jones' Farm (September 30, 1864)

Pegram's Farm (October 1, 1864)

Harman Road (October 2, 1864)

Sayler's Creek (April 6, 1865)

Appomattox Court House (April 9, 1865)

381.   VIRGINIA 48TH INFANTRY REGIMENT

Organization: Organized for one year on September 20, 1861. Reorganized on April 21, 1862. Field consolidation with 21st, 25th, 42nd, 44th and 50th Infantry Regiments from May 14, 1864, to April 9, 1865. 50th Infantry Regiment detached from this field consolidation prior to July 9, 1864. Surrendered at Appomattox Court House, Virginia, on April 9, 1865.

First Commander: John A. Campbell (Colonel)

Field Officers: James C. Campbell (Major)

Robert H. Dungan (Lieutenant Colonel, Colonel)

Wilson Faris (Major)

Thomas S. Garnett (Lieutenant Colonel, Colonel)

David B. Stewart (Major)

Oscar White (Major, Lieutenant Colonel)

Assignments: Burks' Brigade, Army of the Northwest (August-November 1861)

Gilham's Brigade, Loring's Division, Army of the Northwest (November-December 1861)

2nd (Burks-Campbell's) Brigade, Valley District, Department of Northern Virginia (December 1861-May 1862)

2nd (Campbell's) Brigade, Jackson's Division, Valley District, Department of Northern Virginia (May-June 1862)

J. R. Jones'-J. M. Jones' Brigade, Jackson's-Trimble's-Johnson's Division, 2nd Corps, Army of Northern Virginia (June 1862-May 1864)

Terry's Consolidated Brigade, Gordon's Division, 2nd Corps, Army of Northern Virginia (May-June 1864)

Terry's Consolidated Brigade, Gordon's Division, Valley District, Department of Northern Virginia (June-December 1864)

Terry's Consolidated Brigade, Gordon's Division, 2nd Corps, Army of Northern Virginia (December 1864-April 1865)

Battles: Kernstown (March 23, 1862)

McDowell (May 8, 1862)

Shenandoah Valley Campaign of 1862 (May-June 1862)

Cross Keys (June 8, 1862)

Seven Days Battles (June 25-July 1, 1862)

Gaines' Mill (June 27, 1862)

White Oak Swamp (June 30, 1862)

Malvern Hill (July 1, 1862)

Cedar Mountain (August 9, 1862)

2nd Bull Run (August 28-30, 1862)

Harpers Ferry (September 12-15, 1862)

Antietam (September 17, 1862)

Fredericksburg (December 13, 1862)

Chancellorsville (May 1-4, 1863)

2nd Winchester (June 14-15, 1863)

Gettysburg (July 1-3, 1863)

Bristoe Campaign (October 1863)

Mine Run Campaign (November-December 1863)

The Wilderness (May 5-6, 1864)

Spotsylvania Court House (May 8-21, 1864)

North Anna (May 22-26, 1864)
Cold Harbor (June 1-3, 1864)
Lynchburg Campaign (June 1864)
Monocacy (July 9, 1864)
3rd Winchester (September 19, 1864)
Fisher's Hill (September 22, 1864)
Cedar Creek (October 19, 1864)
Petersburg Siege (from December 1864) (June 1864-April 1865)
Fort Stedman (March 25, 1865)
Appomattox Court House (April 9, 1865)
Further Reading: Chapla, John D., *48th Virginia Infantry.*

382.   VIRGINIA 49TH INFANTRY REGIMENT

Organization: Organization for one year commenced in July 1861 and was completed in August 1861. Reorganized on May 1, 1862. Surrendered at Appomattox Court House, Virginia, on April 9, 1865.
First Commander: William Smith (Colonel)
Field Officers: Charles B. Christian (Major, Lieutenant Colonel)
Jonathan C. Gibson (Lieutenant Colonel, Colonel)
Edward Murray (Lieutenant Colonel)
Caleb Smith (Major)
Assignments: Cocke's Brigade, Army of the Potomac (July 1861)
Cocke's Brigade, 1st Corps, Army of the Potomac (July-October 1861)
Cocke's Brigade, Longstreet's Division, 1st Corps, Army of the Potomac (October 1861)
Garrison of Manassas, Potomac District, Department of Northern Virginia (January-March 1862)
G. B. Anderson's Special Brigade, Department of Northern Virginia (March-April 1862)
Featherston's Brigade, D. H. Hill's Division, Department of Northern Virginia (April 1862)
Featherston's Brigade, Rains' Division, D. H. Hill's Command, Department of Northern Virginia (April-May 1862)
Featherston's Brigade, D. H. Hill's Division, Army of Northern Virginia (May-June 1862)
Mahone's Brigade, Huger's-Anderson's Division, Army of Northern Virginia (June-July 1862)
Mahone's Brigade, Anderson's Division, 1st Corps, Army of Northern Virginia (July-August 1862)
Early's-Smith's-Pegram's Brigade, Ewell's-Early's Division, 2nd Corps, Army of Northern Virginia (September 1862-June 1864)

Pegram's Brigade, Ramseur's-Pegram's Division, Valley District, Department of
   Northern Virginia (June-December 1864)
Pegram's-Walker's Brigade, Pegram's Division, 2nd Corps, Army of Northern
   Virginia (December 1864-April 1865)
Battles: 1st Bull Run (three companies) (July 21, 1861)
Yorktown Siege (April-May 1862)
Williamsburg (May 5, 1862)
Seven Pines (May 31-June 1, 1862)
Seven Days Battles (June 25-July 1, 1862)
King's School House (June 25, 1862)
Brackett's (June 30, 1862)
Malvern Hill (July 1, 1862)
2nd Bull Run (August 28-30, 1862)
Antietam (September 17, 1862)
Fredericksburg (December 13, 1862)
Chancellorsville (May 1-4, 1863)
2nd Winchester (June 14-15, 1863)
Gettysburg (July 1-3, 1863)
Bristoe Campaign (October 1863)
Mine Run Campaign (November-December 1863)
The Wilderness (May 5-6, 1864)
Spotsylvania Court House (May 8-21, 1864)
North Anna (May 22-26, 1864)
Cold Harbor (June 1-3, 1864)
Lynchburg Campaign (June 1864)
Monocacy (July 9, 1864)
Fort Stevens (July 11, 1864)
3rd Winchester (September 19, 1864)
Fisher's Hill (September 22, 1864)
Cedar Creek (October 19, 1864)
Petersburg Siege (from December 1864) (June 1864-April 1865)
Hatcher's Run (February 5-7, 1865)
Appomattox Court House (April 9, 1865)

383.   VIRGINIA 50TH INFANTRY REGIMENT

Organization: Organized with 10 infantry companies and three cavalry companies for one year on July 3, 1861. Cavalry Company B mustered out on
September 26, 1861. Cavalry Companies A and C became Companies A and
B, 8th Virginia Cavalry Regiment, respectively, in October 1861. Company L
organized on October 7, 1861, and transferred to the 23rd Infantry Battalion
on January 15, 1862. Regiment reorganized with nine companies on May 25,

1862. 2nd Company G organized on August 26, 1862. Field consolidation with 21st, 25th, 42nd, 44th and 48th Infantry Regiments from May 14, 1864, to prior to July 9, 1864. Dispersed at Waynesborough on March 2, 1865.

First Commander: Alexander W. Reynolds (Colonel)

Field Officers: William W. Finney (Lieutenant Colonel)

Lynville J. Perkins (Major)

Thomas Poage (Colonel)

Logan H. N. Sayler (Major, Lieutenant Colonel)

Charles E. Thorburn (Major)

Alexander S. Vandeventer (Lieutenant Colonel, Colonel)

Assignments: Army of the Kanawha (August-December 1861)

Floyd's Division, Central Army of Kentucky, Department #2 (January-February 1862)

McCausland's Brigade, Floyd's Division, Central Army of Kentucky, Department #2 (February 1862)

McCausland's Brigade, Army of the Kanawha (February-May 1862)

McCausland's Brigade, Department of Southwestern Virginia (May-September 1862)

Unattached, Elzey's Command, Department of North Carolina and Southern Virginia (December 1862)

Colston's Brigade, Elzey's Command, Department of North Carolina and Southern Virginia (December 1862)

Colston's-Pryor's Brigade, French's Command, Department of North Carolina and Southern Virginia (December 1862-February 1863)

Wharton's Brigade, Department of Western Virginia (April-June 1863)

J. M. Jones' Brigade, Johnson's Division, 2nd Corps, Army of Northern Virginia (June 1863-May 1864)

Terry's Consolidated Brigade, Gordon's Division, 2nd Corps, Army of Northern Virginia (May-June 1864)

Terry's Consolidated Brigade, Gordon's Division, Valley District, Department of Northern Virginia (June 1864)

Wharton's-Forsberg's Brigade, Wharton's Division, Valley District, Department of Northern Virginia (July 1864-March 1865)

Battles: Carnifax Ferry (September 10, 1861)

Fort Donelson (February 12-16, 1862)

Kanawha Campaign (September 1862)

Kelly's Store (January 30, 1863)

Blackwater River (January 30, 1863)

Gettysburg (July 1-3, 1863)

Bristoe Campaign (October 1863)

Mine Run Campaign (November-December 1863)

The Wilderness (May 5-6, 1864)
Spotsylvania Court House (May 8-21, 1864)
North Anna (May 22-26, 1864)
Cold Harbor (June 1-3, 1864)
Lynchburg Campaign (June 1864)
Monocacy (July 9, 1864)
3rd Winchester (September 19, 1864)
Fisher's Hill (September 22, 1864)
Cedar Creek (October 19, 1864)
Waynesborough (March 2, 1865)

384. VIRGINIA 51ST INFANTRY REGIMENT

Organization: Organized for one year at Wytheville ca. August 1861. Company L enlisted on August 22, 1861. Company L became Company D, 23rd Infantry Battalion, on January 15, 1862. Reorganized on May 26, 1862. Most of the unit dispersed at Waynesborough on March 2, 1865; a detachment joined Lee's army for its final operation.

First Commander: Gabriel C. Wharton (Colonel)

Field Officers: William T. Akers (Major)

George A. Cunningham (Major, Lieutenant Colonel)

Stephen M. Divkey (Major)

Augustus Forsberg (Lieutenant Colonel, Colonel)

David P. Graham (Major)

James W. Massie (Lieutenant Colonel)

Samuel H. Reynolds (Lieutenant Colonel)

John P. Wolfe (Lieutenant Colonel)

William A. Yonce (Major)

Assignments: Army of the Kanawha (August-December 1861)

Floyd's Division, Central Army of Kentucky, Department #2 (January-February 1862)

Wharton's Brigade, Floyd's Division, Central Army of Kentucky, Department #2 (February 1862)

Wharton's Brigade, Floyd's Division, Fort Donelson, Department #2 (February 1862)

Wharton's Brigade, Army of the Kanawha (February-May 1862)

Wharton's Brigade, Army of the Kanawha, Department of Southwestern Virginia (May-September 1862)

Wharton's Brigade, Department of Western Virginia (February-October 1863)

Wharton's Brigade, Ransom's Division, Department of Western Virginia and East Tennessee (October-November 1863)

Wharton's Brigade, Ransom's Division, Department of East Tennessee (November 1863-March 1864)

Wharton's Brigade, Department of Western Virginia (March-May 1864)

Wharton's Brigade, Breckinridge's Division, Army of Northern Virginia (May-June 1864)

Wharton's-Forsberg's Brigade, Breckinridge's-Wharton's Division, Valley District, Department of Northern Virginia (June 1864-March 1865)

Battles: Gauley River (September 10, 1861)

Carnifax Ferry (September 11, 1861)

Buffalo Mountain (December 13, 1861)

Fort Donelson (February 12-16, 1862)

Lewisburg and Clarksville (February 18, 1862)

Mercer and Princeton (May 17-18, 1862)

Lewisburg, West Virginia (August 28, 1862)

Kanawha Campaign (September 1862)

Fayetteville, West Virginia (September 10, 1862)

Charleston, West Virginia (September 25, 1862)

Pikeville, Kentucky (April 15, 1863)

Chancellorsville (May 1-4, 1863)

Hanover, Pennsylvania (July 1, 1863)

Chattanooga Siege (September-November 1863)

Knoxville Siege (November-December 1863)

Knoxville (February 1, 1864)

New Market (May 15, 1864)

North Anna (May 22-26, 1864)

Totopotomoy Creek (May 30, 1864)

Cold Harbor (June 1-3, 1864)

Lynchburg Campaign (June 1864)

Frederick, Maryland (July 7-8, 1864)

Monocacy (July 9, 1864)

Fort Stevens (July 11, 1864)

Rockville (July 13, 1864)

Kernstown (July 24, 1864)

Winchester (August 17, 1864)

3rd Winchester (September 19, 1864)

Fisher's Hill (September 22, 1864)

Harrisonburg (September 23, 1864)

Brown's Gap (September 26, 1864)

Cedar Creek (October 19, 1864)

Leetown, West Virginia (December 1, 1864)

Fisherville (January 7, 1865)

Waynesborough (March 2, 1865)
Ivory Creek (March 3, 1865)
Charlottesville (March 6, 1865)
Union Furnace (detachment) (March 27, 1865)
Fort Stedman (detachment) (March 25, 1865)
Further Reading: Davis, James A., *51st Virginia Infantry.*

385.   VIRGINIA 52ND INFANTRY REGIMENT

Organization: Organized in state service for one year on August 19, 1861.
Reorganized in Confederate service for three years on May 1, 1862. Surrendered
at Appomattox Court House, Virginia, on April 9, 1865.
First Commander: John B. Baldwin (Colonel)
Field Officers: Michael G. Harman (Lieutenant Colonel, Colonel)
John D. Lilley (Major, Lieutenant Colonel)
John D. Ross (Major, Lieutenant Colonel)
James H. Skinner (Lieutenant Colonel, Colonel)
Thomas H. Watkins (Major, Lieutenant Colonel)
Assignments: H. R. Jackson's Brigade, Army of the Northwest (August 1861-
    November 1861)
Johnson's Brigade, Jackson's Division, Army of the Northwest (November-De-
    cember 1861)
Army of the Northwest (March 1862)
Scott's Brigade, Army of the Northwest (May 1862)
Scott's-Steuart's-Scott's Brigade, Ewell's Division, Valley District, Department
    of Northern Virginia (May-June 1862)
Elzey's-Early's-Smith's-Pegram's Brigade, Ewell's-Early's-Ramseur's Division,
    2nd Corps, Army of Northern Virginia (June 1862-June 1864)
Pegram's Brigade, Ramseur's-Pegram's Division, Valley District, Department of
    Northern Virginia (June-December 1864)
Pegram's-Walker's Brigade, Pegram's Division, 2nd Corps, Army of Northern
    Virginia (December 1864-April 1865)
Battles: Camp Alleghany, West Virginia (December 13, 1861)
McDowell (May 8, 1862)
Shenandoah Valley Campaign of 1862 (May-June 1862)
Cross Keys (June 8, 1862)
Port Republic (June 9, 1862)
Seven Days Battles (June 25-July 1, 1862)
Gaines' Mill (June 27, 1862)
Malvern Hill (July 1, 1862)
Cedar Mountain (August 9, 1862)
Bristoe and Manassas Junction (August 26-27, 1862)

2nd Bull Run (August 28-30, 1862)
Chantilly (September 1, 1862)
Harpers Ferry (September 12-15, 1862)
Antietam (September 17, 1862)
Fredericksburg (December 13, 1862)
Chancellorsville (May 1-4, 1863)
2nd Winchester (June 14-15, 1863)
Gettysburg (July 1-3, 1863)
Bristoe Campaign (October 1863)
Mine Run Campaign (November-December 1863)
The Wilderness (May 5-6, 1864)
Spotsylvania Court House (May 8-21, 1864)
North Anna (May 22-26, 1864)
Totopotomoy Creek (May 30, 1864)
Cold Harbor (June 1-3, 1864)
Lynchburg Campaign (June 1864)
Monocacy (July 9, 1864)
Fort Stevens (July 11, 1864)
3rd Winchester (September 19, 1864)
Fisher's Hill (September 22, 1864)
Cedar Creek (October 19, 1864)
Petersburg Siege (from December 1864) (June 1864-April 1865)
Appomattox Court House (April 9, 1865)
Further Reading: Driver, Robert J., Jr., *52nd Virginia Infantry*.

386.   Virginia 53rd Infantry Regiment

Organization: Organized by the consolidation of Montague's and Tomlin's Infantry Battalions and Waddill's Infantry Company on December 1, 1861, per S.O. #214, Adjutant and Inspector General's Office, dated November 9, 1861. Reorganized in May 1862. Those men liable to conscription in the 5th Infantry Battalion assigned to this regiment per S.O. #209, Adjutant and Inspector General's Office, dated September 6, 1862. Surrendered at Appomattox Court House, Virginia, on April 9, 1865.

First Commander: Carter L. Stevenson (Colonel)
Field Officers: William R. Aylett (Major, Lieutenant Colonel)
Henry A. Edmondson (Major)
John R. Grammer, Jr. (Major, Lieutenant Colonel, Colonel)
William Leigh (Major)
Rawley W. Martin (Major, Lieutenant Colonel)
Edgar B. Montague (Lieutenant Colonel)
John C. Timberlake (Major, Lieutenant Colonel)

Harrison B. Tomlin (Colonel)

George M. Waddill (Major, Lieutenant Colonel)

Assignments: Wise's Brigade (September-October 1861)

Rains' Division, Department of the Peninsula (January-April 1862)

McLaws' Division, Department of the Peninsula (one company) (January-April 1862)

Williamsburg and Spratley's (B. S. Ewell's Command), Department of the Peninsula (January-April 1862)

Armistead's Brigade, Huger's-Anderson's Division, Army of Northern Virginia (June-July 1862)

Armistead's Brigade, Anderson's Division, 1st Corps, Army of Northern Virginia (July-September 1862)

Armistead's Brigade, Pickett's Division, 1st Corps, Army of Northern Virginia (September 1862-February 1863)

Armistead's Brigade, Pickett's Division, Department of Virginia and North Carolina (February-April 1863)

Armistead's Brigade, Pickett's Division, Department of Southern Virginia (April-May 1863)

Armistead's Brigade, Pickett's Division, 1st Corps, Army of Northern Virginia (May-September 1863)

Armistead's-Barton's Brigade, Pickett's Division, Department of North Carolina (September-October 1863)

Barton's Brigade, Department of North Carolina (December 1863-February 1864)

Barton's Brigade, Department of Richmond (February-May 1864)

Barton's-Steuart's Brigade, Pickett's Division, 1st Corps, Army of Northern Virginia (May 1864-April 1865)

Battles: Yorktown Siege (April-May 1862)

Williamsburg (May 5, 1862)

Seven Pines (May 31-June 1, 1862)

Seven Days Battles (June 25-July 1, 1862)

King's School House (June 25, 1862)

Malvern Hill (July 1, 1862)

2nd Bull Run (August 28-30, 1862)

South Mountain (September 14, 1862)

Antietam (September 17, 1862)

Shepherdstown Ford (September 20, 1862)

Fredericksburg (December 13, 1862)

Suffolk Campaign (April-May 1863)

Gettysburg (July 1-3, 1863)

Chester Station (May 10, 1864)

Drewry's Bluff (May 16, 1864)
North Anna (May 22-26, 1864)
Cold Harbor (June 1-3, 1864)
Petersburg Siege (June 1864-April 1865)
Chaffin's Farm (September 29, 1864)
Five Forks (April 1, 1865)
Sayler's Creek (April 6, 1865)
Appomattox Court House (April 9, 1865)

387. VIRGINIA 54TH CONSOLIDATED INFANTRY BATTALION

Organization: Organized with nine companies by the consolidation of the 54th and 63rd Infantry Regiments at Smithfield, North Carolina, on April 9, 1865. Surrendered at Durham Station, Orange County, North Carolina, on April 26, 1865.

First Commander: Connally H. Lynch (Lieutenant Colonel)

Assignment: Pettus' Brigade, Stevenson's Division 2nd Corps, Army of Tennessee (April 1865)

Battle: Carolinas Campaign (February-April 1865)

388. VIRGINIA 54TH INFANTRY REGIMENT

Organization: Organized with only four companies in state service for one year on September 10, 1861. Companies B and G organized on September 16, 1861. Companies D, H and I organized on October 1, 1861. Company K organized on October 10, 1861, completing the regimental organization. Regiment reorganized on May 13, 1862. Mustered into Confederate service for the war on May 13, 1862. Consolidated with the 63rd Infantry Regiment at Smithfield, North Carolina, and designated as the 54th Consolidated Infantry Battalion on April 9, 1865.

First Commander: Robert C. Trigg (Colonel)

Field Officers: John S. Deyerle (Major)
Henry A. Edmundson (Lieutenant Colonel)
Austin Harman (Major)
William B. Shelor (Major, Lieutenant Colonel)
James C. Taylor (Major)
John J. Wade (Major, Lieutenant Colonel)

Assignments: Wise's Brigade (September-October 1861)
Marshall's Brigade, Army of Eastern Kentucky, Department #2 (February-May 1862)
District of Abingdon (May 1862)
District of Abingdon, Department of Southwestern Virginia (May-September 1862)

Unattached, Elzey's Command, Department of North Carolina and Southern Virginia (December 1862)

Colston's Brigade, Elzey's Command, Department of North Carolina and Southern Virginia (December 1862)

Colston's-Pryor's-Colston's Brigade, French's Command, Department of North Carolina and Southern Virginia (December 1862-March 1863)

Unattached, Department of East Tennessee (April 1863)

Unattached, Department of Southwestern Virginia (April 1863)

Trigg's Brigade, Preston's Division, Buckner's Corps, Army of Tennessee (September-October 1863)

Trigg's Brigade, Buckner's Division, 1st Corps, Army of Tennessee (October-November 1863)

Reynolds' Brigade, Stevenson's Division, 1st Corps, Army of Tennessee (November 1863-February 1864)

Reynolds' Brigade, Stevenson's Division, 2nd Corps, Army of Tennessee (February-September 1864)

Reynolds' and Brown's Consolidated-Palmer's Brigade, Stevenson's Division, 2nd Corps, Army of Tennessee (September 1864-April 1865)

Battles: Middle Creek, Kentucky (January 10, 1862)

Wolf Creek, West Virginia (May 15, 1862)

Princeton, West Virginia (May 15-17, 1862)

Kelly's Store (January 30, 1863)

Chickamauga, Georgia (September 19-20, 1863)

Chattanooga Siege (September-November 1863)

Chattanooga (November 23-25, 1863)

Atlanta Campaign (May-September 1864)

Kolb's Farm (June 22, 1864)

Peach Tree Creek (July 20, 1864)

Atlanta (July 22, 1864)

Atlanta Siege (July-September 1864)

Carolinas Campaign (February-April 1865)

Bentonville (March 19-21, 1865)

389. VIRGINIA 55TH INFANTRY REGIMENT

Organization: Organized for one year by the addition of three companies to the Essex and Middlesex Infantry Battalion (Major William N. Ward) in September 1861. Companies I, K and L assigned in April 1862. Company B became the Middlesex Artillery Battery on April 28, 1862. Reorganized on May 1, 1862. Company F, 5th Alabama Infantry Battalion, assigned as Company M on June 10, 1862. Field consolidation with 47th Infantry Regiment from

February 1865 to April 9, 1865. Surrendered at Appomattox Court House, Virginia, on April 9, 1865.

First Commander: Francis Malory (Colonel)

Field Officers: Robert H. Archer (Lieutenant Colonel)

Thomas M. Burke (Major)

William S. Christian (Major, Lieutenant Colonel, Colonel)

Robert B. Fauntleroy (Major)

Charles N. Lawson (Major)

Evan Rice (Major, Lieutenant Colonel)

Andrew D. Saunders (Major)

William N. Ward (Major)

Assignments: Department of Fredericksburg (September-October 1861)

Unattached, Aquia District, Department of Northern Virginia (October 1861-March 1862)

Field's Brigade, A. P. Hill's Division, Army of Northern Virginia (May-June 1862)

Field's Brigade, A. P. Hill's Division, 1st Corps, Army of Northern Virginia (June-July 1862)

Field's Brigade, A. P. Hill's Division, 2nd Corps, Army of Northern Virginia (July 1862-May 1863)

Field's-Walker's Brigade, Heth's Division, 3rd Corps, Army of Northern Virginia (May 1863-January 1865)

Mayo's-Barton's Brigade, Department of Richmond (January-March 1865)

Barton's Brigade, G. W. C. Lee's Division, Department of Richmond (March-April 1865)

Barton's Brigade, G. W. C. Lee's Division, Army of Northern Virginia (April 1865)

Battles: US occupation of Fredericksburg (April 19, 1862)

Seven Days Battles (June 25-July 1, 1862)

Gaines' Mill (June 27, 1862)

Cedar Mountain (August 9, 1862)

2nd Bull Run (August 28-30, 1862)

Harpers Ferry (September 12-15, 1862)

Antietam (September 17, 1862)

Shepherdstown Ford (September 20, 1862)

Fredericksburg (December 13, 1862)

Chancellorsville (May 1-4, 1863)

Gettysburg (July 1-3, 1863)

Bristoe Campaign (October 1863)

Mine Run Campaign (November-December 1863)

The Wilderness (May 5-6, 1864)

Spotsylvania Court House (May 8-21, 1864)
North Anna (May 22-26, 1864)
Cold Harbor (June 1-3, 1864)
Petersburg Siege (June 1864-April 1865)
Squirrel Level Road (September 29, 1864)
Jones' Farm (September 30, 1864)
Pegram's Farm (October 1, 1864)
Harman Road (October 2, 1864)
Sayler's Creek (April 6, 1865)
Appomattox Court House (April 9, 1865)

390.   VIRGINIA 56TH INFANTRY REGIMENT

Organization: Organized for one year on September 23, 1861, per S.O. #285, Adjutant and Inspector General's Office. Reorganized on May 3, 1862. Surrendered at Appomattox Court House, Virginia, on April 9, 1865.

First Commander: William D. Stuart (Colonel)

Field Officers: William E. Green (Major, Lieutenant Colonel)
John B. McPhail, Jr. (Major)
Philip E. Slaughter (Lieutenant Colonel, Colonel)
Timoleon Smith (Major, Lieutenant Colonel)

Assignments: Wise's Brigade (September-October 1861)
Wharton's Brigade, Floyd's Division, Central Army of Kentucky, Department #2 (January-February 1862)
Wharton's Brigade, Floyd's Division, Fort Donelson, Department #2 (February 1862)
Pickett's Brigade, Longstreet's Division, Army of Northern Virginia (June 1862)
Pickett's Brigade, Longstreet's Division, 1st Corps, Army of Northern Virginia (June-August 1862)
Pickett's Brigade, Kemper's Division, 1st Corps, Army of Northern Virginia (August-September 1862)
Pickett's Brigade, D. R. Jones' Division, 1st Corps, Army of Northern Virginia (September 1862)
Pickett's-Garnett's Brigade, Pickett's Division, 1st Corps, Army of Northern Virginia (September 1862-February 1863)
Garnett's Brigade, Pickett's Division, Department of Virginia and North Carolina (February-April 1863)
Garnett's Brigade, Pickett's Division, Department of Southern Virginia (April-May 1863)
Garnett's-Hunton's Brigade, Pickett's Division, 1st Corps, Army of Northern Virginia (May-September 1863)

Hunton's Brigade, Department of Richmond (September 1863-May 1864)
Hunton's Brigade, Pickett's Division, 1st Corps, Army of Northern Virginia
 (May 1864-April 1865)
Battles: Fort Donelson (February 12-16, 1862)
Seven Days Battles (June 25-July 1, 1862)
Gaines' Mill (June 27, 1862)
Frayser's Farm (June 30, 1862)
2nd Bull Run (August 28-30, 1862)
South Mountain (September 14, 1862)
Antietam (September 17, 1862)
Fredericksburg (December 13, 1862)
Gettysburg (July 1,3-, 1863)
North Anna (May 22-26, 1864)
Cold Harbor (June 1-3, 1864)
Petersburg Siege (June 1864-April 1865)
Chaffin's Farm (September 29, 1864)
Five Forks (April 1, 1865)
Sayler's Creek (April 6, 1865)
Appomattox Court House (April 9, 1865)

391. VIRGINIA 57TH INFANTRY REGIMENT

Organization: Organized by the addition of five companies to Keen's Infantry
Battalion on September 23, 1861, per S.O. #285, Adjutant and Inspector
General's Office. Reorganized on May 7, 1862. Surrendered at Appomattox
Court House, Virginia, on April 9, 1865.
First Commander: Lewis A. Armistead (Colonel)
Field Officers: George W. Carr (Lieutenant Colonel, Colonel)
David Dyer (Major, Lieutenant Colonel, Colonel)
Clement R. Fontaine (Major, Colonel)
Garland B. Hanes (Major)
David P. Heckman (Major)
Waddy T. James (Lieutenant Colonel)
Elisha F. Keen (Major, Lieutenant Colonel, Colonel)
John B. Magruder (Major, Lieutenant Colonel, Colonel)
William H. Ramsey (Lieutenant Colonel)
Andrew J. Smith (Major)
Benjamin H. Wade (Major, Lieutenant Colonel)
Assignments: Army of the Kanawha (November 1861)
Armistead's Brigade, Huger's-Anderson's Division, Army of Northern Virginia
 (April-July 1862)

Armistead's Brigade, Anderson's Division, 1st Corps, Army of Northern Virginia (July-September 1862)

Armistead's Brigade, Pickett's Division, 1st Corps, Army of Northern Virginia (September 1862-February 1863)

Armistead's Brigade, Pickett's Division, Department of Virginia and North Carolina (February-April 1863)

Armistead's Brigade, Pickett's Division, Department of Southern Virginia (April-May 1863)

Armistead's Brigade, Pickett's Division, 1st Corps, Army of Northern Virginia (May-September 1863)

Armistead's-Barton's Brigade, Pickett's Division, Department of North Carolina (September-October 1863)

Barton's Brigade, Department of North Carolina (December 1863-February 1864)

Barton's Brigade, Department of Richmond (February-May 1864)

Barton's Brigade, Ransom's Division, Department of North Carolina and Southern Virginia (May 1864)

Barton's-Steuart's Brigade, Pickett's Division, 1st Corps, Army of Northern Virginia (May 1864-April 1865)

Battles: Seven Days Battles (June 25-July 1, 1862)

Malvern Hill (July 1, 1862)

2nd Bull Run (August 28-30, 1862)

Antietam (September 17, 1862)

Shepherdstown Ford (September 20, 1862)

Fredericksburg (December 13, 1862)

Suffolk Campaign (April-May 1863)

Gettysburg (July 1-3, 1863)

Chester Station (May 10, 1864)

Drewry's Bluff (May 16, 1864)

North Anna (May 22-26, 1864)

Cold Harbor (June 1-3, 1864)

Dinwiddie Court House (March 31, 1865)

Five Forks (April 1, 1865)

Sayler's Creek (April 6, 1865)

Appomattox Court House (April 9, 1865)

Further Reading: Sublett, Charles W., *57th Virginia Infantry.*

392.   VIRGINIA 58TH INFANTRY REGIMENT

Organization: Organized for one year on October 13, 1861. Reorganized on May 1, 1862. Surrendered at Appomattox Court House, Virginia, on April 9, 1865.

First Commander: Edmond Goode (Colonel)
Field Officers: Francis H. Board (Lieutenant Colonel, Colonel)
George E. Booker (Major)
Stapleton Crutchfield (Major, Lieutenant Colonel)
John G. Kasey (Major, Lieutenant Colonel)
Samuel H. Letcher (Lieutenant Colonel, Colonel)
Edward T. Walker (Major)
Assignments: Scott's Brigade, Army of the Northwest (May 1862)
Scott's-Steuart's-Scott's Brigade, Ewell's Division, Valley District, Department of Northern Virginia (May-June 1862)
Elzey's-Early's-Smith's-Pegram's Brigade, Ewell's-Early's-Ramseur's Division, 2nd Corps, Army of Northern Virginia (June 1862-June 1864)
Pegram's Brigade, Ramseur's-Pegram's Division, Valley District, Department of Northern Virginia (June-December 1864)
Pegram's-Walker's Brigade, Pegram's Division, 2nd Corps, Army of Northern Virginia (December 1864-April 1865)
Battles: McDowell (May 8, 1862)
Shenandoah Valley Campaign of 1862 (May-June 1862)
Harrisonburg (June 6, 1862)
Cross Keys (June 8, 1862)
Port Republic (June 9, 1862)
Seven Days Battles (June 25-July 1, 1862)
Gaines' Mill (June 27, 1862)
Malvern Hill (July 1, 1862)
Cedar Mountain (August 9, 1862)
Bristoe and Manassas Junction (August 26-27, 1862)
2nd Bull Run (August 28-30, 1862)
Chantilly (September 1, 1862)
Harpers Ferry (September 12-15, 1862)
Antietam (September 17, 1862)
Fredericksburg (December 13, 1862)
Chancellorsville (May 1-4, 1863)
2nd Winchester (June 14-15, 1863)
Bristoe Campaign (October 1863)
Mine Run Campaign (November-December 1863)
The Wilderness (May 5-6, 1864)
Spotsylvania Court House (May 8-21, 1864)
North Anna (May 22-26, 1864)
Totopotomoy Creek (May 30, 1864)
Cold Harbor (June 1-3, 1864)
Lynchburg Campaign (June 1864)

Monocacy (July 9, 1864)
Fort Stevens (July 11, 1864)
Winchester (July 20, 1864)
3rd Winchester (September 19, 1864)
Fisher's Hill (September 22, 1864)
Cedar Creek (October 19, 1864)
Petersburg Siege (from December 1864) (June 1864-April 1865)
Fort Stedman (March 25, 1865)
Appomattox Court House (April 9, 1865)

393. VIRGINIA 59TH INFANTRY REGIMENT

Nickname: 2nd Infantry Regiment, Wise Legion

Organization: Organized for one year on August 8, 1861, per S.O. #290, Headquarters, Wise's Brigade. Much of the regiment captured and paroled at Roanoke Island, North Carolina, on February 8, 1862. Portion that avoided capture became the 26th Infantry Battalion and never rejoined the regiment. Portion that had been captured declared exchanged about September 1862. Merged with the 28th Infantry Battalion as the 59th Infantry Regiment on November 1, 1862. Surrendered at Appomattox Court House, Virginia, on April 9, 1865.

First Commander: Charles F. Henningsen (Colonel)

Field Officers: Frank P. Anderson (Lieutenant Colonel)

Joseph Jones (Lieutenant Colonel)

John Lawson (Major)

Robert G. Mosby (Major)

William B. Tabb (Colonel)

Assignments: District of the Albemarle (Wise's Brigade), Department of Norfolk (December 1861-February 1862)

Wise's Brigade, Department of Northern Virginia (May 1862)

Wise's Brigade, D. H. Hill's Division, Army of Northern Virginia (May-June 1862)

Wise's Brigade, Army of Northern Virginia (June-July 1862)

Wise's Brigade, D. H. Hill's Division, Army of Northern Virginia (July 1862)

Wise's Brigade, Unattached, Department of North Carolina and Southern Virginia (August-December 1862)

Wise's Brigade, Elzey's Command, Department of North Carolina and Southern Virginia (December 1862-April 1863)

Wise's Brigade, Department of Richmond (April-September 1863)

Wise's Brigade, 1st Military District of South Carolina, Department of South Carolina, Georgia and Florida (September-October 1863)

6th Military District of South Carolina, Department of South Carolina, Georgia and Florida (October-November 1863)

Wise's Brigade, 6th Military District of South Carolina, Department of South Carolina, Georgia and Florida (December 1863-February 1864)

District of Florida, Department of South Carolina, Georgia and Florida (February-April 1864)

Wise's Brigade, Johnson's Division, Department of North Carolina and Southern Virginia (May-October 1864)

Wise's Brigade, Johnson's Division, 4th Corps, Army of Northern Virginia (October 1864-April 1865)

Battles: Scarey Creek, West Virginia (July 17, 1861)

Hawk's Nest, West Virginia (September 2, 1861)

Roanoke Island (February 8, 1862)

Seven Days Battles (June 25-July 1, 1862)

Olive Branch Church, Virginia (skirmish) (four companies) (February 7, 1863)

Williamsburg (skirmish) (March 29, 1863)

Charleston Harbor (August-September 1863)

Nottoway Bridge (May 8, 1864)

Petersburg Siege (June 1864-April 1865)

The Crater (July 30, 1864)

Sayler's Creek (April 6, 1865)

Appomattox Court House (April 9, 1865)

394. VIRGINIA 60TH INFANTRY REGIMENT

Nickname: Virginia 3rd Infantry Regiment, Wise Legion

Organization: Organized for one year on August 13, 1861. Company L assigned ca. September 29, 1861. 1st Company H transferred to the 59th Infantry Regiment and Company L became 2nd Company H on November 5, 1861, per S.O. #206, Adjutant and Inspector General's Office. Reorganized on April 27, 1862. Dispersed at Waynesborough on March 2, 1865.

First Commander: William E. Starke (Colonel)

Field Officers: James L. Corley (Lieutenant Colonel)

William A. Gilliam (Lieutenant Colonel)

George W. Hammond (Major, Lieutenant Colonel)

Buehring H. Jones (Lieutenant Colonel, Colonel)

William S. Rowan (Major)

James W. Spalding (Lieutenant Colonel)

John C. Summers (Major, Lieutenant Colonel)

James W. Sweeney (Major, Lieutenant Colonel)

Jacob N. Taylor (Major)

Assignments: District of Cape Fear, Department of North Carolina (April 1862)

Field's Brigade, A. P. Hill's Division, Army of Northern Virginia (June 1862)

Field's Brigade, A. P. Hill's Division, 1st Corps, Army of Northern Virginia (June-July 1862)

McCausland's-Smith's Brigade, Department of Western Virginia and East Tennessee (February 1863-September 1864)

Smith's Brigade, Wharton's Division, Valley District, Department of Northern Virginia (September 1864-March 1865)

Battles: Sewell Mountain (September 27, 1861)

Seven Days Battles (June 25-July 1, 1862)

Gaines' Mill (June 27, 1862)

Cloyd's Mountain (May 9, 1864)

Piedmont (June 5, 1864)

Cedar Creek (October 19, 1864)

Waynesborough (March 2, 1865)

395. VIRGINIA 61ST INFANTRY REGIMENT

Organization: Organized at Petersburg by the increase of the 7th Infantry Battalion to a regiment on May 22, 1862. Organization not finalized until October 1, 1862. Was originally intended to be a regiment of heavy artillery for the defense of Portsmouth and Norfolk. After their fall, the War Department determined to turn the regiment into an infantry unit. Surrendered at Appomattox Court House, Virginia, on April 9, 1865.

First Commander: Samuel M. Wilson (Colonel)

Field Officers: Virginia D. Groner (Colonel)

Charles R. McAlpine (Major)

William F. Niemeyer (Lieutenant Colonel)

William H. Stewart (Major, Lieutenant Colonel)

Assignments: Unattached, Department of North Carolina (July-August 1862)

Mahone's Brigade, Anderson's Division, 1st Corps, Army of Northern Virginia (September 1862-May 1863)

Mahone's-Weisiger's Brigade, Anderson's-Mahone's Division, 3rd Corps, Army of Northern Virginia (May 1863-April 1865)

Battles: Antietam (September 17, 1862)

Catlett's Station (September 29, 1862)

Fredericksburg (December 13, 1862)

Zoah Church (April 30, 1863)

Chancellorsville (May 1-4, 1863)

Gettysburg (July 1-3, 1863)

Bristoe Campaign (October 1863)
Bristoe Station (October 14, 1863)
Mine Run Campaign (November-December 1863)
The Wilderness (May 5-6, 1864)
Spotsylvania Court House (May 8-21, 1864)
North Anna (May 22-26, 1864)
Totopotomoy Creek (May 30, 1864)
Cold Harbor (June 1-3, 1864)
Frayser's Farm (June 13, 1864)
Petersburg Siege (June 1864-April 1865)
Wilcox's Farm (June 22, 1864)
Gurley House (June 23, 1864)
The Crater (July 30, 1864)
Johnson's Farm (August 19, 1864)
Reams' Station (August 25, 1864)
Burgess' Mill (October 27, 1864)
Hatcher's Run (February 5-7, 1865)
Cumberland Church (April 7, 1865)
Appomattox Court House (April 9, 1865)
Further Reading: Trask, Benjamin H., *61st Virginia Infantry*. Stewart, William H., *A Pair of Blankets*.

396. VIRGINIA 62ND INFANTRY REGIMENT

Nicknames: Virginia 1st Cavalry Regiment Partisan Rangers
62nd Virginia Partisan Rangers Regiment
Virginia 62nd Cavalry Regiment
Organization: Organized for the war with a mixture of infantry and cavalry companies on September 9, 1862. Companies 1st D, 1st G, 1st H, 1st L, 1st M, N, O, P and Q transferred to the 18th Cavalry Regiment ca. December 15, 1862. 2nd Companies A, B, F and I assigned from the 25th Infantry Regiment ca. January 25, 1863. 1st Company A became Staunton Artillery Battery in about February 1863. Regiment mounted in late 1863. Company C, 41st Cavalry Battalion, assigned as 2nd Company L. 2nd Company M assigned September 18, 1864. Apparently disbanded in April 1865.
First Commander: John D. Imboden (Colonel)
Field Officers: Robert L. Doyle (Lieutenant Colonel)
Samuel H. Hall (Major)
George W. Imboden (Major)
David B. Lang (Major, Lieutenant Colonel)
George H. Smith (Colonel)

Assignments: Northwestern Virginia Brigade, Department of Northern Virginia (March-July 1863)

Valley District, Department of Northern Virginia (July-December 1863)

Imboden's Command, Valley District, Department of Northern Virginia (December 1863-January 1864)

Northwestern Virginia Brigade, Department of Northern Virginia (February-June 1864)

Imboden's Brigade, Ransom's-Lomax's Cavalry Division, Valley District, Department of Northern Virginia (June 1864-April 1865)

Battles: Imboden's Expedition into Tucker County, West Virginia (November 8-14, 1862)

Jones'-Imboden's West Virginia Raid (April 1863)

Gettysburg (July 1-3, 1863)

Greencastle, Pennsylvania (July 5, 1863)

Williamsport (July 5, 1863)

New Market (May 15, 1864)

Lynchburg Campaign (June 1864)

Monocacy (July 9, 1864)

near Bunker Hill (September 5, 1864)

3rd Winchester (September 19, 1864)

Fisher's Hill (September 22, 1864)

Woodstock (September 23, 1864)

Cedar Creek (October 19, 1864)

Further Reading: Delauter, Robert U., Jr., *62nd Virginia Infantry.*

397.   VIRGINIA 63RD INFANTRY REGIMENT

Organization: Organized for three years or the war on May 24, 1862. Consolidated with the 54th Infantry Regiment at Smithfield, North Carolina, and designated as the 54th Consolidated Infantry Battalion on April 9, 1865.

First Commander: John J. McMahon (Colonel)

Field Officers: David C. Dunn (Lieutenant Colonel)

James M. French (Major, Colonel)

Connally H. Lynch (Lieutenant Colonel)

Assignments: Williams' Brigade, Army of the Kanawha, Department of Southwestern Virginia (August-September 1862)

Unattached, Elzey's Command, Department of North Carolina and Southern Virginia (January-December 1862)

Colston's Brigade, Elzey's Command, Department of North Carolina and Southern Virginia (December 1862)

Colston's-Pryor's-Colston's Brigade, French's Command, Department of North Carolina and Southern Virginia (December 1862-March 1863)

Williams' Brigade, Department of Western Virginia (April-May 1863)
Unattached, Department of Southwestern Virginia (April 1863)
Kelly's Brigade, Preston's Division, Buckner's Corps, Army of Tennessee (September-October 1863)
Kelly's Brigade, Buckner's Division, 1st Corps, Army of Tennessee (October-November 1863)
Reynolds' Brigade, Stevenson's Division, 1st Corps, Army of Tennessee (November 1863-February 1864)
Reynolds' Brigade, Stevenson's Division, 2nd Corps, Army of Tennessee (February-September 1864)
Reynolds' and Brown's Consolidated-Palmer's Brigade, Stevenson's Division, 2nd Corps, Army of Tennessee (September 1864-April 1865)
Battles: Kanawha Campaign (September 1862)
Chickamauga (September 19-20, 1863)
Chattanooga Siege (September-November 1863)
Chattanooga (November 23-25, 1863)
Atlanta Campaign (May-September 1864)
Kolb's Farm (June 22, 1864)
Peach Tree Creek (July 20, 1864)
Atlanta (July 22, 1864)
Atlanta Siege (July-September 1864)
Carolinas Campaign (February-April 1865)
Bentonville (March 19-21, 1865)

398. VIRGINIA 64TH INFANTRY REGIMENT

Nickname: Virginia 64th Cavalry Regiment
Organization: Organized by the consolidation of the 21st and 29th Infantry Battalions on December 14, 1862. Mounted in late 1863. Much of the regiment captured at Cumberland Gap on September 9, 1863. Presumably disbanded in April 1865.
First Commander: Campbell Slemp (Colonel)
Field Officers: Harvey Gray (Major)
Auburn L. Pridmore (Lieutenant Colonel, Colonel)
James B. Richmond (Major, Lieutenant Colonel)
Assignments: District of Abingdon, Department of Western Virginia (December 1862-January 1863)
District of Abingdon, Department of East Tennessee (January-July 1863)
Marshall's-Preston's Brigade, Army of East Tennessee, Department of East Tennessee (July-August 1863)
Williams'-Giltner's Cavalry Brigade, Ransom's Division, Department of East Tennessee (November 1863-February 1864)

Williams' Cavalry Brigade, Department of East Tennessee (February-March 1864)

Giltner's Brigade, Vaughn's Division, Cavalry Corps, Department of East Tennessee (March-April 1864)

Jones' Brigade, Cavalry, Department of East Tennessee (April-May 1864)

Jones' (old) Cavalry Brigade, Department of Western Virginia and East Tennessee (May-August 1864)

Giltner's Cavalry Brigade, Department of Western Virginia and East Tennessee (November 1864-April 1865)

Battles: Cumberland Gap (September 5, 1863)

Knoxville Siege (November-December 1863)

Rogersville, Tennessee (November 6, 1863)

Jonesville, Virginia (January 3, 1864)

Coalsmouth, West Virginia (skirmish) (detachment) (September 30, 1864)

Flat Top Mountain (October 1, 1864)

Laurel Gap (October 1, 1684)

Saltville (October 2, 1864)

399. VIRGINIA AMBULANCE INFANTRY COMPANY

Organization: Organized for emergency service at Richmond in 1861.
First Commander: John Dooley (Captain)
Battles: Petersburg Siege (June 1864-April 1865)
Roper's Farm (September 30, 1864)

400. VIRGINIA AVERETT'S INFANTRY BATTALION RESERVES

Organization: Organized with five companies on August 9, 1864. Consolidated with Farinholt's Infantry Battalion Reserves on August 12, 1864, and designated the 1st Infantry Regiment Reserves per S.O. #48, Adjutant and Inspector General's Office.
First Commander: C. E. Averett (Major)
Assignment: Unattached, Department of Richmond

401. VIRGINIA COHOON'S INFANTRY BATTALION

See: NORTH CAROLINA 6TH INFANTRY BATTALION

402. VIRGINIA ESSEX AND MIDDLESEX INFANTRY BATTALION

See: VIRGINIA WARD'S INFANTRY BATTALION

403. VIRGINIA FARINHOLT'S INFANTRY BATTALION RESERVES

Nickname: Staunton River Battalion

Organization: Organized with five companies on July 18, 1864. Consolidated with Averett's Infantry Battalion Reserves on August 12, 1864, with the companies becoming Companies A-E in the new regiment. Officially designated as the 1st Virginia Infantry Regiment, Reserves, per S.O. #48, Adjutant and Inspector General's Office, on February 27, 1865.
First Commander: Benjamin L. Farinholt (Lieutenant Colonel)
Assignment: Unattached, Department of Richmond (July-August 1864)

404. VIRGINIA FONTAINE'S INFANTRY REGIMENT, STATE LINE
Organization: Failed to complete its organization.
First Commander: Winston Fontaine (Colonel)

405. VIRGINIA FRENCH'S INFANTRY BATTALION
Also Known As: French's Infantry Regiment
Organization: Failed to complete its organization in the spring of 1863.
First Commander: James M. French (Major)

406. VIRGINIA GREEN'S INDEPENDENT INFANTRY REGIMENT, WISE LEGION
Organization: Organized with four North Carolina companies at Richmond in late 1861. Failed to complete its organization on November 1, 1861. The four companies were then assigned to the 2nd North Carolina Infantry Battalion.
First Commander: Wharton J. Green (Colonel)

407. VIRGINIA HOOD'S INFANTRY BATTALION RESERVES
Organization: Organized with six companies at Petersburg on August 6, 1864. (Actually the battalion had been formed by June 1864.) No record found subsequent to October 5, 1864.
First Commander: William H. Hood (Major, Lieutenant Colonel)
Field Officer: Thomas H. Bond (Major)
Assignment: 1st Military District, Department of North Carolina and Southern Virginia (June-October 1864)
Battle: Petersburg Siege (June 1864-April 1865)

408. VIRGINIA KEEN'S INFANTRY BATTALION
Organization: Organized as a temporary field organization with five companies in the summer of 1861. Increased to a regiment and designated as the 57th Infantry Regiment on September 23, 1861, per S.O. #285, Adjutant and Inspector General's Office.
First Commander: Elisha F. Keen (Major)

409.   VIRGINIA MONTAGUE'S INFANTRY BATTALION

Organization: Organized with five companies ca. May 1861. Temporarily attached to the 32nd Infantry Regiment. Consolidated with Tomlin's Infantry Battalion and Waddill's Infantry Company and designated as the 53rd Infantry Regiment on December 1, 1861, per S.O. #214, Adjutant and Inspector General's Office, dated November 9, 1861.
First Commander: Edgar B. Montague (Major)
Assignment: B. S. Ewell's Brigade, Department of the Peninsula (October-December 1861)

410.   VIRGINIA MUNFORD'S INFANTRY BATTALION, LOCAL DEFENSE TROOPS

Organization: Apparently failed to complete its organization in Richmond with only three companies reported.
First Commander: William Munford (Major)

411.   VIRGINIA PRESTON'S INFANTRY BATTALION RESERVES

Organization: Organized with seven companies on August 27, 1864. Increased to a regiment on November 24, 1864, per orders from Headquarters, Department of Western Virginia and East Tennessee, dated September 20, 1864.
First Commander: Robert T. Preston (Lieutenant Colonel)
Assignment: Unattached, Department of Western Virginia and East Tennessee (August-November 1864)

412.   VIRGINIA SCOTT'S INFANTRY BATTALION

Organization: Failed to complete its organization.

413.   VIRGINIA TOMLIN'S INFANTRY BATTALION

Organization: Organized with four companies ca. July 1861. Consolidated with Montague's Infantry Battalion and Waddill's Infantry Company and designated as the 53rd Infantry Regiment on December 1, 1861, per S.O. #214, Adjutant and Inspector General's Office, dated November 9, 1861.
First Commander: Harrison B. Tomlin (Major)
Assignment: B. S. Ewell's Brigade, Department of the Peninsula (October-December 1861)

414.   VIRGINIA VMI INFANTRY BATTALION

Organization: Organized with four companies. Called into active service by Major General Thomas J. Jackson, commanding the Valley District, Department of Northern Virginia, on April 30, 1862. Returned to studies on May 18, 1862. Again called into active service by Major General John C. Breckinridge, commanding the Department of Western Virginia, on May 11, 1864. Furloughed at Lexington June 27, 1864, following the burning of the Virginia Military Institute, until September 1, 1864. On active service in October 1864. Again in active service in March-April 1865. Disbanded at Richmond on April 2, 1865.

First Commander: Francis H. Smith (Colonel)

Field Officer: Scott Shipp (Major)

Assignments: Unattached, Valley District, Department of Northern Virginia (May 1862)

Unattached, Department of Southwestern Virginia (May 1864)

Unattached, Breckinridge's Division, Army of Northern Virginia (May-June 1864)

Local Defense Brigade, Department of Richmond (one company) (October 1864)

Unattached, Department of Richmond (March-April 1865)

Battles: Shenandoah Valley Campaign of 1862 (May-June 1862)

New Market (May 15, 1864)

Cold Harbor (June 1-3, 1864)

Lynchburg Campaign (June 1864)

Petersburg Siege (June 1864-April 1865)

Roper's Farm (September 30, 1864)

415. VIRGINIA WADDILL'S INFANTRY COMPANY

Nickname: Charles City Southern Guards

Organization: Organized on May 9, 1861. Became Company K, 53rd Infantry Regiment, upon consolidation with Montague's and Tomlin's Infantry Battalions on December 1, 1861, per S.O. #214, Adjutant and Inspector General's Office, dated November 9, 1861.

First Commander: George M. Waddill (Captain)

Assignment: B. S. Ewell's Brigade, Department of the Peninsula (October-December 1861)

416. VIRGINIA WARD'S INFANTRY BATTALION

Nickname: Essex and Middlesex Battalion

Organization: Organized by the detachment of four companies of the 47th Infantry Regiment on August 16, 1861, per S.O. #252, Adjutant and Inspector General's Office. An additional company assigned later in the month. Increased to a regiment and designated as the 55th Infantry Regiment in September 1861. Does not appear in the *Official Records*.

First Commander: William N. Ward (Major)

417.   VIRGINIA WISE LEGION INFANTRY LEGION

See: VIRGINIA 46TH INFANTRY REGIMENT, VIRGINIA 59TH INFANTRY REGIMENT, VIRGINIA 60TH INFANTRY REGIMENT

418.   VIRGINIA WISE'S INFANTRY BATTALION

Organization: Organized as a temporary field organization with two companies in June 1861. Became 1st Companies A and B, 59th Infantry Regiment, on August 8, 1861.
First Commander: O. Jennings Wise (Captain)
Assignment: Troops in Kanawha Valley (June-August 1861)

BIBLIOGRAPHY

Amman, William. *Personnel of the Civil War.* 2 volumes. New York: Thomas Yoseloff, 1961. Provides valuable information on local unit designations, general officers' assignments and organizational data on geographical commands.

Boatner, Mark Mayo III. *The Civil War Dictionary.* New York: David McKay Company, 1959. Provides thumbnail sketches of leaders, battles, campaigns, events and units.

Bowman, John S. *The Civil War Almanac.* New York: Facts On File, 1982. Basically a chronology; it is valuable for its 130 biographical sketches, many of them military personalities.

Daniel, Larry J. *Cannoneers in Gray: The Field Artillery of the Army of Tennessee, 1861-1865.* University, Ala.: University of Alabama Press, 1984. An excellent study of the artillery in the western theater.

Evans, Clement A., ed. *Confederate Military History.* 13 volumes. Atlanta: Confederate Publishing Company, 1899. Each volume of this series primarily provides the histories of one or two states. Each state military account was written by a different participant in the war, and they vary greatly in quality. All accounts, however, include biographies of the generals from their state. The lack of a comprehensive index is the major drawback of this work. Volume III, the Virginia volume, is by Major Jed. Hotchkiss.

Freeman, Douglas Southall. *Lee's Lieutenants: A Study in Command.* 3 volumes. New York: Charles Scribner's Sons, 1941-1946. The premier narrative study of the organizational and command structure of the Army of Northern Virginia.

———. *R. E. Lee: A Biography.* 4 volumes. New York: Charles Scribner's Sons, 1934-1935. Also provides organizational information on the Army of Northern Virginia.

Johnson, Robert Underwood, and Buel, Clarence Clough, eds. *Battle and Leaders of the Civil War.* 4 volumes. New York: The Century Company, 1887.

Reprinted 1956. Exceptionally valuable for its tables of organization for major engagements.

Krick, Robert K. *Lee's Colonels: A Biographical Register of the Field Officers of the Army of Northern Virginia*, 2nd edition. Dayton, Ohio: Press of Morningside Bookstore, 1984. Brief but very informative sketches of the 1,965 field-grade officers who at one time or another served with the Army of Northern Virginia but never achieved the rank of brigadier general. The second edition also includes a listing by name and unit of those field-grade officers who never served with Lee.

Long, E. B., and Barbara. *The Civil War Day by Day: An Almanac 1861-1865*. Garden City, N.Y.: Doubleday, 1971. An excellent chronology of the conflict, with much information on the organizational changes command assignments.

Lonn, Ella. *Foreigners in the Confederacy*. Chapel Hill: University of North Carolina, 1940. Accounts of the foreign-born contribution to the Confederacy.

National Archives, Record Group 109. Microfilm compilation of the service records of every known Confederate soldier, organized by unit. The caption cards and record-of-events cards at the beginning of each unit provide much valuable information on the unit's organizational history.

Scharf, J. Thomas. *History of the Confederate States Navy: From Its Organization to the Surrender of Its Last Vessels*. Albany: Joseph McDonough, 1887. A rather disjointed narrative that provides some insight into questions along the southern coast and on the inland waterways. Unfortunately, it lacks an adequate index.

Sifakis, Stewart. *Who Was Who in the Civil War*. New York: Facts On File, 1988.

———. *Who Was Who in the Confederacy*. New York: Facts On File, 1989. Together both works include biographies of over 1,000 participants who served the South during the Civil War. The military entries include much information on the regiments and higher commands.

U.S. Navy Department. *Official Records of the Union and Confederate Navies in the War of the Rebellion*. 31 volumes. Washington: Government Printing Office, 1894-1927. Provides much valuable information on the coastal and riverine operations of the Civil War.

U.S. War Department. *The War of the Rebellion: A Compilation of the Official Records of the Union and Confederate Armies*. 70 volumes in 128 books divided into four series, plus Atlas. Washington: Government Printing Office, 1881-1901. While difficult to use, this set provides a gold mine of information. Organized by campaigns in specified geographic regions, the volumes are divided into postaction reports and correspondence. The information contained in the hundreds of organizational tables proved invaluable for my purposes.

Wakely, Jon L. *Biographical Dictionary of the Confederacy*. Westport, Conn.: Greenwood Press, 1977. Short biographies of 651 leaders of the Confederacy. However, the selection criteria among the military leaders are somewhat haphazard.

Wallace, Lee A., Jr. *A Guide to Virginia Military Organizations 1861-1865*. Lynchburg, Va.: H. E. Howard, 1986. An excellent compilation of the organizational details of the Virginia units and their officers.

Warner, Ezra. *Generals in Gray: Lives of the Confederate Commanders*. Baton Rouge: Louisiana State University Press, 1959. Sketches of the 425 Southern generals. Good coverage of pre- and postwar careers. The wartime portion of the entries leaves something to be desired.

Wise, Jennings Cropper. *The Long Arm of Lee: The History of the Artillery of the Army of Northern Virginia*. Lynchburg, Va.: J. P. Bell Co., 1915. Reprinted 1959. An excellent study of Lee's artillery, providing valuable information on batteries and their commanders and organizational assignments.

Wright, Marcus J. *General Officers of the Confederate Army*. New York: Neale Publishing Co., 1911. Long the definitive work on the Confederate command structure, it was superseded by Ezra Warner's work.

PERIODICALS

Civil War Illustrated, its predecessor *Civil War Times*, *American History Illustrated* and *Civil War History*. In addition, the *Southern Historical Society Papers* (47 vols., 1876-1930) are a gold mine of information on Confederate units and leaders.

BATTLE INDEX

References are to record numbers, not page numbers.

NAME INDEX

References are to record numbers, not page numbers.

Stewart Sifakis, a free-lance writer on historical topics, has been a Civil War enthusiast since childhood. He studied history and politics at the American College in Paris and at George Washington University. He has worked for the National Archives and is the author of *Who Was Who in the Civil War*. Originally from New York City, he currently resides in Gettysburg and works for the Adams County Library System.

Other books by the author:

Compendium of the Confederate Armies: Alabama

Compendium of the Confederate Armies: Florida and Arkansas

Compendium of the Confederate Armies: Kentucky, Maryland, Missouri, The Confederate Units and The Indian Units

Compendium of the Confederate Armies: Louisiana

Compendium of the Confederate Armies: Mississippi

Compendium of the Confederate Armies: North Carolina

Compendium of the Confederate Armies: South Carolina and Georgia

Compendium of the Confederate Armies: Tennessee

Compendium of the Confederate Armies: Texas